BARRON'S BUSINESS LIBRARY

Selling and Sales Management

Robert D. Hisrich, Ph.D.
Bovaird Chair, Entrepreneurial Studies
Professor of Marketing
College of Business Administration
University of Tulsa

Ralph W. Jackson, Ph.D.
Associate Professor of Marketing
Chairman, Department of Management
    and Marketing
College of Business Administration
University of Tulsa

BARRON'S

General Editor for *Barron's Business Library* is George T. Friedlob, professor in the school of accountancy at Clemson University.

All inquiries should be addressed to:
Barron's Educational Series, Inc.
250 Wireless Boulevard
Hauppauge, New York 11788

Library of Congress Catalog Card No. 92-36070

International Standard Book No. 0-8120-4693-5

Library of Congress Cataloging-in-Publication Data

Hisrich, Robert D.
     Selling and sales management / Robert D. Hisrich, Ralph
W. Jackson.
        p.   cm. — (Barron's business library)
     Includes index.
     ISBN 0-8120-4693-5
     1. Selling. 2. Sales management. I. Jackson, Ralph W.
II. Title. III. Series.
HF5438.25.H57   1992   92-36070
658.8'1—dc20   CIP

PRINTED IN ITALY
3456 9929 987654321

Contents

Preface

In the decade of the 90s, the United States faces significant challenges and opportunities. The hypercompetition of products from the European Community, Japan, and other countries of the Pacific Rim, the new trade treaty between the United States, Mexico, and Canada, significant new markets being opened in selected countries in the former Eastern and Central Europe and the USSR, and the need for innovation in all areas of business in the United States, will increase the focus on better and more effective personal selling and sales management.

While the momentum of United States business following World War II has slowed, there is an international market opportunity today that was not available just three years ago. This and other international and national opportunities have spurred increased interest in business activities with new customers. Concurrent with this is an increasing emphasis on *partnering*, or developing long-term relationships between suppliers and customers. These trends necessitate a new understanding of the role and application of personal selling and sales management.

This book provides an indepth, practically-oriented presentation of personal selling and sales management. Each of the twenty chapters presents one aspect of this area as an important creative activity that affects the transactions and success of businesses each day. To make the book meaningful, and to assist the reader in applying the concepts presented, each chapter begins with an introduction to the material and the main points covered, discusses the theory along with numerous practical applications, and concludes with a summary of the key concepts.

Many individuals have made this book possible. A listing of all the numerous sales executives, students, professors, and editorial staff whose comments, insights, and examples were invaluable, would take far too many pages. Special thanks goes to Sandy Hughes, without whom this manuscript would not have been typed in a timely manner, and to Troy Bradley, Todd Willmann, Shelley Skyrmes, and Thayla Painter for providing research material and editorial assistance.

We are deeply indebted to Tina Hisrich and daughters Kary, Katy, and Kelly, and to Gary Jackson and Debra Cain to whom this book is dedicated. Their patience, support, and understanding were instrumental in bringing this work to fruition.

The Selling Process and Management

INTRODUCTION AND MAIN POINTS

Regardless of your present position and background, you, and everyone else in the world, have done some form of selling. This may have occurred when you obtained the job you have now. You did some form of selling when asking for a new assignment. You used a form of selling to obtain your last raise. Each of us employs varying degrees of personal selling in our daily activities.

Personal selling can be defined as a formal, paid-for, personal presentation of aspects of a company to an individual or group. It is important to understand the aspects of personal selling and how to manage it, to be able to live and perform more effectively.

After reading the material in this chapter:

━━ You will understand the nature of the selling process and the aspects of its management.

━━ You will appreciate the relationship between personal selling and marketing.

━━ You will understand the role of selling in the organization.

━━ You will know the emerging issues in selling.

━━ You will know the aspects of sales as a career.

NATURE OF THE SELLING TASK

Personal sales and making personal presentations are the most important, and most expensive, stimulants for a company's sales and profits. They require that each person involved in the selling task be well trained in aspects of the company and its products, as well as in presentation skills. The salesperson interacts with the prospect or customer and provides a more personal touch than other aspects of the marketing effort: good products, attractive packaging, and informative advertising. Given the hypercompetitive environment of today's business world, first-hand contact and knowledge of customer needs and attitudes is essential to the overall marketing effort. Listening to and understanding the customer and then delivering a product or service can result in customer satisfaction.

It is no longer possible to be successful in personal selling by being brash or pushy or by making grandiose claims. While personality and other individual characteristics will always be factors in successful selling, this aspect alone does not complete a sale. A successful sale requires that a salesperson understand thoroughly the company's products and how these fulfill the needs of the customer.

The selling task increases in complexity as the technology of the products and services becomes more complex and as customers become more knowledgeable and better informed. It is often further complicated by shared decision-making in many buying decisions, which requires interaction among individuals at various levels of the buying and selling organizations.

A salesperson is developed, not born. A successful salesperson usually combines innate ability and acquired skills. Customers appreciate a salesperson who is reliable, credible, and professional and who has integrity and knowledge of the product or service.

Knowledge of the attributes and qualities of a product and the skill necessary to present the product effectively require extensive training and practice. Many companies now have schools for training and management. Xerox in Virginia, IBM in New York, and AT&T in Colorado each has its own corporate school.

Salespeople's Time

The professionalism of each salesperson is particularly significant when considering the use of time during a typical week. In an average forty-seven-hour sales work week, a salesperson spends 50 percent in selling—30 percent (14.1 hours) selling face-to-face and 20 percent (9.4 hours) selling over the telephone. The rest is spent traveling and waiting (23 percent, 10.8 hours); handling administrative tasks (14 percent, 6.6 hours); and making service calls (13 percent, 6.1 hours). Given the high cost of a single sales call and the amount of time spent in nonselling activities, it is imperative that a salesperson be professional in selling, whether face-to-face or over the telephone.

Importance and Role of the Salesperson

The fact that companies are willing to establish their own schools and programs attests to the importance of personal selling. Personal selling is labor intensive and the most expensive way to contact a customer and market the company's products. Personal selling accounts for about 58 percent of the total sales expense of a company. More than 10 percent of the labor force in the United States—over 7.5 million people—are in personal sales. This alone indicates the recognition by business of the importance of a close relationship with the customer. It is the most flexible, personal, yet most costly method possible for communicating information about a company's products and services. Personal selling allows products and services to be tailored to the unique needs of a particular market, even the needs of an individual customer.

To the customer, the salesperson is the personification of the company. The salesperson is often the only representative of a company with whom the customer comes in contact. The salesperson significantly enhances (or detracts) from the company's image. Although the salesperson is usually blamed for unfilled or inappropriately filled orders, billing errors, late delivery, and faulty products, he or she is also given the credit for all the good aspects of the company, particularly all the services.

The Professional Salesperson

Each year the level of professionalism needed to be a success increases. *Professionalism* is the ability of the salesperson to perform in a businesslike manner in all dealings with a customer or prospect. The increasing level of customer knowledge, as well as expectations, has radically changed the selling task. Salespeople call on customers at all levels of management and must be able to handle themselves accordingly. Some companies, such as IBM and Xerox, now refer to sales representatives as "market representatives." This title change emphasizes that their market representatives receive intensive training and retraining, ensuring that the proper presentation is made to the customer and that the appropriate company image is projected.

Progressive companies increasingly recognize the need to be represented by talented, professional salespeople. Since negative word of mouth by previous customers who have switched to competing companies can have a significant negative impact on sales, management recognizes the need for good hiring, training, and compensation of the sales force.

RELATIONSHIP BETWEEN PERSONAL SELLING AND MARKETING

Salespeople are becoming more oriented to the market and the customer, trying to make sure that each customer is satisfied.

Marketing is part of a developed society, affecting the lives of everyone. It is not an isolated function within a firm, but begins and ends in the changing external environment, starting with the idea for a product or service and finishing after the consumer is satisfied with the purchase. Marketing is a process of making decisions in a completely interrelated business environment about all activities that satisfy targeted groups of customers.

Marketing and the Marketing Process

Marketing has an increasing impact on the decisions being made, not only by the buyer and seller but other groups, including politicians and even the clergy. For example, a small business owner may be trying to decide to allocate a small promotional budget. Should an expensive newspaper advertisement be used, should there be radio spots, or would additional flyers placed in various locations throughout the city be a better use of available money? Other decisions need to be made on how the business owner should spend the time. Should personal calls be made on key accounts or should attempts be made to ensure the product is well displayed in retail stores? These and other basic marketing decisions are routinely made by every business.

Purchasing managers or buyers of industrial goods are confronted with related yet different aspects of marketing. Should sources of supply be switched because of the superior quality and lower price of a new supplier? Will a new firm consistently supply the quantity needed at the right price? Will the new supplier deliver the product on time to avoid costly plant shutdowns? An industrial buyer or purchasing manager must carefully weigh many aspects of marketing in selecting the correct product and supplier.

Consider the small specialty store manager trying to decide what merchandise to carry. Should a more complete line of long sleeved men's shirts be carried or a smaller line, along with short sleeved shirts? Should an advertisement be placed in a local paper? Should a spring clearance sale be held? Should the store sponsor the local basketball team?

Marketing: An Integrated Definition

The definition of marketing depends on individual perspective. Law, finance, economics, operations, and consumers all view marketing from different vantage points.

In this ever-changing environment, the following definition of marketing is applicable. *Marketing* is the process of making decisions in an interrelated environment and all the activities that satisfy a targeted group of customers and accomplish the firm's objectives.

This definition has four aspects. First, how does the *decision-making process* impact the accomplishment of the *defined objectives*? Specific objectives vary from firm to firm, as well as from product to product, but it is impossible for good marketing decisions to be made without defined objectives. The basic objective of a profit organization is to make a profit. This objective may not occur in the short run or for all of the firm's products. Overall, however, each firm must make a profit in the long run to exist. Obtaining this objective under the *going concern concept*—the organization plans to do business with the same or similar customers year after year—means that profits cannot be obtained by sacrificing customers. The going concern concept can be defined as a goal of the organization when it prefers to do business with the same or similar customers year after year.

The second part of the definition is the satisfaction of the target group of customers. This requires that the customer be the focus of all the firm's activities. The customer's wants and needs are constantly analyzed, enabling the firm to offer exactly what the customer desires. This is the essence of the marketing concept. Without this focus, a customer can choose an alternative from a competitor.

All activities that facilitate exchange, the third part of the definition, are the controllable marketing elements used for customer satisfaction. *Facilitating exchange* means that the customer gives something up (usually money) for what the firm offers.

These controllable marketing elements that comprise the firm's offering can be classified in four areas: product, price, distribution, and promotion. Each element has its strategic decision mix needed to achieve customer satisfaction.

1) The *product area* includes all aspects of the physical product or service being offered. Decisions involve quality, assortment, the breadth and depth of the line, warranties, guarantees, service and packaging. All these aspects make the final product or service more (or less) appealing to the target market.

2) Closely related to product and mix is price. The least understood of these elements, price greatly influences the image of the product as well as whether it will be purchased. Price takes

into consideration the three C's: Cost, competition, and the consumer.

3) Distribution covers two different areas. *Channels of distribution* involves wholesalers and retailers that handle the product between the firm and the consumer. *Physical distribution* deals physically moving the product from the firm to the consumer. This includes warehousing, inventory, and transportation.

4) *Promotion* involves policies and procedures related to four areas:

A. *Personal selling:* Policies and procedures related to the personal presentation of the product or service.

B. *Advertising:* Policies and procedures related to budget, message, and media.

C. *Sales promotions:* Policies and procedures related to nonrecurring promotional activities such as trade promotions and displays.

D. *Publicity:* Policies and procedures related to a comprehensive program for good media coverage and a strong company image.

The final part of the marketing definition indicates that marketing exists in a changing environment. Decisions in other areas of the firm, as well as those made by competing firms, affect marketing, as do variables in the external environment.

The Marketing Concept

More than any other functional business area, marketing develops the goals and direction of an organization. The basic philosophy of the firm's management should center on the satisfaction of the target customer. This is the heart of the marketing concept. Under the marketing concept, the consumer is the focus with all the resources and activities of the firm directed at customer satisfaction primarily.

Adopting a marketing concept was precipitated in U.S. business by several factors. First, there has been an increase in the intensity of competition in both national and international markets, forcing organizations to place greater emphasis on consumer satisfaction.

A second factor forcing adoption of a marketing concept is consumer knowledge and sophistication. Consumers are more aware of product alternatives and price than ever before. As consumers become increasingly aware of various options, only products and services that are recognized as "need satisfying" will be purchased.

An increase in production capabilities in conjunction with the development of worldwide mass markets has also led to the adoption of the marketing concept. This *increased production capacity*—the ability to produce more and more units at a decreased per unit product cost—dramatically increases the total number of units available for sale. These can only be sold successfully, reaching more and larger markets, only by focusing on customer satisfaction.

Finally, the need for survival forces firms to place the customer first. Just a simple count of the number of times you have heard the phrase "new and improved" should indicate the size of the consumer appetite for new and supposedly better products. Yet between 80 and 90 percent of all new products fail.

A key ingredient to successful new product introduction is knowing the needs and buying habits of the *target group* of customers, those identified and selected as the customers who should receive the thrust of the marketing activity. This concept is important in personal selling and sales management. A salesperson wants to ensure that a customer is satisfied and purchases only those goods and services needed in the correct amount. This helps to establish customer rapport, which, in the long run, results in continuous sales.

Under a philosophy of knowing the needs and buying habits of consumers and satisfying them, the customer is not blamed for problems in the sales cycle.

Without this philosophy, salespeople might think that customers always have a list of objections just to annoy the sellers and make them miserable. Under the marketing concept, a salesperson views questions and objections differently and tries to determine why customers have these objections. Is it because they do not have enough information? Is it because there are problems with the product? Or is it because there is not enough customer service in the selling process?

ASPECTS OF SALES MANAGEMENT WITHIN MARKETING

For an effective selling effort, good sales management is required. A sales manager can have a narrow or a broad spectrum of responsibilities, including the following:

- Estimate demand and prepare sales forecasts.
- Establish sales force objectives and quotas.
- Prepare sales plans and budgets.
- Establish the size and organization of the sales force.
- Recruit, select, and train the sales force.

■ Compensate the sales force.
■ Control and evaluate sales performances.

These activities are critical to any firm, as sales directly generate income, without which the firm cannot survive.

The exact responsibilities of the sales manager vary greatly with the industry and even within a given industry, depending on the nature of the product and the firm and the attitude of top management about selling. In some firms the sales manager is a supervisor of the sales force and in other firms a sales manager performs all the preceding activities. The latter definition is frequently the case in small, growing firms that are opportunity rich and cash poor.

The responsibilities of a sales manager also vary depending on the level of the position within the organization. The highest level of sales executive is typically the vice president of sales, who usually reports to the vice president of marketing and sometimes even to the president of the company. This position involves long-range planning and developing and implementing the sales portion of the marketing strategy. In companies with no vice president of marketing, the position includes responsibility for all marketing activities. The next highest sales management position is the national sales manager. This position provides a link between upper level management and the sales force and provides the sales force with the necessary guidance and strategic plan to carry out the marketing strategy.

Below the national sales manager are often two middle-level supervisory positions: Middle-level sales managers and first-level sales managers. Middle-level sales managers, also called regional, divisional, or zone sales managers, are responsible for line sales activities in a designated geographic area. Zone sales managers report to divisional sales managers, who in turn report to regional sales managers when all three levels exist within a company. Below middle-level sales managers are first-level sales managers, frequently called field sales managers or sales supervisors. These individuals are responsible for the daily activities of the salespeople in their area.

The final area of sales force management is the key account or national account manager. This position involves selling to a few major customers; for example, selling to the central buying offices of major chains, such as Kroger, K-Mart, Wal-Mart, Sears, J. C. Penney, or IGA. Usually a salesperson is assigned to call on individual stores in the chain.

SALES CAREERS

As a career, sales can be diverse, challenging, exciting, and financially rewarding. A sales career is hardly ever boring: It involves dealing with different individuals and their changing wants, needs, and behavior patterns. Depending on the compensation method, a sales career provides the security of working for a company and the freedom and independence associated with being your own boss. Given its direct impact on sales and profits, a good salesperson has a significant amount of job security and often job opportunities as well.

Shortage of Good Salespeople

There are many job opportunities in sales as well as a relatively high level of compensation. There is always a shortage of qualified salespeople. Not counting replacement hires, more than 400,000 new salespeople are needed each year. This shortage is compounded by the inefficiency of many salespeople already working, which also results in a high turnover rate. The majority of actual sales are made by a small number of salespeople. Many salespeople operate inefficiently, not planning or organizing their sales efforts well, which results in wasted time and calls to potential customers who are not likely to make a purchase.

Career Path

Besides a career in sales itself, sales can quickly lead to an upper level management position. Many executives in various management positions in Fortune 500 companies started their careers in sales. This reflects the importance of learning the business from the perspective of those who ultimately determine the success or failure of a business or product—the customer.

Benefits

A sales career offers income possibilities and perquisites that are at least as good as any other business career. Salespeople are among the most highly paid in business. Salespeople working for industrial products companies are generally paid salary plus commissions. They earn more than those working for consumer products or service companies, who are generally paid on a straight-salary basis. Many salespeople on a straight-commission and bonus compensation plan earn more than $100,000, and some straight-commission salespeople earn more than their sales managers. In some companies, a salesperson is expected to earn at least $50,000 shortly after the training period. Since success can be directly measured, salespeople and sales executives are usually objectively evaluated and compensated based on performance. This performance measurement leads to significant job security and opportunity. Even during times of personnel cutbacks, sales personnel are among the last to be severed. Eliminating a sales position usually means the loss of sales and revenues.

In addition to substantial income, a salesperson also has good perquisites. An expense account, benefits of entertaining potential and present customers, as well as a car, membership dues, and an office at home enhance the earned income.

Sales Careers for Women

Sales career opportunities for women have dramatically increased over the past two decades. Previous myths about women not being reliable, suitable, or strong enough to deal with customers have been laid to rest even in high-technology industries. More and more women are in sales and have key selling and sales management positions in industries ranging from retailing, steel, and life insurance to pharmaceutical, brewing, and biotechnology.

In many progressive companies, women outperform men in equivalent sales positions for several reasons, such as: Women are generally better listeners than men; women may be more easily remembered than men with a positive recall being transferred to the product(s) being sold; and women are better able to obtain time with some buyers. However, in some industries, sales people are most often men. This occurs more often in industrial selling situations and particularly those that are more technically oriented. A woman sales person in this type of situation is an anomaly and can therefore use this to obtain time with some buyers. This situation is changing in these industries as more women become engaged in the sales area, in a fashion similar to what occurred previously in other industrial areas.

Sexual overtures and problems involving entertaining customers are decreasing. Today, women face about the same problems as men in sales. Saleswomen can get advice and help from professional organizations, such as the National Association of Business and Industrial Saleswomen and the National Association for Professional Saleswomen.

Sales Careers for Minorities

Accompanying the increasing number of women in sales careers is an increase in the number of blacks, Hispanics, Asians, and

Native Americans. While strong legal and moral pressures under civil rights law are contributing to this, the increased business abilities of minorities has also positively affected the number of sales positions available to them. In addition, companies have found that some sales positions are more productive when filled with a minority salesperson. A minority person can be particularly effective when calling on the minority buyers. The increasing impact of the National Association for the Advancement of Colored People (NAACP) and the Urban League, coupled with the law enforcement and noncompliance actions of the Equal Employment Opportunity Commission (EEOC), have created expanding opportunities for minorities in sales.

EMERGING ISSUES IN SELLING AND SALES MANAGEMENT

It appears that the importance of the salesperson in the overall marketing strategy of the firm will continue to increase. Sales is already the most critical aspect of a successful marketing mix in many companies. Salespeople are receiving increased responsibilities and need more education and training to compete effectively in the marketplace. Salespeople benefit from higher compensation, more prestige and security, and more opportunities for advancement. In the past, a college degree was not necessary for sales, but this is often not the case today. A college education helps broaden a person and provides confidence, better analytic, communication, and personal skills. It is too bad that many college students have a negative stereotype of salespeople based on the stereotype of contact used car dealers or door-to-door salespeople.

Yet, interest in sales and sales management continues to increase. Sales is rapidly being recognized as an excellent entry-level position. Sales and sales management positions are changing significantly and will continue to do so in the future because of several factors. First, there is continually an increase in consumer expectations. Consumers are becoming less tolerant of faulty products, as well as product and service limitations. Rapport and loyalty can be established by any competent salesperson, but a dissatisfied customer will quickly switch to a better alternative. Firms must place more emphasis on innovations and quality in the product and service mix. This requires the sales organization to be even more aware of customer needs, level of satisfaction, complaints and to report these regularly and systematically.

A second factor contributing to the increased interest in sales is buyer expertise. With tighter budgets and increasing profit squeezes, buyers are becoming adept at obtaining value for their dollars. Buying committees are used more frequently to ensure that the purchase has input from many different perspectives. Consumers now treat an increasing number of purchase decisions as long-term investments. This places more responsibility on salespeople to develop long-term relationships with their customers by having a thorough understanding of the buying process. Professional salespeople who focus on consultancy, not persuasive selling, are needed to an increasing extent.

The effects of these two factors on the future of personal selling and sales management is compounded by a third factor, international competition. The large U.S. market, with its significant purchasing power, attracts quality, cost-competitive products from all over the world. This requires that salespeople and salesmanagers offer quality and be sensitive to customer needs.

The final factor affecting the future of salespeople and their managers is the electronic revolution in communications and computer technology. Today, salespeople and sales managers alike can use personal computers for order entry and customer and sales analysis. Variations in sales performance can be quickly identified, and various "what-if" scenarios can be run to determine the impact on sales territory adjustments or reassignment of salespeople.

Sales presentations are becoming more vivid and realistic through videotape presentations. A company's products can demonstrate attributes not visible in catalogue pages or product brochures. Videotapes are also useful for the sales manager to communicate a message to all the salespeople in the field.

To minimize travel time and costs, videoconferencing is also used. This allows a professional presentation to be made and any concerns to be handled efficiently at a distance.

Automobile telephones and electronic beepers are common in sales and allow the sales manager to make instant contact with salespeople in the field. These devices also allow salespeople to warn a customer about a delay in an appointment.

CHAPTER PERSPECTIVE

Personal selling can be defined as a formal, paid-for, personal presentation of aspects of a company to an individual or group. Selling requires a professional person who takes initiative to satisfy the customer. A successful salesperson requires a thorough understanding of the company's products and how these products fulfill the needs of the customer. With hard work, salespeople develop selling skills that combined with innate character traits to heighten selling strength. Most buyers note reliability, credibility, professionalism, integrity, and product knowledge as a salesperson's most desirable traits. This list not only shows the traits desired, but also points out that the salesperson is the personification of the company. Because of their importance, salespeople can enhance or detract from the company's image.

A salesperson needs to use time-management skills. Given the high cost of a sales call and the amount of time spent in non-selling activities, it is imperative that a salesperson be professional in selling, whether face-to-face or by telephone, to be successful in making sales and profits.

A key ingredient to successful product introduction and sales is knowing the needs and buying habits of consumers. This data is usually collected at the sales management level. The planning, directing, and monitoring of personal selling activities aids in estimating demand and preparing sales forecasts. A sales manager establishes sales force objectives and quotas, prepares sales plans and budgets, and helps to determine sales force compensation. These factors help ensure that a sales career is diverse, challenging, exciting, and financially rewarding.

More and more women and minorities are pursuing sales careers. With this growing variety of salespeople, an individual company's selling techniques are increasingly diverse. Companies use state-of-the-art training ideas to sharpen sales strategies. Also, many companies take advantage of modern advances, such as videoconferencing and electronic beepers, to complement sales. Sales presentations are becoming more vivid and realistic, making a sales career even more exciting.

Recruiting and Selecting Salespeople

CHAPTER

2

INTRODUCTION AND MAIN POINTS

A major part of the sales manager's job is building a sales force that provides the representation the company needs in the marketplace. This means locating and recruiting salespeople who can relate to customers and provide the level of service they need; who have the intelligence to learn about the product line as well as the desire to continue learning about changes in technology; and who possess the attributes, skills, and knowledge necessary to ensure a reasonable chance of success. With many people available in the job market it seems that this would be one of the easier sales manager's tasks.

The general view is that a good salesperson is anyone who is talkative, with a firm handshake and a ready smile. Related is the view that a successful salesperson is one who possesses an ephemeral quality; who goes through life without making any real contribution to anyone or anything. The salesperson's job consists chiefly of cajoling customers and moving on before customers have time to think logically about the purchase decision and can change their minds. For people who take this view, "salespeople are born, not made."

In reality, we know this view of the successful salesperson is terribly inaccurate. However, the myth of the "perfect salesperson," a person who exists somewhere, who possesses a particular set of characteristics, who looks and acts a certain way, and who is always successful, persists. The myth goes on to suggest that "if I had some kind of device that would measure every applicant who comes through the door and indicate if he or she is that perfect type, my problems would be solved." Well, unfortunately, perfect types do not exist, and even if they did your competition would probably hold the patent on the machine that spots them.

After reading this chapter:

▬ You will understand the characteristics of good salespeople.

▬ You will have some insight into the best approaches to locating a viable set of candidates.

▬ You will better understand the tools available to the sales manager to screen candidates.

CHARACTERISTICS OF SUCCESSFUL SALESPEOPLE

Although we cannot say that successful salespeople possess a specific set of characteristics and that those who are unsuccessful do not, we can say that successful salespeople have some qualities in common. A number of research studies have been conducted that address what it is that sets good salespeople apart from average and poor. Although there is some variation in the findings, in general there is agreement on the traits that characterize good salespeople. These traits can be placed in one of three categories:

Attributes: Specific personality characteristics.

Skills: Specific talents that set them apart.

Knowledge: Specific information that sets them apart.

The number of attributes that have been found repeatedly in studies of successful salespeople is relatively small. Among the most commonly mentioned is *empathy* (Lamont and Lundstrom, 1977; Greenberg and Greenberg, 1983). *Empathy* is the ability to understand the situation from the other person's perspective. This is critical because the salesperson attempts to build a relationship with the buyer.

Probably the second most commonly found attribute is *ego drive* (Greenberg and Greenberg 1983). *Ego drive* is the quality of a salesperson whose self-image is inextricably tied to success in making a sale. In other words, the person who possesses this attribute wants to succeed at selling because there is an identification with the job.

Ego strength or *resilience* is the ability to "bounce back" from defeat. For the salesperson, defeat comes when he or she is turned down in a sales call. Obviously, salespeople hear "no" more times than they hear "yes." Better salespeople do not let such refusals shake them. They stay with the fundamentals of selling and are able to put such refusals behind them.

In a recent study that asked sales managers about the traits of good salespeople, honesty was ranked first (the study of sales managers conducted by Conrad N. Jackson and Ralph W. Jackson is in the form of a working paper). Although this attribute is included in only a few studies (e.g., Plotkin, 1986), it may be growing in importance, given the increased emphasis on the importance of building trust. Sales managers are beginning to recognize that honesty and integrity are the cornerstones of trust.

A number of other attributes have been discussed in various studies as being important. Among these are the following:

> Self-discipline
> Intelligence
> Creativity
> Flexibility
> Self-motivation
> Persistence
> Personableness
> Dependability

Although the necessary attributes vary from sales job to sales job, those discussed here appear to form the basis for a successful sales career. The first four should be considered especially essential.

Possessing certain attributes is not enough. Successful salespeople use particular skills more effectively than those who are not as successful. A number of studies have found certain skills that seem to predominate in successful salespeople. The following are some of the most commonly reported skills found in recent studies:

1) Communication skills
2) Analytical skills
3) Organization skills
4) Time management skills

Most people think that the communication skills needed in selling require salespeople to be "good talkers." However, communication (Chapter 4), is a two-way street. It involves listening as well as talking. Talks with sales managers from various types of companies indicates that listening is perhaps the paramount skill of good salespeople. One manager said, "Over the years, I sold more products by listening than I ever did by talking."

Analytic skills are important especially in today's selling climate with its emphasis on consultative selling. It has been said that "a problem well-defined is half-solved." Good salespeople have the ability to go beyond the symptoms and to get to the heart of the matter. Additionally, good analysis means that the salesperson possesses an adequate understanding of the customer's business and needs.

Organizational and time management skills are related. Organizational skills are important because of the tremendous amount of information the typical salesperson is called upon to handle. The salesperson must deal with information about each customer, the product line, the general economy, the industry and his or her company. This must be organized into a usable format. There is, after all, a difference between data and information. Simply loading the customer with an endless array of data is not the same as informing the customer. Unfortunately, too many salespeople believe that, "If I can't dazzle them with my brilliance, I'll baffle them with my ...." You know the rest.

Time management skills are critical for two reasons (McCollough, 1979; Smith, 1979; Raphel, 1981; Korschun, 1982). First, the typical salesperson spends only about one-third of the time in front of the customer. Anything the person can do to spend more time with the customer means an increase in sales. In addition, as we mentioned previously, the old *80:20 principle* works in selling: In general, about 80 percent of sales come from 20 percent of customers. Better salespeople allocate their time so they can spend most of it with this 20 percent. Yet they do not ignore those smaller customers because they represent future earning potential.

The third category of traits that set good salespeople apart from average and poor is *knowledge*. The following are the major types of knowledge most often mentioned as needed by salespeople:

1) Product knowledge
2) Customer knowledge
3) Knowledge of the industry
4) Knowledge of the competition
5) Knowledge of the company

THE RECRUITING AND SELECTING PROCESS

Even though there are characteristics common to successful salespeople, every company and sales job is different, and the sales manager needs to examine those factors specifically related to the particular job before hiring a person to fill a slot. This is where a formal job description comes in handy. Often an organization develops a job description and never bothers to review it. If there have been changes in the organization, the job description for the salesperson probably needs some adjustment. Often, people other than the sales manager take part in the hiring process. Human resource personnel may not realize that a job description is out of date and often look for people who fit the old job description. The people they consider may not be qualified for the position. Job analysis must consider a number of factors:

The market: Who will the salesperson call on? Does the market consist of wholesalers or end users?

The product line: How technical is the product line? How many different products will one person be responsible for?

Tasks and responsibilities: Does the job require any special skills, and does it have physical requirements beyond the typical white-collar job? Does the salesperson perform certain service tasks that require a particular skill?

The degree of autonomy: How much freedom does the person have in making decisions? How often does the person interact with his or her superiors?

Sources of Candidates

Once the set of job requirements is determined and the job description is drawn, the next issue is where to recruit qualified candidates. Certainly the job description establishes where to find the best recruits. In general, however, there are several viable sources for prospective salespeople. Table 2-1 presents the positive and negative aspects of recruiting from these various sources.

Reaching Recruits

A parallel issue to determining the best source of candidates is the question of how best to reach these candidates. Among the factors to be considered when selecting the source is the amount of time the sales manager has to get a salesperson in place and how much time can be devoted to the task of recruiting. Second is the question of how much labor can be spared for recruiting. Additionally, there is the issue of the amount of money available for recruiting.

One of the more commonly used media for reaching candidates is *advertising*. The obvious advantage of using this approach is the wide exposure. When using advertisements, there are three major questions to be answered. First, will the company advertise in newspapers, magazines, and/or trade journals? Second, which specific publications will be used? Finally, will the company use "open" or "blind" ads? The advantage of magazines and trade journals is that they are *targeted media:* They usually reach a specific audience and therefore many nuisance responses are eliminated. With newspapers, the advantage is that a wider audience is reached: However, with this wider audience a number of less-than-qualified candidates will respond.

Table 2-1
Sources for Recruiting

Source	Positive Aspects	Negative Aspects
Within the Company	Candidates are familiar with the product line.	There may not be candidates who are qualified for the position.
	Candidates are familiar with company procedures.	Candidates who are considered and then turned down for the position may become dissatisfied.
	Candidates tend to be more loyal to the company.	
	It is less expensive than external recruiting.	Candidates may have a mistaken perception of the sales job.
	It provides the chance for advancement within the company.	Candidates may have a difficult time making the transition to the sales job.
	There is already some information on candidate's abilities and work habits.	
Colleges and Universities	There is a large pool of qualified candidates in one place.	Candidates tend to lack experience and may not fully understand the requirements of the sales career.
	Candidates are in a learning mode and, hence, are more easily trained.	Candidates may be somewhat immature.
	Candidates are eager to start their careers and the enthusiasm carries over into the job.	There tends to be a higher turnover rate for younger salespeople than for veterans.
	Candidates have demonstrated the ability to establish and accomplish a goal.	Candidates may shop companies that recruit: they may interview with some companies for which they have no intention of working.

Usually the pay scale is lower for new graduates than for veteran salespeople.

Generally, the candidates are younger and have more physical energy to devote to the job.

Recent graduates are often more mobile and willing to relocate.

Recent graduates usually enjoy the travel involved in a job more than veteran salespeople.

Competitors		
The prospects are veterans and know their industry.	The candidates are more expensive to hire.
The candidates understand the type of customers that buy from your firm.	They may not be loyal to one company: if you hired them, someone else can.
The candidates have a realistic understanding of the sales job.	If the other company has a different way of doing things, they may be difficult to "untrain."
They have established accounts and may bring some of their customers with them.	If they leave, they may take your customers.
They have a track record that can be evaluated.	They are likely less mobile than younger salespeople.
The prospects probably have some knowledge of your product line.	

Other industries	These prospects are veterans who require less training on how to sell.	These candidates are relatively expensive to hire compared to college students.
	They may bring a fresh perspective.	They may find that they do not like selling in your industry.
	They have an established record that can be evaluated.	They may have certain ways of doing things and will need to be "untrained."
	These candidates have a good understanding of the sales career.	They may have a "prima donna" attitude.
	Generally they bring a certain enthusiasm, given their willingness to change industries.	
Professionals from a nonsales background	These candidates have some knowledge of the business world.	They may be impatient with the process of building a sales career.
	They tend to have a mature outlook.	They may not have a realistic view of the sales profession.
	The prospects are probably enthusiastic and willing to learn.	They may experience a good deal of stress brought about by a career change.
	They may introduce a fresh perspective to the sales job.	They may be expensive to hire.
	Generally, the candidates are willing to work hard to get established in a sales career.	

The specific publication or combination of publications is a function of the characteristics and location of preferred prospects. Newspapers give wide coverage in a specific geographic area; however, even with national magazines a company can restrict the geographic coverage to a certain extent. If a firm wants to hire salespeople for its southwestern region, it can run an ad only in the southwestern issue of a given national magazine. If the firm wants to hire a sales engineer, it can run an ad in trade publications aimed at engineers. Generally, any magazine will provide a profile of its readers upon request. Additionally, the firm can refer to *Standard Rate and Data* (SRDS) for a synopsis of readers of various magazines. This publication should be available in the local public library.

Once the specific media have been selected, the question of whether to use open or blind ads arises. *Open ads* are those that identify the company doing the recruiting. *Blind ads* are those that provide only a post office box number to which the candidate sends his or her resume. The advantage of open ads is that they eliminate those individuals who may not want to work for your company. However, they mean more *drop-ins,* people who come to the office in hope of obtaining an interview.

Another avenue for reaching prospective candidates is the *employment agency.* The advantage of using headhunters is that they screen candidates for you. Additionally, they know what questions to ask and generally what to look for in selecting a pool of applicants. There are a couple of disadvantages to using employment agencies. First, most professional positions are fee paid—the recruiting company pays the agency a percentage of the position's salary. These fees can be quite high. The second major drawback to agencies is the complaint that they are mainly interested in earning the fee, and hence send out applicants who are less than satisfactory. However, if the recruiting company does a good job of specifying exactly what it is looking for in its candidates, is careful in selecting which agency to use, and develops a long-term relationship with an agency, much of this problem can be alleviated.

When recruiting on the university campus, three major avenues can be followed. Probably the most commonly used is the university placement center. *Placement centers* specialize in trying to match graduating students with interested firms. The main advantage of going through the placement center to reach candidates is that this resource is widely used by the student body. This is also perhaps the major disadvantage: The recruiter may have to speak to a number of students who do not fit the profile of the company. Another disadvantage arises from the magnitude of demands placed on placement centers by students. Placement centers often use some kind of "bid system" to match students with recruiting companies.

Given that one company can allocate only so many slots for interviews, the center selects students for these slots by giving each student a specific number of points. The students then "bid" for the chance to interview with a particular company. The students with the highest bids for the company get the time slots. The problem for the recruiter is that often he or she does not have the opportunity to interview other candidates who might be qualified for the job.

A trend that seems to be growing on college campuses is the job fair, typically a forum for interested companies to set up information booths or tables on campus and dispense information. It provides the chance to see a wider spectrum of students than is possible through the placement center. Generally, a number of students, when they have the chance to find about a company, discover that it is one for which they might enjoy working.

Furthermore, students who are interested in a particular company can make contact with the company and perhaps start the recruitment process at the fair. In conjunction with such a fair, individual companies often hold a reception for interested candidates, which provides the chance for more personal contact and more in-depth information about the company.

A final avenue to reach college students is through faculty members. Although it is sometimes difficult to establish contact with the right faculty member, once the relationship is developed, the faculty member(s) can provide not only names of prospective students, but also in-depth information about them. If a particular university offers a sales or sales management course, the company should attempt to establish contact with the person(s) teaching that course.

A factor of particular importance when recruiting on campuses is the person sent to do the recruiting. Several studies have dealt with the issue of which characteristics are necessary for college recruiters to be effective (Cherrington 1987):

- Recruiters need to demonstrate an interest in and appreciation for students as individuals.
- Recruiters need to show enthusiasm and make the job sound inviting.
- Students seem to prefer recruiters who are between 35 and 55

years of age. Younger recruiters lack credibility in the eyes of students, and older recruiters are not perceived as understanding students.

■■ Effective recruiters take time both to talk and to listen. Students want the opportunity to tell the recruiter what they have to offer and want the chance to find out about the firm.

■■ Effective recruiters build rapport with students. They do not use stress interviews, nor do they try to put students on the spot.

Tools of Recruitment and Selection

The process of recruiting and selecting salespeople can be greatly simplified and improved by using quality instruments and well-designed processes (for a more in-depth discussion, see French, 1990). In general, these must possess three characteristics if they are to be useful:

1. *Validity* has to do with whether the device measures what it is that we want to measure or how well it relates to the requirements of the job.
2. *Reliability* has to do with the consistency or stability of the results. In other words, does the device yield similar results with similar people? Also, do two people who are objectively equal receive a similar evaluation in terms of desirability for hiring?
3. *Job relatedness* has to do with whether the instrument or process is relevant to the job. For example, a typing test has job relatedness for a secretary but not for salespeople.

It is not enough that these characteristics were present when these tools were devised. The sales manager must ensure that the instruments are updated.

Legal Issues

It is virtually impossible for any one individual to understand all the legal ramifications of making a hiring decision. Especially for the sales manager, who has so many other concerns, attempting to keep up with the changing world of equal employment and opportunity is out of the question. This is why companies involve human resources personnel, who have legal expertise in the hiring process. However, there are some basic areas the sales manager must understand that will help prevent problems. Based on the Civil Rights Act of 1964 and other laws that followed it, there are two basic principles for the sales manager to remember when setting out to fill a position.

First, when a plaintiff brings a discrimination charge against a company, he or she is not required to show intention to discriminate, only that the practice has a disproportionate impact on a protected group.

In other words, for a sales manager to plead that there is no intention to discriminate is not a defense in court.

Second, once the impact is demonstrated, the burden of proof shifts from the plaintiff to the defendant (the company). The plaintiff does not need to establish how the discrimination was carried out or who exactly was involved, but only that it took place. After this is done, the defendant must prove that, in fact, discrimination did not take place.

Generally speaking, discrimination against a person because of age, sex, race, national origin, religion, ethnic background, handicaps and so forth, is strictly forbidden. The exception is if the discrimination is justified by business necessity. This exception is referred to as a *bonafide occupational qualification* (BFOQ) (for a further explanation, see Clark and Kinder, 1986). If the requirements of the job necessitate that certain limitations be placed on the type of person who fills it, this constitutes a BFOQ.

It should be noted, however, that in no case has race been found to be a BFOQ, although both age and sex have been. For example, if a dressmaker is looking for models for the spring dress line, he or she can specify that a female model is needed. The dressmaker cannot, however, specify that the model be white or follow a particular religion. If the job requires skill and dexterity levels for purposes of safety, the employer may specify that applicants be below a certain age level.

For instance, an airline company may refuse to hire a pilot who is 60 years of age as a trainee, given the number of years required to become a first officer and the issue of passenger safety. However, the same airline company cannot refuse to hire a person who is female or Asian. In short, a BFOQ is a very restrictive classification and there must be a clear-cut relationship between it and the performance of the job in question.

In general, there almost seem to be more things you cannot ask on an application or in an interview than you can ask. Basically, any question regarding the demographic background of the individual, unless it is related to a BFOQ, is legally suspect. The following are subjects you cannot ask about:

1) Sex
2) Religion

3) Race
4) Ethnic background
5) National origin
6) Type of discharge from the military
7) Arrest record
8) Weight and/or height
9) Credit history
10) Marital status
11) Whether the individual has children
12) Whether the individual is handicapped

It is advisable, if one is unsure about the legality of a particular question, to seek the advice of an expert in EEOC (Equal Employment Opportunity Commission) matters.

Some have attempted to circumvent the law by asking for information indirectly. Also, some have asked discriminatory questions very innocently. The reasoning is that if the interviewer is not directly asking for information concerning the preceding categories, there is no violation of the law. However, remember that the intention to discriminate is not a requisite to being guilty of discrimination. Any attempt to ascertain this information is considered discriminatory, however. The following questions or requests for information would probably be illegal:

Please enclose a photo with the application.
When did you graduate from high school?
What is your hometown?
How old are your kids?
Would your minister mind providing a reference?
Are you planning on getting married anytime soon?
Are you looking forward to Christmas?
What are some of your hobbies?
Do you own or rent your home?
When did you get your honorable discharge?
Please list any arrests you have had along with the reason.
How long have you been in this country?
Will you provide a credit history?

Even though this list might contain some questions that seem innocuous, each is related to some aspect of discrimination. For example, arrest rates are higher among black youths than white, and hence questions about arrests indirectly get at race. The questions about hobbies might be a way of getting at national origin or religion. Certainly, asking about whether one is looking forward to Christmas is a way of finding out about a person's religious preference.

Application Forms

Application forms are used in the vast majority of organizations ` operating today. Given their pervasiveness and that once they are devised they are rarely changed, often the forms are either inappropriate or illegal, or both. Therefore, these forms must be reviewed periodically to ensure that the questions are valid, reliable, job-related, and legal.

The forms usually address four basic areas: Personal data, such as name, address and phone number where the person may be reached, and Social Security Number; education data; experience, including where the applicant has worked and the types of jobs he or she has held; and general health questions. Typically, the applicant is asked to sign the form to verify the accuracy of the information and to allow the company to conduct a background check.

Some companies use a weighted application form in which different pieces of information are given more importance and an overall numerical score is calculated to indicate the relative qualifications of the applicant. This is an attempt to make the selection process more *objective*—to ensure minimal interviewer bias. The usefulness of the weighted form in accomplishing this end is, frankly, questionable.

A well-designed application not only provides information useful in the selection process, but is also useful in the interview. It helps keep the interviewer on track and provides insights into the areas that may need to be probed more deeply. Additionally, it can assist the interviewer in making the applicant feel more relaxed during the interview.

Interviews

The interview is an indispensable part of the recruitment and selection process. The interview process not only acts to verify the information in the application form or resume, it can provide meaningful insight into the candidate as a person. For instance, the interviewer can ask about the person's goals or perhaps what the person has accomplished. This gives a clue to what is important to the individual and provides insight as to whether there is a "fit" between the applicant and the firm. Often the recruiting process involves several interviews. The initial interview is a screening interview, and as the process continues, the interviews become more in-depth and deal with issues that are progressively more pertinent to the job.

There are four general types of interviews. The *structured interview* consists of using a questionnaire with a specific set of questions. Of the following answers, which one describes the major reason you are attracted to sales:

▬ I like to work with people.
▬ I enjoy persuading others to do what I want them to.
▬ The job involves knowing and doing several things.
▬ A person can make a lot of money in sales.
▬ There are always new challenges in sales.

The candidate is read the question and must choose which of the five best tells about him or her. It ensures more consistency than the other types of interviews and does not call for the interviewer skill level of the other approaches. However, it obviously restricts the information received and does not allow any variation in the questions.

The *semistructured interview* consists of the interviewer using a questionnaire with specific questions, but the questions are often open ended and the interviewer has the option of probing more deeply into certain areas depending upon the candidate's response.

What is it about sales that attracts you?

How does a career in sales fit in with your overall goals?

These types of questions allows the candidate to talk more than in the structured interview but guides the direction of what is said. The interviewer must be adept at picking up on information that needs further clarification.

The *unstructured interview* consists of the interviewer asking an open-ended question and allowing the candidate to talk extensively. The interviewer encourages the candidate by active listening and providing occasional feedback. The process provides insight into the candidate's ability to "think on his feet." It often causes discomfort on the part of candidates because they must be able to determine what information is pertinent and present it in a clear fashion. It calls for a high level of expertise on the part of the interviewer. The following are sample questions used in this approach:

Tell me about yourself.

Where do you want to be five years from now?

Obviously, these questions have the potential to yield answers that are fairly far afield of anything to do with sales. However, a skilled interviewer has the ability to focus and direct the interview without taking it over.

The fourth type is the *problem-solving interview,* and it consists of presenting the candidate with an issue or a problem to solve. The candidate goes through the process of resolving the problem and answers questions by the interviewer. In sales, this approach often involves role playing by the candidate during which the candidate is asked to sell a particular item. At times, this takes the form of a stress interview in which the candidate is placed in a problem-solving situation, must devise a solution to the problem, and then must defend the solution. Although this form has been criticized because it creates unproductive stress for the candidate, in general the problem-solving interview has been useful.

Tests

Many types of tests can be used to screen and select candidates:

Aptitude tests examine an individual's capacity to perform a particular type of job or to learn how to perform that job.

Intelligence tests measure the overall mental capacity of the person. These deal with the person's ability at logic and reasoning, use of language and mathematics, and the ability to understand spatial relationships.

Knowledge or proficiency tests assess the amount of information possessed about a subject.

Personality tests attempt to categorize people using a personality profile. They attempt to measure the inherent traits of a person.

Honesty tests attempt to assess the inherent honesty of the individual. These tests attempt to uncover the person's ethical value system and judgment of situations in which honesty is an issue.

Although these tests have often proven to be useful, they are not without problems. There is the underlying legal issue involved with the use of tests: The company must be able to show that performing in a particular fashion on these tests is related to performing well on the job. If this cannot be proven statistically, the test should not be used. Second, a number of court cases have found certain of these tests, particularly intelligence and personality tests, to be discriminatory. A solution is to use a testing service specializing in administering, scoring, and validating these tests. The service has developed the data base necessary to demonstrate the validity and reliability of any test it uses.

It is worthwhile to note that the use of polygraph tests was outlawed by the Employee Polygraph Protection Act of 1988. This outlaws the use of such tests for the purpose of hiring, except for government employees and employees of security firms and pharmaceutical companies. If the firm suspects economic loss because of the actions of its employees, the use of a polygraph is generally acceptable. Some firms attempt to use honesty tests to replace the polygraph; however, the validity of such tests is suspect.

It should be recognized that tests are also limited by the process itself. Candidates, particularly those who have some behavioral science education, can often "knock off" employment tests—they can determine the answers acceptable to the company and simply give these responses rather than what might have been the "true" response.

Reference Checks

Historically, it has been the practice of companies to perform reference checks on prospective employees. It is generally a given that letters of reference come only from persons who are predisposed to give a favorable report of the candidate, and therefore their usefulness has been questioned. However, references often provide insights into just why they think a particular candidate is worth considering.

Although reference checks are sometimes viewed as an "exercise in futility," it is estimated that between 20 and 25 percent of all resumes contain fabrications (French, 1990). It should be recognized that with the growing number of cases in which former employees are successfully suing companies for giving out negative information about them, many firms today only verify dates of employment and job title. The information to be gleaned from reference checks is therefore limited. However, a background check can serve to verify basic information given by the candidate, such as length of employment, the position occupied at a former company, and salary information.

It is also advisable, given the growing number of applicants who indicate they possess a degree, when in fact they do not, that the company request official transcripts from the applicant's university. The reason we specify "official" transcripts is that they are stamped by the registrar's office and are less likely to be forged. Furthermore, it is advisable to obtain a written release from the candidate before checking references.

Physical Examinations

Typically, the final step in the hiring process is a physical examination by a qualified physician. These serve the purpose of screening out employees with health problems that might lead to a high rate of absenteeism. Also, such exams often negate insurance company claims of preexisting conditions should the person have medical problems later. Physical exams, however, are not very good predictors of future health (Cherrington, 1987). As with the other tools of recruitment and selection, physical exams must pass the test of job relatedness.

CHAPTER PERSPECTIVE

Various factors are important to consider in the recruitment and selection process: The traits a firm should consider when hiring salespeople and the various issues that affect the process. A number of pitfalls are related to the process of seeking out and hiring prospective salespeople, and there is no sure fire method of doing so with 100 percent success. However, if the company carefully reviews what it needs in a salesperson, attempts to seek out this type of person in the appropriate places, and uses up-to-date approaches to screening, the chance of success is greatly enhanced. Hiring is a mine field, and only by careful attention to details can a manager avoid making a serious mistake.

REFERENCES

Cherrington, David J. (1987), *Personnel Management,* Dubuque, IA: William C. Brown Publishers.

Clark, Lawrence S., and Peter D. Kinder (1986), *Law and Business,* New York: McGraw-Hill Book Company.

French, Wendell L. (1990), *Human Resources Management,* Boston: Houghton Mifflin Company.

Greenberg, Herbert M., and Jeanne Greenberg (1983), "Job Matching for Better Performance," *Harvard Business Review,* 58(Sept.-Oct.), 128-133.

Korschun, Alan M. (1982), "Success Is Only One Degree Away," *American Statesman,* 27, 13-16.

Lamont, Lawrence M., and William J. Lundstrom (1977), "Identifying Successful Industrial Salesmen by Personality and Personal Characteristics," *Journal of Marketing Researeh,* 14(Nov.), 517-529.

McCollough, Rose V. (1979), "Evaluate Your Sales Personality," *Rough Notes,* 122(June), 80-86.

Plotkin, Harris M. (1986), "Taking the Guesswork out of Hiring Successful Salespeople," *Sales and Marketing Management,* (Dec.), 72-73.

Raphel, Murray (1981), "Ten Characteristics of Top Salesmen," *Direct Marketing* (Nov.-Dec.), 102-103, 121.

Smith, Fran (1979), "The Profile of a Successful Salesperson," *Sales & Marketing Management in Canada* (July-August), 14-15.

The Organizational Buyer and the Buying Process

INTRODUCTION AND MAIN POINTS

Salespeople who will continue to enjoy success are those who understand buyers and buying organizations. Buyers and buying organizations are those people within a company who are in charge of procuring the products necessary to operate an organization. In the past, organizational buyers were viewed as "cogs in the wheel" who followed the "rational" approach to buying decisions: The thought that buyers invariably made choices based on a set of established criteria, buying at the lowest price. In reality, buying organizations and individual buyers had little impact on buying decisions, and they were viewed as mechanics.

Today, it is more accurate to say that the buying process is a rationalized process. In other words, buyers are given guidelines on carrying out their jobs, but like salespeople, they are increasingly professional in their orientation and today enjoy a fair amount of latitude in their buying decisions. Buyers are people too, and subject to many of the same influences affecting consumers. The successful salesperson recognizes this and acts accordingly.

After reading the material in this chapter:

■ You will understand the human factors that affect the buying decision.

■ You will understand the organizational factors affecting the decision and how they influence it. You will appreciate the organizational buying process and how this process varies among different organizations.

■ You will be able to segment the organizational market based on the unique characteristics of the organization.

FACTORS AFFECTING ORGANIZATIONAL BUYER BEHAVIOR

At any given time, organizational buyers are affected by a number of internal and external factors. External forces have an impact on internal forces. In turn, these directly influence buyer behavior. These forces are interrelated and dynamic.

Internal Forces

The internal forces that affect buyer behavior include factors that shape thoughts and actions. These internal forces develop over a person's life and are dynamic. The salesperson must recognize that buyers' decisions are based on complex web of influences that may change over time.

Organizational buyers make purchasing decisions to satisfy their own needs and those of the organization. This is important because salespeople often assume that all they need to address are organizational needs, such as providing a product that meets a particular set of specifications. (The assumption is that if they meet these needs, they will get the order.)

Although a firm's needs determine the type of product and a general set of suppliers, the buyer's needs decide which specific vendors are asked to offer a quote. For example, when the buyer purchases a lathe for a specific manufacturing application, the lathe meets the needs of the company for precise metal fabrication. However, the buyer decides on a particular vendor because that supplier is reliable and offers a reasonable price.

An organizational buyer is usually not noticed until something goes wrong. Generally, the buyer is not rewarded for taking risks even if those risks save the company money. In this case, personal need is the avoidance of risk and the buyer is likely to stay with the supplier representing the lowest risk. The salesperson whose company is the "new kid on the block" must not only provide a good product and price, but also must overcome buyer hesitation.

Another internal force is *personality*. When a salesperson faces a buyer, he or she must recognize that the personality of the buyer determines: The type of information that is important for a decision to be made; how that information will be processed; and the readiness to make a purchasing decision.

Only by understanding personality does the salesperson avoid taking the wrong approach with a particular buyer. Schiffman and Kanuk (1991, p. 100) define personality as "those inner psychological characteristics that both determine and reflect how a person responds to his or her environment." Personality makes us act in a reasonably consistent fashion.

In the organizational setting, buyers learn not only from past experience but also from other buyers, supervisors, and even salespeople. Learning about a supplier sometimes begins even before the first contact by a salesperson. *Learning* is the manner in which our thoughts, beliefs, and attitudes are shaped. Individuals continually learn. The reputation of the supplier and other people's experience powerfully shape the image a buyer holds of a company. When the buyer has no previous knowledge of a vendor, the initial contact by a salesperson forms the framework in which learning takes place.

First impressions are important because when a person is faced with a new situation, that person goes through the *associative thinking process,* the process of making sense of a new situation and making a value judgment by recalling similar incidents or situations from the past. The person, either consciously or subconsciously, asks, "What have I seen like this before?" If the association is positive, there is a tendency to have a positive view of the person and the company.

For the salesperson, *impression formation,* or helping the buyer to form the correct perception, is important. We are often tempted to think that if we are doing a good job, this is enough, and customers should realize we are doing a good job for them. However, a "good job" is often not noticed until it is not done. Salespeople must do a good job, but they should also let the buyer know what a good job they are doing. This does not mean the salesperson should brag, as though the customer is privileged to do business with this party. It does mean that salespeople show concern for the customer, that they should conduct themselves professionally, follows up on orders, and pay attention to details.

Attitude is the element that directs us to think and react in a particular fashion. In the words of Schiffman and Kanuk (1991, p. 227), "... attitude is a learned predisposition to behave in a consistently favorable or unfavorable way with respect to a given object. In other words, attitude guides our reaction to a given object, idea, person, or activity. Attitude can be thought of as setting the boundaries of our reaction to a particular situation.

Another internal force is *motive.* For the professional buyer, motives are usually external: They need to make a purchase. What may not be as readily evident is that the decision about who to buy from is also affected by motive. In other words, a salesperson must be aware that often there are more reasons not to buy from a given source than to buy from that source. The salesperson must continually provide the buyer with reasons to choose his or her company. Although some argue that attitudes and motives are the same, they are different. Attitudes create a predisposition to act or behave in a certain way; motives provide the reason for acting. Often, "out of sight, out of mind" is the prevailing rule, no matter how professional the buyer.

External Forces

The external forces specific to an organization are types of organizations, organizational culture, and buying situation.

Types of Organizations

Although it is perhaps overly simplistic, organizations can be classified into three major groups: Commercial, governmental, and institutional. Each of these can be further subdivided into more specific groups.

Commercial Organizations are defined as those organizations that exist to make a profit. The operation of their business depends on achieving a return on their investments and, generally, a primary concern is the allocation of resources to obtain the best possible return. In general, a guiding principle is the efficient use of funds. Although commercial organizations share some common characteristics, there are three types, and each has some unique properties. Users purchase a product for the purpose of using it in the operation of their business. These items become part of overhead—the cost of doing business. When an organization buys the product as a user, cost is a primary concern. By cost we mean not only the money it takes to buy the item, but other costs associated with it, such as opportunity costs. The salesperson must be able to justify the cost to the buyer in terms of how this purchase decision will contribute to the firm's efficient operation.

Producers purchase a product to include it in whatever they are producing. If the producer is a manufacturer, the product may be a component part or raw material. If the producer is a construction firm, the product may be a building material. The items producers buy represent direct costs. Certainly the cost of the item is a concern, but for the producer quality is likely to be the major consideration. This is true because customers will blame the producer if the product fails or, conversely, praise the producer if it works. Customers may recognize that the producer did not actually make all the components that are part of its products; however, that is of little comfort if the product fails. The producer, then, recognizes that its product is "only as strong as its weakest part."

The job of the salesperson in this case is to help the buyer to determine not only what component part will perform the function needed, but also how the buyer's product is positioned in the market in terms of quality. The salesperson must then offer a product that provides appropriate quality at the best possible price.

Additionally, when the salesperson is selling to a producer, he or she needs to understand the production process and what approach the producer wishes to take in terms of stocking that component. With more producers adopting versions of JIT systems, the salesperson who is able to adapt to the delivery needs of the customer will be successful.

Resellers buy products to resell them. Included in this group are both wholesalers and retailers. Resellers view themselves as purchasing agents for their customers, and, therefore, their main goal is to provide what their customers need and want. Resellers are concerned with margin and turnover. The salesperson, in this case, must be knowledgeable enough of the resellers' customers and be able to show that the product will justify the allocation of shelf space in terms of margin and turnover.

Governmental Organizations are the next major category of organizations. Although it might be instructive to discuss the different types of governments, given the limitations on space, our discussion will be about governments in general. Whereas commercial organizations are profit-driven, government organizations could be said to be budget-driven. Government organizations exist for the purpose of serving the public and, hence, are supported by the public through taxes. Their revenues do not result from the profit created through enterprise, which is only restricted by the success of the enterprise. Their revenues flow from the public's ability and willingness to pay taxes. Given that both ability and willingness are limited, governments are limited in the amount of revenue to which they have access. The budget, then, becomes the guidance mechanism.

The salesperson's job in dealing with governments is somewhat different than when selling to commercial organizations. The salesperson must keep abreast of the purchasing procedures of the government and ensure that his or her organization is in full compliance with those procedures. Governments generally use a formalized bidding process; therefore, price is again a major factor. Perhaps almost as important is ensuring that the product conforms to government specifications and is delivered in the time promised. Failure to deliver on time often results in the cancellation of orders, and sometimes, in the assessment of a penalty.

Institutional Organizations, like governments, tend to be budget-driven. Institutions are constrained by their funding agencies. Because institutions, like governments, tend to be rather bureaucratic, they often have fairly strict procedures to follow. So, one of the salesperson's responsibilities involves ensuring compliance with procedures.

Institutions are unique in that often purchase decisions are made by people considered to be professionals, but who are not experts in purchasing. This means that the salespersons must convey that they are knowledgeable and be able to communicate on a professional level if they are to gain the trust and respect of the professional. The salesperson, however, must not ignore the buyer during the selling process.

Organizational Culture

Organizational culture is an external element that determines the "atmosphere" within which the buyer operates. Some organizations have rigid structures with specific procedures and demand a particular approach to decision making. Others are much less formal and the approach to decision making is fluid. The salesperson who adapts this approach to the particular culture is more successful than one who does not.

Buying Situation

By *buying situation* we mean the various characteristics of a given purchase. Purchases fall into three types (for a full explanation, see Robinson et al., 1967):

1) *Straight rebuy:* The item being purchased is bought on a repetitive basis. There is little or no searching on the part of the buyer, and few people are involved.

2) *Modified rebuy:* The item has been modified or is no longer available from old sources. More searching behavior and possibly more people are involved in the process.

3) *New task purchase:* The item is either completely changed or is entirely new. This involves the determination of specifications and extensive searching on the part of the buyer. Generally, several persons are involved in the buying process.

Another aspect of the buying situation is the composition of the group of people who have an impact on the buying decision. This group of people collectively is the *buying center*. The buying center typically consists of six roles:

1) *The initiator:* Detects the need for a purchase and begins the process, such as a shop foreman.
2) *The influencer:* Has an impact on the decision process because of specialized information; for example, an engineer.
3) *The gatekeeper:* Controls the flow of information and/or access to others in the organization; such as a secretary.
4) *The decider:* Actually makes the final decision on what to buy or from whom to buy, for example, the vice president of purchasing.
5) *The buyer:* Actually issues the purchase order.
6) *The user:* Makes use of the item purchased, either using it in the operation of the firm or adding it to the product being produced; that is, maintenance personnel or machinists.

The salesperson must recognize that each person within the buying center has different concerns. The salesperson must address the concerns of each member of this buying center. In the purchase of a major piece of machining equipment for a manufacturing company, for instance, not only is the buyer involved but the firm may also assign a mechanical engineer to incorporate the machine into operations and to work with the supplier.

During the vendor selection process, this engineer is interested in the technical aspects of the equipment and plays the part of influencer. The vice president of finance may also be involved and makes the ultimate decision about whether the firm can financially justify the purchase. This person may be interested in the life cycle costing of the equipment and in the payoff period. In this case, the end user is the shop foreman, who wants to know how the machine operates, how efficient it is, and how much downtime can be expected. The salesperson must work with the buyer, who controls the access to each of these other people.

Salespeople often make two mistakes in this situation. The first is to assume that if he or she puts together a packet of materials for each member of the buying center, the buyer will deliver the material in such a way as to get the attention it deserves. This is not true because *buyers are not salespeople!*

The salesperson should try to get direct access to each member of the buying center. Unfortunately, this often leads to the second mistake: The salesperson bypasses the buyer in the process. Buyers are protective of their turf and they have a right to be. When a purchase is made and something goes wrong with the product, the buyer will probably take the blame, regardless of how much he was involved. Salespeople often try to circumvent the buyer. The salesperson's assumption is that the buyer performs only a mechanical function. If a decision is made by "higher-ups," the buyer acts passively. In reality, there are dozens of ways the buyer can affect the decision even after the purchase is "settled." If a buyer feels cut out of the process, the effect generally is negative. Even if the buyer proceeds with the purchase in accordance with the wishes of superiors, the relationship between the buyer and the salesperson may be spoiled and future dealings may be impossible.

The Organizational Purchasing Process

The purchasing process basically involves six steps. These are depicted in Figure 3-1. The figure shows a generalized purchasing process model. This model depicts the purchasing for a new task of perhaps a modified rebuy purchase. Obviously, the process will vary depending on the type of purchase. The process begins with the recognition of a need.

In different organizations and with different purchasing situations, the manner in which needs are recognized will vary. Purchasing organizations today make heavy use of computers in the purchasing process (Jackson and Pride, 1986). In many manufacturing organizations, the computer keeps track of inventory level and scheduling, and when stock levels reach a certain point, the computer notifies the materials control department. In some cases, the need is formally recognized with the signing of a contract for a product or construction project. In this case, often a person in the engineering or in the drafting department completes a material take-off, i.e., a list of items needed to complete the product or project.

The second step in the process is developing a set of specifications for the product to be purchased and issuance of a requisition. If the need arises as the result of a stock-out, the specifications are already spelled out, and do not require development. However, with a new task or modified rebuy purchase, the development of specifications can be a very involved process, calling on people from engineering, production, purchasing, and marketing. Once the requisition is drawn up, it is forwarded to the purchasing department.

The third step in the process involves selecting vendors from which to request quotations and sending out the Request for Quotation (RFQ). Just as the process of developing specifications will vary with the type of purchase, so too will the extent of search behavior required by the buyer.

Increasingly, firms use formalized Approved Vendor Lists (AVLs) from which suppliers must be drawn. When extended search behavior is required by the buyer, suppliers names must be readily available to the buyer. Buyers make heavy use of such sources as the Thomas Register (Jackson and Pride, 1986).

Professional directories such as these and ads in trade publications provide leads for the selling firm and thereby supplement the sales effort. When the buyer does not need to engage in extended search behavior, the task of the selling organization is to not only be included on the AVL, but also to make sure that the customer associates the firm with a reasonably high level of service.

FIGURE 3-1
STEPS IN THE PURCHASING PROCESS

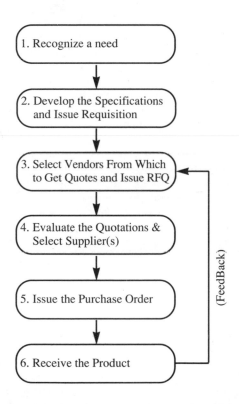

Evaluation of the quotations and the selection of supplier(s) is the next step in the process. Although price is probably the main determinant at this point, other factors are also important. The promised delivery date and quality are often as critical as the price and, at times, each of these will serve as major criteria. Other factors, such as payment and delivery, are evaluated because they represent a cost for the buyer's firm.

As mentioned earlier, the importance of the criteria vary from company to company and in different purchasing situations. At this point, the salesperson's role is extremely critical. The sales job takes on a different purpose. Until this time, the sales message revolved around the reliability of the supplier and its products, and the object was to convince the buyer that he or she needs what the salesperson has to offer. At this juncture, however, the selling job becomes one of arriving at mutually acceptable terms.

The buyer is already convinced that a need exists for the salesperson's product, and must now be convinced that the best possible terms have been offered. Buyers understand the selling firm must make a profit; however, their job is to see that the profit is reasonable and that the purchase contributes toward the goals of their firm.

Placement of the purchase order is the next step in the process. This is generally a fairly mechanical one. The ease with which this is accomplished directly relates to the quality of the quotations supplied by the selected vendor. By this we mean that errors often arise at this point because a clause is not properly spelled out in the RFQ and is subject to misinterpretation. Although the buyer should catch any discrepancy, it is typically a buying clerk who actually types the purchase order. This person may not be familiar enough with the genesis of the order to know when mistakes are present. Buyers generally have a tremendous amount of work to do and sometimes miss details that may be important later.

The final step in the process involves receipt of the material. Although many salespersons consider the sale closed when they receive the purchase order, the buyer does not consider the sale closed until the product is received in good order and at the right time. Monitoring the order and a follow-up phone call will go a long way toward cementing the relationship between the buyer and the seller. The information received concerning conformity to specifications, quality, and the condition of product received—and whether the order was received on schedule—provides feedback for the buyers and affects decisions concerning the selection of vendors from which to solicit quotations in the future.

CHAPTER PERSPECTIVE

The major influences affecting the organizational buyer and the buying process interact to determine the outcome of a given purchase decision. Astute salespeople need not be psychologists or experts in purchasing, but they must be aware of the complex nature of organizational buying. The salesperson must be able to relate to the buyer, empathize, and be flexible enough to meet the needs of the buyer insofar as possible. In short, the salesperson's principal job is to solve the problems of the buyer.

REFERENCES

Jackson, Ralph W. (1988), "The Effect of Approved Vendors Lists on Industrial Marketing," in Arch G. Woodside (ed.), *Advances in Business Marketing,* Vol. 3, 79-94.

Jackson, Ralph W., and William M. Pride (1986), "The Use of Approved Vendors Lists," *Industrial Marketing Management,* Vol. 15, 165-169.

Robinson, Patrick J., Charles W. Faris, and Yoram Wind (1967), *Industrial Buying and Creative Marketing,* Boston, MA: Allyn & Bacon, Inc.

Schiffman, Leon G., and Leslie L. Kanuk (1991), *Consumer Behavior,* Englewood Cliffs, NJ: Prentice-Hall, Inc.

Communication in Sales

INTRODUCTION AND MAIN POINTS

Since the beginning of time, human beings have interacted. It seems that at some point people would have learned how to communicate, yet we know that one of the most difficult things for people to do is to express themselves precisely. Sales is a process of communication that involves informing, persuading, and reminding. Communication is a two-way process that involves not only speaking but also listening. An assumption often made about the sales profession is that the successful salesperson is the one who is a "good talker," who has developed storytelling to an art. It may be true that speaking helps a person communicate effectively, but this is not the premier skill in communication. In fact, speaking is less important than listening. Even if we train someone to speak well, this person will not communicate effectively if he or she does not develop other skills necessary to the complex process of communication.

Communication is the drive gear of effective selling. The drive gear has five spokes (see Figure 4-1):

1) State the message clearly.
2) Listen to the customer.
3) Observe the surroundings.
4) Ask open-ended questions.
5) Present the product.

Each of these spokes has its part in the sales process, and all are important, but those that help the salesperson better understand and relate to the customer are often the most neglected and perhaps the most critical in successful selling.

After reading the material in this chapter:

■ You will understand that communication is a complex process of conveying meaning.

■ You will understand the different ways in which people communicate.

FIGURE 4-1
Communication: The Drive Gear of Personal Selling

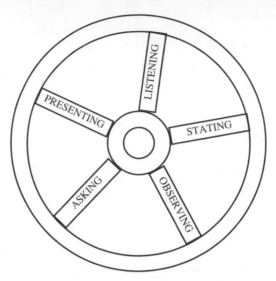

━━ You will recognize that a number of skills are required to communicate effectively.

━━ You will be able to develop strategies for communicating with customers and subordinates.

COMMUNICATION INVOLVES THE VERBAL AND THE NONVERBAL

A wise person once stated, "Words don't mean, people do." Communication is the process of conveying a message from one person or group to another. The message can include facts, feelings, beliefs, desires, and fears. The message a person wants to give to another first exists as a mental image. It is impossible to convey this raw mental image directly to the other person, so the person who wishes to transmit this message must translate it into symbols that he or she believes the other will understand. These symbols can be generally classified as:

1) Words
2) Objects
3) Actions

Less than half of our communication is through the written or spoken word. Even though words are not used as often as non-verbal communication (objects and actions), we sometimes make the implicit assumption that they are the most precise mean of communicating. However, when one considers the connotations that words may acquire over time or the different uses of words in different parts of the country, the precision of words quickly comes into question. For example, the simple word *dog* has a number of different meanings, both good and bad. It can mean the mammal considered "man's best friend." Used as a colloquial expression, it can also mean a car that does not run well, a poorly performing stock, a mechanical device for holding something, or an ugly person.

Even when both parties in the conversation know we are using *dog* to mean the mammal, this can represent something different to each. For the person who likes dogs, the image is positive, but if the other person does not like dogs, the image is very different. If we move outside our culture, the differences may be even more pronounced and cause problems in communication.

Objects have always been used to convey meaning. The king's scepter and robe convey authority. Even the automobile, which was developed as a means of efficient and effective transportation, is also a means to convey status. In the business world, we read such books as *Dress for Success* because we recognize the power of clothes to communicate status. Often, by observing the trappings of a person's office, we can learn a great deal about the individual because people tend to surround themselves with items that enhance their sense of identity.

Actions are an important part of the communication process. Within the word actions we include gestures, facial expressions, body language, and nonverbal sounds. Certain actions, such as "thumbing a ride," have very specific meaning in our culture. Actions often are used to supplement the meanings of words. For example, if a person has a smirk on his face as he says, "I sure like the way he handled that problem!," this completely alters the meaning. The speaker's smirk deliberately altered the meaning of his words. Many times, however, we do not consciously control our actions and yet these still convey meaning.

The salesperson needs to recognize the power of symbolic communication. Not only what the salesperson says, but how it is said communicates a message to a customer, and vice versa. The communication process involves not only speaking and hearing what another says, but also observing what is done.

THE COMMUNICATION PROCESS IN PERSONAL SELLING

For a more accurate picture of communication in the personal selling situation, the classic model needs modification. The *source* has a piece of information to convey. The person must *encode* the information, put it into a form that is transmittable. The appropriate *medium* is selected to convey the encoded information. The *receiver* must then *decode* the information, or, translate it into something meaningful. The classic model includes a feedback loop in which the receiver conveys a reaction to the source. "Noise" can affect the process at any point along the way and can distort the message if the noise level is high enough.

Also in this model are fields of experience and the common field. The *field of experience* has to do with an individual's sociopsychological background. Background is unique to every individual and forms the basis of his or her personality and outlook on life. When fields of experience overlap there is a common field and the possibility for effective communication and interaction. The greater this overlap—the larger this common field—the more easily two persons or groups communicate. Salespeople cannot possibly have a large common field with all the clients with whom they interact, but the more they understand the existence of individual fields of experience and the more this understanding is incorporated into the selling experience, the more effective they will be in selling.

Listening as a Selling Skill

People often act as though they communicate only when speaking. The inference is that listening is passive. If communication is a two-way process, however, listening should also be considered active. Typically we assume that speaking is the more difficult of the two skills to master, and often we erroneously believe that listening is something we do naturally.

Why do people not listen better than they do? First, in reality, listening is hard work. When a person "actively listens," his or her metabolic processes increase slightly, causing a slight rise in body temperature, and the pupils of the eyes tend to dilate slightly. This indicates that real listening is anything but passive. A person who truly listens pays close attention to what is conveyed and provides the speaker with affirmation that he or she is tuned into what is being said.

People often use the time when they are not speaking to "rest" and simply act as though they are listening: They look at the other person, nod their heads, and may even give some verbal indication that they understand, when in reality they are rehearsing what they are going to say next or thinking about a discussion they had that morning. Active listening means concentrating, and concentrating is hard work.

A second reason salespeople fail to listen well is because they feel uncomfortable when not talking. Salespeople often contend that they do not want to "lose control of the interview." They feel that if they are not speaking, they are not selling, and that they need to provide the buyer with as much information as possible in order to sell the product.

Recently, one of the authors was shopping for a whirlpool spa for his home. He had done some preliminary research about the product and was trying to evaluate different brands. At one outlet, he encountered a salesperson who, in response to a specific question, spoke nonstop for fifteen minutes, explaining the features of various models. After a couple of attempts at posing the question in other ways, the author decided to observe this salesperson to see what would happen. At the end of the spiel, the salesperson asked if he had any questions. The only one the author had (yet refrained from asking), was whether the salesperson thought he had delivered an effective presentation.

The need for providing adequate information is paramount, but salespeople, particularly new salespeople, often attempt a *core dump,* that is, to give the customer all the information the sellers possess about a product. The fear is that if they fail to do so, an important fact will be omitted. In discussing the attributes that distinguish good from average and poor salespeople, sales managers from a variety of companies overwhelmingly indicate that *listening* is the key skill. Sales managers need to train salespeople to listen well in addition to training them to make presentations.

Elements in Active Listening
There are two basic elements in active listening:

1) *Paraphrasing* summarizes the speaker's expressed thoughts, as they were understood by the listener, or puts what the speaker has said into the listener's own words. It often begins with phrases like "I hear you saying that..." and "So, in your opinion..."

2) *Perception checking* describes what the listener perceives to be the unspoken feelings (emotions) or wants of the speaker. This description is offered tentatively and nonevaluatively. It often begins with phrases like: "I get the impression that..." and "It sounds like you felt..."

Both elements are important for a variety of reasons. First, they enable the salesperson to understand what the buyer is really attempting to convey. Again, "words don't mean, people do." *Active listening* provides the salesperson with either new information or confirmation of information already gathered. Paraphrasing helps the listener ensure that he or she understands what has just been said.

If the listener summarizes the information incorrectly, the speaker seldom fails to correct the impression. Perception checking helps the listener to go beyond what is being said to what the listener believes the speaker thinks. Often, the speaker either is hesitant to say what is really being thought or has been unable to put those feelings into words.

In addition to helping the salesperson ensure that he or she understands what the customer is communicating, active listening helps to *earn the right to speak* and to have the customer listen to what the salesperson has to say. Every effective salesperson believes that, given the chance for a complete hearing of the facts, the product can be sold. Salespeople who are so intent on what they have to say and who exclude listening to what the customers say, short-circuit the sales process and make it harder on themselves.

Open-Ended Questions

One of the spokes on the gear of communication is the *open-ended question*. We specify the open-ended question as opposed to a yes-no format because it invites the customer to provide more complete information. A question like, "How well does your current system allow you to make adaptations in the product?" invites the customer to provide extra information. Often the additional information gleaned through open-ended questions is more important than the information originally sought. Additionally, this approach tends to create a more relaxed atmosphere, putting the customer more at ease. Yes-no questions, on the other hand, make the interview sound like an interrogation.

Often salespeople ask yes-no questions because they think they are open ended. For example, the question, "Does your current system allow you to make adaptations in the product?" is an open-ended question stated in a yes-no format. Some people take great delight in answering such a question with a simple yes or no, knowing well that the salesperson intended it to be open ended. They particularly enjoy engaging in this sport with new salespeople, especially when the sales manager is with them.

Stating the Message

Although we have spent a great deal of space discussing the importance of listening and understanding the customer, being able to present material in a cogent and concise manner is also a critical factor in successful selling. (The art of the sales presentation is discussed in detail in Chapter 7.) Doing so requires a few key elements:

- Know beforehand what information is important to the buyer.
- Determine the most effective order of presentation.
- Devise an approach to which the buyer can relate.
- Speak to the buyer, not over or around the party.
- Tie together the elements of the message.

It is important to remember that every day the buyer is bombarded by a tremendous number of sales and promotional messages. The buyer also faces the same "story" from every salesperson:

Our company is the best.
Our products are the finest.
Our prices are the lowest.
We love you the most!

Think about what your salespeople can do to stand out from the others and still deliver the right message to the buyer. This is where creativity comes into play.

The salesperson who is able to paint "word pictures" for the buyer conveys information much more effectively than the person who simply states facts. This does not mean that the salesperson should have the ability to "turn a phrase," but rather the salesperson should recognize that there are various ways one can say something and do so in an interesting fashion.

Effective Approaches to Presentations

Confucius is purported to have said:

I hear and I forget,
I see and I remember,
I do and I understand.

This truth certainly applies to a selling situation because it represents "awareness progression." As a person moves from hearing to seeing to doing, that person moves to a greater level of awareness.

The effective sales presentation incorporates this *awareness progression* and includes the following elements:

- State the sales message effectively and appropriately.
- Use sales aids, such as pictures, written testimonials, and

charts.

▬ Include, when possible, a demonstration of the product, benefit, and/or concepts.

Presentations represent the salesperson's chance to build a case for the company and the products. The best way to obtain and hold the buyer's interest is to involve the buyer in the process. The buyer becomes part of the presentation. It is no longer the salesperson's words, but rather the buyer's own experience, that contributes to the persuasive content of the presentation.

What Buyers Buy

One of the most important lessons for any salesperson to remember is that "People buy benefits, not features." Often the salesperson is tempted to dwell on the technical aspects of the product, but buyers make purchases based on what the product or the company can do for them and their organizations.

There are three elements in any product purchased (see Figure 4-2). The *core product* consists of the benefits the product represents for the buyer. These are the reasons the person decides to buy. Charles Revson, founder of Revlon, said it this way: "In the factory we make cosmetics, in the drugstores we sell hope."

An effective salesperson understands the complexity of the product's benefits to the buyer and sets out to communicate these benefits because they are the basis of the purchasing decision. The statement, "The fans on our heat exchangers have fiberglass blades and use gear drives" contains some interesting facts, but does not list any benefits. "Because of the components we use in the fans on our heat exchangers, they have a longer life and operate more efficiently than competing brands" presents a benefit that forms the basis for a buying decision.

The *formal product* is the actual product being purchased. As shown in Figure 4-2, it includes the brand, style, options. In the presentation, the salesperson should discuss the features and advantages of the product with the prospect. However, these must be tied to the benefits they offer. If not, they become a litany of facts and figures that does little to persuade the customer that one product offers more than another. Develop a visual prop that delineates the advantages and features of the product and links these to a set of benefits for the customer.

The *ancillary product* is the element of the product that helps the buyer better use the product. It includes warranty, installation, service packages, and financing. These may seem minor at first, but they are often the only real difference between various com-

FIGURE 4-2
What People Buy

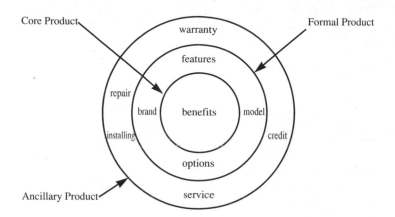

peting products. For example, both Whirlpool and Kenmore washers and driers are manufactured by Whirlpool. Given that people generally prefer to buy the national brand product rather than a private brand, it would seem that Whirlpool would be the unit of choice. However, people often prefer to buy the Kenmore precisely because of the ancillary products, such as credit and delivery. Sears has successfully built a major portion of its business around the ancillary product. Salespeople need to understand the role of ancillary products in the buyer's decision process and communicate the ancillary elements of their own products.

These three elements form what we call the product. Each has a place in the buyer's decision. Effectively communicating about the product requires that the salesperson break the product down into these elements and deal with each separately.

CHAPTER PERSPECTIVE
Given that sales is principally a communication process, a thorough understanding of the process is essential. Communication is the symbolic conveyance of meaning. Symbols can take the form of words, objects, and actions. Some contend that about 60 percent of our communication is nonverbal, so the last two types of symbols are much more important than we might at first think. It is important for the salesperson to understand the buyer's frame of reference so that he or she can facilitate the communication process.

Often, when people think of the communication process in sales, they only consider the speaking side of communication. In reality, probably the most important part of the process is effective listening. While this is contrary to the stereotype of salespeople, and probably contrary to selling historically, listening is nonetheless emerging as the chief skill in sales.

In addition to listening, the chapter discussed the importance of careful observation in gaining an understanding of the buyer. Finally, when a salesperson engages the buyer in a sales presentation, he or she must remember that the product is not simply what is picked up off the shelf, but rather a complex of benefits, features and options. To communicate in such a way that the buyer listens, the salesperson should speak of the needs that the company and its products provide. As salespeople approach the selling process, one of the goals should be effective communication, which is more than simply being able to speak well.

Prospecting for Potential Sales

CHAPTER 5

INTRODUCTION AND MAIN POINTS

Selling requires that a salesperson develop a systematic approach adapted to each customer type and situation. This chapter deals with one of the most important, yet unrewarding, parts of this approach—prospecting. If a salesperson wants to increase and, more importantly, maintain sales volume, new customers must continually be identified and sold. More time is needed for prospecting than for any other step in selling.

After reading this chapter:

■ You will be able to identify a prospect.

■ You will learn how to use different prospecting methods and strategies.

■ You will learn about the variety of information sources.

■ You will learn how to turn a lead into a prospect.

GENERAL ROLE OF PROSPECTING

As is indicated in Figure 5-1, the selling process is composed of a series of seven steps, modified for each client: Prospecting, preapproach, sales presentation, handling objections, closing the sale, and servicing after the sale.

Prospecting, the act of obtaining the names of potential customers, receives little attention. Although prospecting does not result in immediate sales, without it new customers cannot be located and future sales cannot be made to replace lost or decreasing sales.

Good prospects are found by *qualifying leads* from a variety of sources, deciding their prospects on the basis of need, ability to purchase, and authority to purchased. When purchasing, a salesperson groups prospects based on relevant demographic information in terms of their potential to buy.

FIGURE 5-1
The Stages in the Selling Process

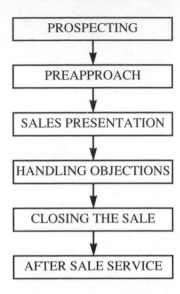

Needs and Wants

Sometimes a salesperson is so involved with the products offered by the company, with meeting sales quotas, or obtaining new customers that the salesperson thinks the product can be sold to everyone. Trying to sell a product or service to someone who does not need it is always a waste of time and effort. (This does not refer to those special times when a salesperson is able to help a person recognize a hidden need that can be fulfilled by the purchase.) Not only is selling products to people who do not need or want them difficult and futile, it violates the basic rule in selling: Customer satisfaction. A salesperson needs to employ the *going concern concept*—continually selling products and services to a satisfied customer so the customer buys again and again.

One way to probe for additional information to generate leads in a selected target group and identify the best prospects for receiving a sales call is *telemarketing*. Given the increasingly high costs of a sales call, telemarketing is being used more and more for this purpose, as well as for actually making the sale.

Identify Those Who Make the Buying Decision

Particularly in industrial sales, it is important for the sales person to identify as early as possible the person or persons in the organization able to make the purchasing decision. It is important to avoid making presentations to people who do not have either the authority or the influence to purchase. Most high-priced industrial sales are decided by a committee of people and involve several people's opinions. The salesperson must make sure everyone involved in the decision process has the necessary information.

For a piece of machinery, such as a bumper welder, the machine operator needs to know the characteristics of operating the machine—for example, its output and ease of operation. At the same time, the plant manager needs to know the relationship of the output of the machine to other aspects of production, the rate of output and the efficiency of the machine, and the way the machine fits into the esthetics of the assembly area. The vice president of production needs to know the efficiency rate and cost per unit of output versus those achieved by other machines. All three individuals need specific information tailored to their area of responsibility for the machine to be the one chosen among alternatives.

Even at the consumer goods level, as in the purchase of a durable good such as carpeting, a purchasing decision can involve several individuals. One partner may decide the color and texture of the carpet and the other the brand to be purchased.

Resources to Make Purchase

When loans and credit are difficult or costly to obtain or during a recession, it is particularly important that the prospect, whether a company or an individual, has the resources to make the purchase. Banks, the Better Business Bureau, other customers, and local credit agencies can provide information on the prospect's financial condition and can indicate any problems previously encountered with late or lack of payment. For most corporations, Dun and Bradstreet can provide information at a reasonable cost on the financial condition of a prospect. Early knowledge of the financial condition of a prospect can allow the salesperson to prepare in advance alternative means of purchase, such as leasing or credit terms, either from the company or from an outside financial institution.

PROSPECTING METHODS

Many different methods of prospecting are listed in Table 5-1. The most commonly used methods include centers of influence,

TABLE 5-1
Prospecting Methods

- Advertising
- Centers of Influence
- Chain of Leads
- Cold Canvassing
- Contests
- Directories and Mailing Lists
- Group Plans
- Information Exchange
- Internal Records
- Observation
- Service Personnel
- Spotters
- Trade Shows

information exchange, trade shows, contests, directories, and mailing lists, even though each of the other methods can also yield good prospects.

Advertising
Amazingly, many companies do not follow up on inquiries by telephone or letter from those interested in the company or its products and services. Every inquiry a company receives should receive *follow-up attention* because these inquiries may become its best prospects. Not responding to inquiries amounts to ignoring a potential customer. A company must establish a systematic approach to handling these inquiries. A typical company approach is to have the telemarketing staff respond to each inquiry and immediately pass the information on to a salesperson in that territory.

Centers of Influence
Contacts at clubs and organizations are one of the best methods for obtaining leads and prospects. Membership in centers of influence—country clubs, fraternal or sororal organizations, service organizations, and professional groups—provide the opportunity to meet various people in a geographic area who, if not prospects themselves, may identify people who are. One professional group every salesperson should join is the local chapter of the American Marketing Association.

In some areas of the country, such as the Southwest, "tips clubs" are popular. The goal of this group, which meets once a month, is to get business leads (tips) from others in the club. Being a member of the local Rotary or the Kiwanis Club is another good method of obtaining leads or prospects. Of course, the salesperson in these clubs or organizations keeps a low profile in terms of being a salesperson to make sure the leads materialize.

Chain of Leads

Current satisfied customers, particularly new customers, can be excellent sources of leads. New customers may be able to provide names of people in previously unexplored areas. These individuals may even provide testimonial letters of referrals upon request. By using referrals from new and satisfied customers, a salesperson can continually update the chain of leads. Sometimes a reward is given if the referral becomes a customer of the company leading oft-times to other leads.

Cold Canvassing

Cold canvassing in person rarely is cost effective prospecting unless the physical product needs to be seen, as in the case of vacuum cleaners and cosmetics, and will be purchased at the time of the presentation. Since these consumer products are sold on a door-to-door basis, cold calls are expected.

With most other products, telephone cold calling is cost effective. A telephone canvassing plan is outlined in Table 5-2.

The first step is to establish the criteria for qualifying the prospects. *Qualifiers* include the type and size of company, the financial condition and creditworthiness of the company, and the company's potential application of the product or service being offered.

Table 5-2
*Telephone Cold Calling
Prospecting Steps*

1. Establish criteria for qualifying the prospects.
2. Develop a list of prospects using the criteria established.
3. Determine each prospect's financial condition and credit worthiness.
4. Establish call objectives.
5. Prepare an opening statement and sales message.
6. Prepare various closes for the sale.
7. Prepare a wrap-up if a sale is made or a request for an early appointment if a sale is not made.

The second step is to develop a list of prospects using the criteria established. This involves using such sources as the Yellow Pages; business directories; local chamber of commerce directories; trade journals; and membership lists in various clubs and organizations, such as Rotary, the Kiwanis Club, and the Elks Club.

Once a list has been established, the financial condition and creditworthiness of each prospect should be determined. This third step can be accomplished with the help of Dun and Bradstreet, a local credit organization, the company's credit department, or checking with other suppliers to the company.

The fourth step—establishing the call objective for each call—is often overlooked. Basic call objectives include gathering prospect information and trying to sell a small order over the telephone. By selling a small order over the telephone, the prospect can be given a company account number and necessary background checks can be performed, facilitating the ordering process once a personal sales call is made.

Basic questions can be used to obtain important prospect information. For example, product use and interest can be obtained by asking, "How would your company use a product like this?" and "Do you currently use the product or a similar one?" In-depth purchasing criteria can also be obtained by asking, "What questions come to mind when thinking about a product like this?" "What benefits do you think you would obtain from using a product like this?" and "What is your usual decision time in purchasing this type of product?"

The fifth step involves preparing the opening statement, the actual sales message, and the close. The *opening statement* is probably the most difficult and most critical in telephone prospecting. Without a good opening, further communication with the prospect will not occur. There are three basic parts of every opening statement:

1) Identify yourself and company: "Good afternoon Mr. Johnson. I hope you are having a good day today. This is Kelly Hisrich of H&B Associates."

2) Make an interest-creating comment: "I understand that Dumas Markt H.K. has just had a record year and is interested in expanding its sales base overseas. I am calling because H&B Associates can assist you and your company in accomplishing this objective."

3) Establish customer rapport: "Given the wide variety of quality products your company is known for throughout

the United States, I am sure you want to continue this image overseas by launching the correct product in the correct market. H&B Associates has helped companies like yours face just such a problem in Europe, Eastern and Central Europe, and the Union of Sovereign States. Given your company's success, I know you are an extremely busy person. Since I do not want to waste my time or yours, I would like to take a few minutes to explain our international program."

A good opening statement must be followed by a strong and succinct sales message, stressing product or service benefits, not features. The benefits are best described using positive, vivid words, words that paint upbeat mental pictures, personal words like "you, me, we, or I," and action-oriented, emotion-creating adjectives. Include in the sales message the material to offset anticipated objections.

Following the sales message is the close; the seventh step in telephone cold call canvassing. The close would naturally follow the sales message. Endeavor to have the client order at least a trial amount, making it easier to pursue larger orders in the future.

The final steps depend on whether the close was successful in obtaining a sale. If success was achieved, the details of order processing and establishing a time for the next call are appropriate. If no sale is made, an appointment needs to be established. A good method uses a strong lead and gives the prospect a choice. "Mr. Johnson, I would like to meet with you for a short time to show you how our program here at H&B Associates can help you and Dumas Markt H.K. achieve profitable sales overseas in a short period of time. Would 10 Wednesday morning or 2 Thursday afternoon be good for you?"

Contests

Contests can be used to obtain inquiries from people who are interested in the company's product or service. When preparing a contest, the prize must be appropriate for the prospect you are attempting to solicit and the contest should be easy to enter. This is a particularly good method for obtaining the names of prospects by mail for real estate, vacation homes, and vacations.

Directories or Mailing Lists

In developed countries like the United States, a mailing list can be compiled for just about any group of people. This list can be developed by various breakdowns with the cost per name and address increasing with each breakdown. The list can be printed on gummed labels at a slightly higher cost for ease in mailing. For example, a list of the ministers presiding over Methodist churches with more than 1,000 members or a list of firms in Massachusetts employing more than 100 people can be obtained.

Most popular and trade magazines sell their subscription lists. Sometimes a mailing list is already compiled in a published directory. Professional groups (such as architects, doctors, lawyers) and specialty subgroups (such as cardiac specialists) often publish directories. Most associations, such as the American Marketing Association, the International Small Business Association, the American Management Association, chamber of commerce membership lists, the Association of Women Entrepreneurs, the Association of Chemical Engineers, and the Association of Certified Financial Planners, have membership directories.

There are also directories of individuals with distinctions, for example, those just graduating from high schools in a particular city, those listed in *Who's Who in America,* or those receiving the Freedom Foundation Award.

Group Plans

Some companies use groups or parties to show and demonstrate their products or services. These are usually done for consumer products, the most familiar being Tupperware, various vitamin companies, and Fuller Brush. This approach can also be used by other companies, particularly when the product is a unique or has a technological advantage over competing products.

Information Exchange

Given the continuing interactions between companies and the salespeople representing these companies, a good way to obtain the names of potential customers is to exchange information with salespeople from noncompeting firms. This can be done on a regular basis with a short initial meeting established between the individuals. For example, a salesperson selling cake mixes to large retail stores notices that the store has a limited assortment of frostings and might inform the sales representative for a company that sells frostings.

Internal Records

An overlooked method for obtaining a mailing list is the internal records of the company. This is particularly fruitful in companies with multiple divisions with similar target markets. Often customers of one division are good prospects for the products of another division. This referral system can be even more effective by establishing a system for referrals between divisions.

Network Marketing

One method of prospecting that every salesperson can do is network marketing—the process of making and using contacts. It involves affiliating with civic, fraternal, professional, religious, or national organizations to develop reference points for expanding social contacts and eventually obtaining prospects. The process involves connecting people with people through their business and social contacts. Some well known national organizations for good network marketing include: the Lions, Kiwanis, Rotary, Chamber of Commerce, and the American Society for Training and Development. Network marketing is a particularly popular prospecting activity for women and small business people.

There are general guidelines that will enhance the prospects from network marketing. First, the salesperson should meet as many people as possible at the social or business meeting. Second, when meeting a prospect, the salesperson should describe what he or she does for a living whenever it is appropriate, as it also becomes a low cost form of advertising. Third, while it may be tempting, the salesperson should refrain from attempting to close the sale at this meeting. Instead, a date should be established for a later meeting where this can be attempted. Finally, appropriate prospects made from network marketing should be screened.

Observation

Prospects can be identified by a salesperson who is observant and who has a systematic method for recording the names of potential leads. A good method is to systematically scan local newspapers for information on real estate transactions, marriages, new residential and commercial construction permits, divorces, fires, accidents, company stories, births, and job promotions. Careful note of any changes seen while driving to a sales call may also produce a prospect.

Reader Service and Referral Cards

Most business and professional journals make available for a fee a referral card service where readers can write for more information about a particular product or service that sounds interesting.

The reader can simply fill out the card with the name and address, requesting additional information, and send it to the company. Usually, these result in good prospect leads because the individual went to the effort of requesting information.

Service Personnel
Service and repair personnel can also be a valuable source of prospects. Those who visit the company regularly know of equipment needs. In addition, automobile mechanics may know who needs a new car or soon will.

Spotters
A *spotter* is an individual who is close to potential prospects and provides information on them for a fee. Retail clerks are close to customers making purchases and can be good spotters. Secretaries are excellent spotters because they know what is taking place in a company or division. These individuals can be the eyes and ears of the salesperson in markets with good potential. The best spotters are satisfied customers who can provide referrals on potential prospects.

Telemarketing
One of the most frequently used methods for identifying prospects is telemarketing. There is nothing new about using the telephone for business in a variety of contexts. The room filled with telephones to solicit contributions for a university or a nonprofit organization has been used for decades. Stockbrokers scan trade journals and newspapers for names of recent promotions and call these prospects. Insurance agents scan lists of wedding announcements in local newspapers and call these newlywed prospects. Telephone lead prospecting has a variety of applications in both consumer and business selling. It can also be used in taking the order for newspaper and magazine subscriptions and trial-examining the first volume in a set of books. A common telephone use is "bird-dogging"—obtaining an appointment (not the final sale) with a prospect. To obtain the appointment, the prospect is often offered a free booklet, a gift, a discount, a calendar, or important information.

Trade Shows and Exhibits
The most widely known method for obtaining a list of prospects is exhibits or demonstrations at trade shows. This is a particularly good method as the trade show attracts individuals who have an

interest in the area. In fact, one purpose of exhibiting at a trade show—even attending one—is to obtain a list of attendees for follow-up sales calls or mailings. For example, the annual computer show is an excellent way to introduce the company's latest software. The annual consumer electronics show provides the names of potential retailers or wholesalers interested in these products.

PROSPECT INFORMATION

Once a prospect has been identified, it is important to obtain as much information as possible. Amazingly, almost all the information obtained about a prospect is useful at some point during the selling process. The name, position, title, authority to buy products, educational background, buying behavior, and important personality traits should be noted. Personal information, hobbies, interests, political views, and life-style are also helpful in obtaining sales.

The salesperson must understand the company and industry environment of the prospect. Understanding the buying situation involves knowing the competitive position of the firm in the industry, the objectives and goals of the company, the company's major customers, and any current problems and opportunities. If the company is publicly held, most of this information is available from the annual report or 10K. The 10K report is the report a publicly traded company files with the Securities and Exchange Commission. Other sources of company information include business guides, government publications, indexes of published information, and trade association directories. These are described in detail in the rest of this chapter.

Business Guides

There are a wide variety of business guides with valuable information on an industry and specific companies in an industry. *Dun and Bradstreet's Reference Book of Corporate Managements* provides information on more than 30,000 executives who are directors and officers of more than 2,000 large corporations. *Moody's Industrial Manual* provides detailed information, such as principal officers and directors, major plants, merger and acquisition activity, and products, and includes seven years of statistical records and financial statements.

Standard & Poor publishes several books that provide valuable information on prospects. One of these, *Standard and Poor's Corporation Services,* has several services, including industry surveys providing weekly stock market information; a stock guide providing data on 5,000 stocks on a monthly basis; and trade and securities, providing statistics on business, finance, foreign trade, productivity, and employment. *Standard and Poor's Register of Corporations* provides a listing of the names and titles of top executives of 36,000 U.S. companies, as well as a list of 75,000 directors and executives in the United States and Canada. Finally, the *Directory of Corporate Affiliations* provides information on the 16,000 divisions, subsidiaries, and affiliates of more than 3,000 parent corporations and cross-references to all of them.

Government Publications

Many government publications provide useful information about potential customers. Most of this information can be found in two publications: The *Monthly Catalogue of United States Government Publications* and the *Monthly Checklist of State Publications.* The first provides a monthly comprehensive list of federal publications by issuing agency. The latter does the same for state publications. The *Survey of Current Business* provides monthly statistics on more than 2,500 different statistical series, including gross national product, national income, employment, construction, real estate, domestic and foreign trade, and balance of payments.

Other extensive sources of government data include the *Census of Retail Trade,* which provides information on the sales, payroll, and personnel of a large number of retail operations by Standard Metropolitan Statistical Area (SMSA); the *Census of Selected Services,* which provides information on various service operations, such as hotels, motels, and beauty parlors; the *Census of Wholesale Trade,* which provides information on a large number of wholesale outlets, such as sales, payroll, and personnel by SMSA; the *Census of Population,* which provides information on the number and demographic characteristics of the population by SMSA; the *Census of Housing,* which provides detailed information on various housing characteristics; and the *Census of Manufacturers,* which provides information on employment, payroll, new capital expenditures, cost of materials, and value of shipments of manufacturers.

Indexes

A wide variety of indexes are available to help the salesperson become familiar with potential customers. One of the most widely used is the *Business Periodicals Index,* a cumulative subject index listing business articles found in more than 175 periodicals. Two

F&S indexes are also widely used—the *F&S Index of Corporations,* which indexes company, product, and company information on U.S. companies from more than 800 newspapers, financial publications, and trade magazines that are business oriented; and the *F&S Index of International Industries,* which provides information on foreign companies classified by SIC code. Another useful index, the *Applied Science and Technology Index,* is a cumulative subject index of articles in various science periodicals.

Trade Association Directories

Trade association directories are a final source of good information on potential prospects. The most widely used directory in this area is the *Encyclopedia of Associations.* This reference book has three volumes that list trade association executives. Another book, the *National Trade and Professional Associations of the United States and Labor Unions,* provides information on more than 50,000 trade associations, professional associations, and labor unions.

CHAPTER PERSPECTIVE

The selling process is a series of seven steps—prospecting, preapproach, sales presentation, handling objections, closing the sale, and servicing. Of these, prospecting is overshadowed by making immediate sales. Information on the needs and wants, ability to purchase, and resources available to purchase should be obtained for each prospect. To obtain this information several prospecting methods can be employed: Advertising, centers of influence, chain of leads, cold canvassing, contests, directories of mailing lists, group plans, information exchange, internal records, observation, service personnel, spotters, and trade shows. Methods should be employed depending on the nature of the industry. Information on prospects can be found through a wide variety of information sources. The four most frequently used information sources are business guides, government publications, indexes of published information, and trade association directories. Regardless of the method or source of information, prospecting is an essential step in the selling process, and without it potential customers cannot be identified.

Preparing the Sales Call

INTRODUCTION AND MAIN POINTS

Once the prospects have been qualified, determine the best method for approaching them. In preparing the sales call, the salesperson uses all the information gathered about the prospect in a call sheet format. This format provides information about the company and the buyer(s), so that the best approach can be determined.

After reading this chapter:

■ You will understand the importance of planning the sales call.

■ You will understand the different methods of approaching a prospect.

■ You will be able to use the elements in planning the sales call.

■ You will understand the mental process of the prospect.

IMPORTANCE OF PLANNING THE SALES CALL

An often overlooked but extremely important step in the selling process is planning the sales call. It is especially important for a prospect that has just been identified, but this planning is also important when calling on established accounts. There is nothing more damaging to a salesperson, or to the company's reputation, than unprepared salespeople. Lack of preparation is all too obvious when this occurs, even to the novice buyer.

There are numerous reasons for planning a sales call. The four most important are that planning reflects professionalism; develops goodwill between buyer and seller; builds the confidence of the salesperson; and increases the probability of making a sale.

Planning Reflects Professionalism

Selling requires good business relationships, relationships established because of the concern of the salesperson and that person's knowledge of the industry, company, competitive products, and company needs. Planning is required to establish these good business relationships. The professionalism shown by planning before the sales call demands specialized knowledge of the salesperson to help solve the customer's problems and needs and ensures that good business relationships are established.

Planning Develops Goodwill

A salesperson who understands a customer's problems and needs and is prepared to discuss and show how the product or service helps fulfill these needs is greatly appreciated and welcomed. (See Figure 6-1 for an example of an account sales plan.) This knowledge of the relationship of the seller's product and service to the buyer's needs develops goodwill between the salesperson and buyer. In time, this leads to trust on the part of the buyer. Without planning, development of goodwill is not possible.

FIGURE 6-1
ACCOUNT SALES PLAN

Date: _____   Salesperson: _____

Customer/Prospect: _____   Address: _____

Telephone: _____   Fax: _____

Objective	Primary Contact	Particular Buyer Characteristics	Benefits Desired	Specific Actions	Achievement Date

Planning Builds the Confidence of the Salesperson

The ability to be professional and build goodwill relies on the confidence of the salesperson. This confidence level significantly increases when the sales call is carefully planned. Since self-confidence is often a prerequisite for an order from a buyer, no other reason is needed for planning.

Planning Increases Sales Probability

A self-confident, well-prepared salesperson who can illustrate how the particular product or service best meets the customer's needs has better sales results than an unprepared salesperson. Planning ensures that the right match between the customer's needs and the company's product and service mix is well thought out and developed into a succinct presentation that is interesting and clearly understood.

STARTING THE PLANNING PROCESS

Given these reasons, it is easy to understand why sales call planning is so important. Now, the question you are asking is: How do I start this important planning process? The best way to start planning for a sales call is to reflect on the prospect and imagine that you actually are the prospect—putting yourself in the prospect's position. When putting yourself in the prospect's shoes, you want to first focus on the questions you, as the prospect, would ask. These questions would probably include: Do I have a particular need or problem? Does this product or service fulfill this need? Is the price right? Is the company one I want to do business with? Is the salesperson all right? Should I purchase the product now or later?

By focusing on these questions, a salesperson is better able to plan an effective sales call, particularly when coming from a problem-solving perspective. These basic questions from the prospect's point of view will guide the development of the presentation plan to address the following:

- How can I quickly identify the prospect's needs?
- How can I best approach the prospect, thereby gaining attention and interest?
- How can I make my presentation to illustrate how my offering will satisfy the customer's needs?
- What are the possible questions the prospect will ask and how will I answer them?
- What is the best method for closing the sale and handling any objections?

Westinghouse Credit Corporation uses telemarketing to qualify leads and develop good prospects for field salespeople. The company's telemarketing center is responsible for determining the interest of a prospect, verifying mailing information, and giving leads to branch offices.

ASPECTS OF SALES CALL PLANNING

There are three basic aspects in planning a sales call: Establish the sales call objective; develop a customer profile and benefits; and develop the sales presentation.

Establish a Sales Call Objective

Every sales call should be based on one or more objectives. The objective needs to be quantifiable, measurable, understandable, and of benefit to the particular buyer. The objective needs to be *quantifiable,* that is, stated in specific numbers, so that specific activities can be developed. Examples of quantifiable objectives are as follows:

- Sell three cases of sixteen-ounce ketchup.
- Sell two cases of a eight-ounce mustard.
- Establish a cooperative advertising agreement.
- Increase the number of shelf facings by one.

Objectives guide the preparation of a specific sales presentation and allow the salesperson to evaluate results. Second, the objective must be measurable. A salesperson develops skills when each sales call is carefully evaluated and the results achieved are compared to the objectives. This can only be accomplished when the objectives are measurable. *Measurable* means that the results of the effort to achieve the objective can be compared to the actual objective. A measurable objective might be to increase the number of new customers by eight during the next month. The actual number of new customers can be compared with the benchmark objective of eight.

Finally, objectives must be *understandable* and *beneficial* to the buyer. If the buyer does not clearly understand how the purchase or any other activity is a benefit, a sale is difficult to make. A useful aid in developing an appropriate objective is a call sheet (see Figure 6-2).

Demographic information, such as buying patterns, specific buying characteristics, and a history of prior purchases, is needed for the salesperson to develop appropriate objectives for the particular customer. It also helps prepare the best sales presentation and most accurate customer profile. The *past purchase history* helps to determine what customers need to reorder. A history also indicates company products not yet purchased.

Once the *sales objective(s)* have been established, the next step is to determine the customer's profile. A *customer profile* includes all available information on the firm, the buyer, and any individuals in the firm who influence the buying decision. These data should be reviewed by the salesperson to develop the best customized presentation possible. A good customer profile indicates:

Who makes the buying decision;

The background of this individual or individuals, as well as the company background;

FIGURE 6-2
EXAMPLE CALL SHEET

Firm: _____

Address: _____

      City, State, and Zip Code: _____

      Telephone: _____ Fax: _____

Primary Buyer: _____

Assistant Buyer: _____

Type of Business: _____

Buying Pattern: ____ Weekly ____Monthly ____As Needed

      ____ Other_____

Specific Buyer Characteristics: _____

_____

_____

Purchases:

Products Bought	Annual Purchases	Company Share	Brand Preferred	Other Suppliers
1.				
2.				
3.				
4.				
5.				
6.				
7.				
8.				

    The desired terms of sale (such as delivery, payment period, and service);

    Past purchasing activity;

    Competitive products purchased.

    This information, as well as specific actions to be taken, can be recorded on the account sales plan.

    Understanding customer benefits is also a critical part of sales call planning. These benefits can be determined by the salesperson, who selects the features, advantages, and benefits of the company's product and service to be presented to a customer. The benefits are determined by answering the question, "Why should the company purchase this particular product?" Because the main reason that the product will be purchased is that it meets the needs or solves a particular problem of the customer, answering this question helps to delineate what should be presented.

The features, advantages, and benefits selected are the basis for developing a marketing plan. The marketing plan shows how the particular product benefits the customer, establishes the price, and indicates the anticipated returns to the company and the payment plan. This is called *delineating the benefits*. The marketing plan helps the salesperson develop a suggested purchase order from the customer. Past analyses can be used as justification for the proposed amount to be purchased by the customer. The suggested purchase order should be complete in terms of the kinds and quantities of each product the salesperson is suggesting that the customer purchase.

Prepare the Sales Presentation

The sales call objective and the customer profile and benefits form the basis for the final aspect of sales call planning: Developing the sales presentation. The sales presentation discussed in Chapter 7 consists of a series of steps—approval, presentation, trial close, and close—that move the buyer from interest to action. In planning the sales presentation, keep in mind the mental process a customer goes through to make (or not make) a purchasing decision.

To sell successfully, a salesperson must understand the buyer's mental process in making a purchase decision. An effective sales presentation moves the buyer through this mental process. The steps in this mental process are attention, interest, desire, conviction, and action (purchase).

Attention: From the moment contact is made with the buyer, a salesperson should obtain and hold the buyer's attention. This can be difficult at times because the salesperson is calling on the buyer in the buyer's own territory. The buyer is often distracted by other responsibilities or by events in the firm and may be interrupted by personnel about problems that need immediate attention. The situation is even more difficult when the buyer has little interest in the product being offered. The goal of the salesperson is to attract initial attention and to move the buyer to the next stage, interest, as quickly as possible.

Interest: It is in the interest stage of the buyer's mental process that delineated buying motives are useful. A salesperson should *link* the purpose of the call and the products being offered with the buyer's needs and interest. Once this link has been made, it is easier to move the buyer through the mental process to a satisfactory conclusion—a sale. If you have not been able to determine the buyer's motives in the planning stage, then you should try to find out by asking questions. Keep in mind that a buyer who enters into a discussion and becomes involved is more likely to maintain a high interest level than one who does not.

Desire: This stage in the mental process occurs when the buyer moves from interest in the product to expressing a wish for a particular or a similar product. The potential buyer questions the salesperson and presents objections during this mental stage in an attempt to determine whether a particular product should be purchased. A salesperson should anticipate the major objections that may be raised and have the answers. These objections should be dealt with in the sales presentation itself. References can then be made to the presentation when the objections are raised. Sometimes objections can be used successfully in the sales presentation as a series of questions most buyers ask.

Conviction: Even though the buyer may want the product being offered, frequently this is not enough for a purchase decision. A buyer's concerns about the purchase must be reduced by convincing the buyer that the product is the right one and the salesperson's company is the best supplier. The buyer is convinced when there are no doubts that the product should be purchased and that it should be purchased from your firm. The extent to which this strong belief can be developed and supported, the easier it is to close the sale and to secure future product sales.

Action (Purchase): Once the stage of conviction is reached, it is important for the salesperson to determine the most appropriate way to ask for action—make the sale. This is perhaps one of the most difficult stages: Many salespeople make good presentations, but fail to close—they fail to ask for the sale. The more skillfully the buyer has been guided through the previous mental stages, the easier it is for action, or purchase, to occur.

CHAPTER PERSPECTIVE

The preparation stage of the selling process begins with planning the sales call. The four most important reasons for planning the sales call are that it indicates professionalism, builds goodwill, builds the salesperson's confidence, and increases the likelihood of a purchase. Planning looks to connect the customer's needs and the company's particular product or service.

The three basic aspects of planning a sales call are establishing a concrete sales objective, developing a customer profile and benefits, and developing the sales presentation. The marketing plan itself shows the ways in which the product benefits the customer.

The mental process a buyer goes through in making a purchase is attention, interest, desire, conviction, and finally action (purchase).

The Sales Presentation

CHAPTER

7

INTRODUCTION AND MAIN POINTS

An effective approach and presentation is the essence of all personal selling. Once the sales call has been planned, it is important that the prospect be approached with the most appropriate presentation. Success in selling occurs when a salesperson understands the prospect's needs, motives, and habits well enough to use the right approach and presentation. Each presentation must be evaluated beforehand in terms of its ability to inform, persuade, and convince the prospect that the product or service should be purchased. Each presentation should also avoid all possible misinterpretation.

After reading the material in this chapter:
- You will understand the various approaches available.
- You will understand the basic aspects of a sales presentation.
- You will understand the basic principles of effective communication.
- You will be able to select the best approach for a particular selling situation.
- You will be able to select the most appropriate type of sales presentation.

APPROACHING THE PROSPECT

The first few minutes of the sales presentation are perhaps the most critical. They determine a buyer's attitude toward the salesperson. This critical period, the *approach,* is so important that it is treated as a separate aspect of the sales presentation. In approaching the potential buyer, it is important to have the right attitude, to understand the situation, and to use the appropriate technique(s).

Attitude During Approach

The attitude of the salesperson, along with his or her appearance, creates the prospect's first impression. This first impression, along with the last, is critical to a successful presentation.

Several factors help create a good first impression, such as wearing appropriate clothing; being neat in dress and grooming; not smoking or chewing gum; standing tall and appearing confident; being enthusiastic and positive; maintaining eye contact; and learning and pronouncing the prospect's name correctly and using it several times throughout the interview.

It is a rare salesperson who does not experience some form of tension in dealing with a prospect. This can be brought on by the salesperson when there are preconceived ideas about the negative characteristics of the prospect and all that may go wrong during the sales call. Successful salespeople have learned to reduce the degree of stress and focus on the positive rather than the negative aspects of the situation. Some use *creative imagery:* First, the worst that can possibly happen in the sales call is envisioned. Then, the salesperson imagines how he or she will react to and even accept this worst case, if it occurs.

The best that can possibly happen is envisioned. Contingency plans are prepared should the selected sales presentation need to be abandoned. Finally, the salesperson focuses on the slim chance (less than 1 percent) that things will really go wrong given the careful planning before the sales call. This means that there is a greater than 99 percent probability that everything will go smoothly.

Situation of the Approach

The situation confronting the salesperson determines the actual approach technique employed to begin the sales presentation. Several variables affect the situation, including the type of product(s) being sold; the degree of knowledge about the customer's needs; the time available for making the presentation; whether the call is the first or a repeat; the sales call objective and customer benefits; and the number of approaches available. These and other variables must be carefully considered by the salesperson in deciding which approach to employ.

Types of Approaches

Depending on the situation, any of several methods can be employed to effectively approach the prospect. These eight approaches are described here.

Compliment approach: When done subtly and sincerely, a compliment can bring about a very positive reaction and establish a pleasant atmosphere for the sales presentation. Most business people are interested in receiving positive feedback about themselves or their company. Usually, an indirect compliment is more effective than a direct approach, which might be viewed as flattery. Some acceptable compliments are as follows:

"Kary, your office has such great decor and your staff is so helpful that it is always a pleasure to make this call.

"Kary, your secretary is just great. She not only switched my appointment because of a problem that came up, but she called me to reconfirm the new date.

"Kary, I understand congratulations are in order on your recent promotion.

"Kary, it is fun dealing with a company like yours, on the cutting edge of technology."

Reference approach: A very good approach is for a salesperson to mention several satisfied customers who are known and respected by the prospect. This approach is even stronger when the reference is an industry leader known for being dynamic and innovative. An example of this approach is, "Your colleague, Barra O'Cinneide, the sales manager at Dumas Markt H.K., an import-export company, has just started buying this product, as have three other leading companies in the area." Whenever possible, a testimonial letter from a satisfied customer is very helpful, not only in the approach but in the presentation itself. A salesperson must be careful that any names mentioned are indeed satisfied customers because the prospect may contact the individual before buying. Some salespeople have obtained good leads by asking each new customer for the names of others who might be interested in the product.

Sample approach: The sample approach has had a long history of establishing goodwill and of approaching a prospect positively. Offering a trial size of the product, a luncheon invitation, a free seminar, or a sample of the services is an excellent way to approach a prospect. One consumer goods salesperson actually took a sample of the product, a piece of cake, when introducing a new cake mix to the trade. It is much easier to consummate a sale when the prospect has already satisfactorily tried the product or service being offered.

Customer benefit approach: Because part of a buyer's job is to solve problems or obtain benefit through the purchase, this approach starts with the most important area: Describing the customer's benefits. Usually only one or two buying motives significantly affect the purchasing decision. These must be identified and referred to whenever possible. Some examples of customer benefit approaches are as follows:

"Kelly, are you aware that our control product reduces the amount of energy lost by 25 percent in only one year?"

"Kelly, did you see in the paper yesterday that an independent research company determined that more consumers preferred this product to any other on the market?"

"Kelly, did you know that your company can ship and deliver your products through Liverpool to London faster using our service than any other?"

Dramatic approach: This approach can be used to gain attention should all other approaches fail. One salesperson placed $5 on the buyer's desk, announcing that the buyer could keep the $5 if the salesperson was not able to show all the benefits of the product within 25 minutes. Vacuum cleaner salespeople often throw dirt on the buyer's carpet and then demonstrate the great way their product picks up the dirt. One salesperson set fire to a $1 bill while saying, "Katy, let me show you how you and your company can stop burning up your profits by using our product in your production process."

Product approach: One good approach is to show the prospect a sample of the product right at the start. This approach allows the prospect to see what is being sold, allowing a smooth transition into the sales presentation. Given that a picture is worth a thousand words, a printout of the new computer program with the name of the prospect's company or a taste of the new food product can significantly affect the reaction to the sales presentation that follows.

Question approach: The question approach involves the prospect in a two-way communication early in the sales presentation. The prospect should be involved in the presentation as soon as possible. Asking questions provides this involvement because responses are required from the prospect. This approach has the added advantage of providing other information, such as the prospect's level of interest, when the buyer responds to the questions asked. Such questions as, "If I can show you how using our product in your production process will provide your company with 5 percent fewer defects per 100 products, would you give me an hour of your time?" will elicit evidence of the prospect's level of interest.

This type of question requires thought on the part of the prospect and can allow an early close with prospects who clearly indicate interest. Prospects with a low degree of interest can receive a different presentation, perhaps shorter, if time is pressing.

A question that helps to identify the prospect's desired benefits is especially good: "What features or benefits are of primary importance when you purchase a product like this?" No matter what question is used, it should be one that elicits a positive, not a negative response. A salesperson should never ask, "May I help you?" because it is all too easy for a prospect to answer quickly, "No," making it difficult to continue the conversation.

Introductory approach: This approach is probably the worst approach a salesperson can use. Because you usually have only one chance to start the presentation positively, a salesperson using this approach should make sure the introductory approach is interesting and flows smoothly into the presentation. Do not follow a bad initial approach with another. A friendly, smiling greeting and a sincere, firm handshake are critical starting points in a good introductory approach. In the introductory approach, a salesperson should indicate his or her name and company: "Good afternoon, Katy, I am Troy Bradley from the Ford Division of Proctor and Gamble, here for our 3 o'clock appointment."

ASPECTS OF THE SALES PRESENTATION

Following the approach, the flavor of the sales presentation depends on the type of selling involved, the nature of the product, and the disposition of the prospect. Each prospect has a unique personality, but prospects generally fall into one of several basic categories: Procrastinating, silent, skeptical, opinionated, impulsive, methodical, talkative, or grouchy. By quickly grasping the particular mood and personality of the prospect, a salesperson can develop the most appropriate sales presentation. Some basic techniques for the sales presentation in each of these categories are detailed in Table 7-1.

TABLE 7-1
Aspects of Sales Presentations for Certain Personality Types

Personality Type	Aspects of Sales Presentations
Procrastinating	Emphasize benefits that will not be obtained if immediate action is not taken; emphasize prospect's ability and position of decision making
Silent	Continually ask questions to get prospect to talk, try to get the prospect to share personal information; be very personal during the entire presentation

Skeptical	Use a conservative presentation filled with facts
Opinionated	Listen attentively to what the prospect says, never directly disagreeing with the views expressed; use features of the product that are in line with his or her opinions whenever possible
Impulsive	Give a short presentation highlighting the most important points and omit lengthy details; close early
Methodical	Make the tempo of the sales presentation fit the prospect's tempo; include many details and support for key points
Talkative	Take care that continuous small talk does not affect your sales presentation; listen attentively, but get the presentation back on track as soon as possible
Grouchy	Do not argue or become defensive; ask questions, and try to understand the nature of the underlying problems and the story behind the disposition; agree as much as possible

A good sales presentation takes account of the personality and mood of the prospect and smoothly and logically moves the prospect from approach to action. Regardless of the objective, each sales presentation must meet the basic requirements briefly introduced in Chapter 6: Obtain the attention of the prospect, arouse the prospect's interest, stimulate desire for the product's benefits, secure the prospect's conviction, and motivate the prospect to take action and buy. Not every presentation requires in-depth concentration on each step, but each step must be incorporated briefly into the sales presentation. The steps themselves can be expanded in numerous ways, depending on the needs of a selling situation.

Obtain Instant Attention
As mentioned earlier, the first few seconds in any sales presentation are the most important. The salesperson must focus the prospect on what is being said. This is sometimes difficult because a prospect may be thinking about something else. No matter what the case, each prospect has one overriding thought: "What's in it for me?"

This question needs to be addressed at the start of the presentation and addressed continually throughout the presentation. One of the best ways to gain a prospect's attention is to relate your product or service to the prospect's needs or problem: "John, did you know that almost every firm in the industry uses our product?"

Create Interest

Once the prospect's attention is obtained, it must be quickly converted into interest. This can be facilitated by writing down, at least in outline form, key selling points built around benefits. This requires that the salesperson thoroughly understand the product and the prospect, and be able to clearly communicate the product's benefits. This approach is often called the feature-advantage-benefit approach.

Feature: A characteristic feature of the product (or service) that produces a benefit.

Advantage: What the feature will do or how it works.

Benefit: Advantage to the prospect of the feature backed up by confirmation.

This approach requires that the salesperson determine the benefits most appealing to the prospect. This determination can be made by finding out what the prospect does and what he or she wants most; relating these desires to the product or service; and selecting the benefits of the product or service that should be of most interest to the prospect and then building appeal around them.

Stimulate Desire

As the salesperson links the prospect's interests to the benefits of the products during the sales presentation, the prospect is thinking, "Why should I believe you? What you're saying sounds good, but how do I know you are telling the truth?" The sales presentation must help the prospect understand that the product or service offered will provide the benefits sought and solve any problems mentioned.

Secure Conviction

As the prospect begins to desire the product or service, it is important that the salesperson transfer this desire to a conviction that the offering being presented is the best possible alternative. Besides questioning the credibility of the salesperson's statements, the prospect is also asking, "How do I know that there is not some alternative that will provide this same benefit more cost effectively?" This question can be answered and the prospect convinced using facts about the product or service being offered, by offering expert evidence in the form of reports of authorities or results of testing, and by giving a guarantee (or warranty) that the product will perform as you have indicated. Any questions or objections by the prospect must be carefully and accurately answered.

Motivate to Action (Purchase)

Motivating the prospect to action, commonly called closing the sale, is the purpose of the sales presentation. It is very difficult for some salespeople to ask the prospect to buy—-obtain the order. Since a prospect seldom indicates outright that to buy the product or service, a salesperson must be able to recognize the opportunity and act upon it immediately with a trial close at any time in the sales presentation. This aspect of the selling process is the focus of Chapter 9.

TYPES OF SALES PRESENTATIONS

There are many different ways to make a sales presentation, but the four most commonly used methods in order of structure are as follows:

1) Memorized (or canned) presentation.
2) Planned (or formula) presentation.
3) Need-satisfaction presentation.
4) The problem-solution (or survey-proposal) presentation.

A sales presentation is a persuasive vocal or visual explanation of a business proposal.

Memorized (Canned) Presentation

Some companies require their salespeople to memorize and follow a well-written and tested canned presentation. These presentations are especially beneficial when the same product is sold over and over again and there is little variation among prospects. These presentations are worded so that a high percentage of closings result from the canned words, which come alive for each prospect.

A memorized sales presentation is based on the stimulus-response method and on these two assumptions: That a prospect's needs can be stimulated by direct exposure to the product through the sale presentation; or that the prospect has already been at least partially stimulated and now needs to be moved into an affirmative response and a purchase request.

In this type of presentation, the salesperson does 80 to 90 percent of the talking, the prospect only occasionally responding to a set question. Since there is no attempt by the salesperson to determine the prospect's needs or to understand what the prospect is thinking, the salesperson concentrates on discussing the product and its benefits and then asking for a purchase request. This presentation method relies on the fact that a convincing presentation of the benefits of the product—the stimulus—causes the prospect to buy—the response.

The memorized presentation is most often used in selling nontechnical items door to door or in telemarketing. It requires limited training time and ensures that all prospects receive the same basic message. Sometimes a company has several standardized sales presentations that can be used as options or parts of the main presentation. When this occurs, each salesperson can then develop particular selling sentences and phrases.

There are several major disadvantages to the memorized sales presentation. First, it allows little if any prospect participation. Second, it can appear to be high-pressure selling because the salesperson moves directly through the presentation, asking for the order at preset times that may not coincide with when the prospect is ready to consider purchasing. Finally, the presentation does not consider the individuality of the prospect and may present features and benefits of little or no interest to the prospect.

Despite its impersonal nature, the memorized presentation has distinct advantages. First, it ensures that each prospect will receive a similar, well-planned presentation. Second, it requires very little training. Finally, it can be used by very inexperienced salespeople to sell nontechnical products, usually on a telemarketing or door-to-door basis.

Planned (Formula) Presentation

When a more personal touch is needed, as well as a very structured approach, the Planned (Formula) presentation may be more appropriate. This type of presentation is by far the most widely used. It presents a carefully planned, personalized sales message.

The salesperson, who knows something about the prospect, uses a less structured, general outline within which the presentation is made. The presentation is based on the assumption that somewhat similar prospects in similar situations can be approached with similar presentations. The salesman follows a general outline. Parts of the script are memorized, and there is constant prospect involvement and interaction. The salesperson maintains control of the conversation, particularly at the beginning, and follows the attention, interest, desire, conviction, and action procedure previously discussed.

Most consumer goods, particularly those that are sold in a repurchase situation, are sold by this method. When the buyer is already aware of the quality of the company and is purchasing (or has previously purchased) some of the company's products, there is no need for a flexible, customized sales presentation. This is the situation for such consumer goods companies as Colgate Palmolive, Quaker Oats, General Foods, H. J. Heinz, Procter and Gamble, Pepsi Cola/Frito Lay, Gillette, Revlon, and Beecham.

A typical sales presentation used by these companies includes the following series of steps in selling process to a retail grocer:

Step 1. Plan the call.
- Review the situation.
- Check the sales plan.
- Establish objectives and modify the plan if necessary.
. Step 2. Check the stock.
- Check shelf facings, and note the appearance on the shelf.
- Note out-of-stocks.
- Straighten the shelf stock.
- Check the backroom for stock.
- Revise the sales plan if necessary.
Step 3. Approach the buyer.
Step 4. Make the presentation
- Use sales tools.
- Make the presentation clear and interesting.
- Tailor the presentation to the specific situation.
Step 5. Close.
- Present and ask for the suggested order.
- Answer questions and handle objections.
- Get the order.
Step 6. Merchandising and records.
- Give the terms of sales.
- Provide a delivery date.
- Build the displays.
Step 7. Reports and call analysis.
- Complete the report immediately after the call.
- Review the call to improve the next presentation.

Whether the approach formula has six, seven, eight, or ten steps, formula selling is a very effective method for calling on customers who are currently buying products from a company. It has a number of advantages. First, it ensures that all information is presented in a clear, logical way while allowing a reasonable amount of buyer interaction. Second, it handles anticipated questions and objections smoothly. As long as the prospect's needs and wants have been correctly identified, there are no major disadvantages to a formula presentation. In a number of more complex selling situations, however, the formula presentation method is not best.

The Need-Satisfaction Presentation

The third type is a relatively flexible, interactive presentation, that is very challenging and creative. The presentation frequently starts with a question such as, "What are you looking for when you purchase this particular type of product?" or "What needs or problems does your company have that I may be able to assist in solving?"

These questions elicit the prospect's needs and provide the salesperson with the opportunity to determine the products that meet these needs or solve the problem identified. Usually the first 50 to 60 percent of the sales call is devoted to determining and discussing the prospect's needs.

In the last part of the presentation, the salesperson takes more control and illustrates how the product will satisfy the prospect's needs. The buyer's response to the final part of the presentation dictates what follows. If an objection is raised, the salesperson can handle it, using one of the methods discussed in Chapter 8.

Care must be taken while determining the prospect's needs in the first part of the presentation: Too many questions alienate the prospect. Many prospects do not initially want to discuss needs or problems with a salesperson. Many salespeople also do not feel comfortable using this sales approach because it is more personal and provides strong control of the presentation situation.

Problem Solving (Survey-Proposal) Presentation

This two-step presentation is frequently used to sell systems or highly complex technical products. It often requires a survey to obtain original data and several sales calls to develop a detailed analysis of the prospect's needs. The prospect often must be convinced that an in-depth study of the present situation and any problems or needs will be beneficial. From this analysis, a carefully written proposal is developed that solves the needs and problems identified. This flexible, customized approach involving a study of needs and a well-planned presentation often proceeds as follows:

1) Propose the analysis to the prospect.
2) Make the analysis.
3) Mutually agree on problems and needs with the prospect.
4) Prepare and present a proposal for solving the prospect's problems and needs.

The proposal is usually presented to a group of managers and can require a selling team, particularly when a technical high-dollar investment is involved. Good team selling requires good interaction and planning. Each team member must have knowledge of effective communication skills.

PRINCIPLES OF EFFECTIVE COMMUNICATION

A basic requirement of making an effective presentation is two-way communication. A salesperson must not only know what a prospect is saying and thinking, but must also be able to communicate a response in the language and at the interest level of the prospect. This requires that the salesperson think and speak clearly in a manner the prospect understands.

Communication Preparation

Communication involves learning to be a good listener and deciding on the appropriate content and length of the presentation. A good way to discover a prospect's needs is to ask good questions. The questions, however, have little value if the salesperson does not carefully listen to the answers. One way to establish rapport with a prospect is to be sincerely interested in what is being said. This is particularly important in successfully handling objections.

Professional selling often involves more careful listening than talking. An effective sales presentation merely explains what a prospect is hearing, seeing, smelling, tasting, or feeling about the product or service.

The best presentation is delivered with maximum effectiveness in the shortest period of time with the prospect's full understanding. Although the exact length of the presentation depends to a large extent on what is being sold, a good salesperson can effectively present some products or service in two to three minutes using 200 to 300 carefully chosen words. The average sales presentation lasts from ten to fifteen minutes, but those of a technical nature last longer. Rarely should a sales presentation last longer than 30 to 40 minutes. The basic rules to follow are, give your presentation; listen, listen, listen; obtain the order; and leave—all in the shortest time possible.

Communication Involves Clear Writing

Since it takes a well-organized, smoothly flowing presentation to obtain a sale, it is effective initially to write out the presentation using a detailed outline in either chart or graph form. A basic concept in any effective written communication is that words create images. A presentation can be very effective when image-producing key words are used to give a prospect a clear mental picture of the selling points and how the product will be of benefit. These key selling points must be organized logically so that they can be remembered. Good grammar, logical organization, and correct technical language must also be used.

Communication Involves Clear Speaking

No matter how carefully planned, an oral presentation is usually only 30 percent effective in conveying an idea accurately. This reflects the fact that both the salesperson and the prospect are communicating in words. Meaning does not exist in specific words, but rather in the significance assigned to the words based on the individual's experience, attitudes, and beliefs. It takes two people to communicate an idea, a sender and a receiver. When there is no mutual understanding between the sender and the receiver, the message is usually not understood. The responsibility for facilitating understanding lies with the salesperson, not the buyer. A salesperson can ascertain whether a prospect clearly understands the message by communicating it and then asking that it be repeated.

In communicating words, voice, body, face, and eyes should be used. Action words and illustrations that create images are best. Speak clearly and positively at a steady pace, varying the pitch, tone and speed. Sit or, whenever possible, stand, conveying confidence and interest. Always smile, letting your face show happiness, confidence, and warmth. Always maintain eye contact, letting your eyes transmit enthusiasm, interest, and sincerity.

Communication Involves Using Tools

Various communication tools can help stimulate all the prospect's senses. They are particularly effective when the prospect participates in the presentation, as in a demonstration of the product or service. Traditional sales aids, such as product samples or models, sales manuals, posters, handouts, and flip charts, should not be overlooked, but many newer visual aids are available: VCRs, slide projectors, and portable computers. Regardless of the communication tool, the most effective will involve the prospect to the greatest extent possible.

CHAPTER PERSPECTIVE

To improve the chances of making a sale, it is important to know how to approach a prospect and make an effective sales presentation. Many approach methods are available: Compliment, customer benefit, dramatic, introductory, product, question, reference, and sample. A particular method should be selected based on the presentation method and the needs of the buyer. Four common presentation methods are memorized, planned, need-satisfaction, and problem-solution. The presentation should guide the prospect logically through the stages of attention, interest, desire, conviction, and action. Good approaches and presentations require effective communication skills and any communication tools that involve the prospect to the greatest extent possible.

Handling Objections

INTRODUCTION AND MAIN POINTS

Rarely does a selling situation not involve handling questions and objections, regardless of the quality of the product or service or the ability of the salesperson. The fourth stage in the selling process—handling objections—is one of the most difficult tasks in sales.

After reading this chapter:

■ You will be able to use questions to obtain a better understanding of the objections being raised.

■ You will be able to ascertain which are the most important objections.

■ You will be able to use various methods for dealing with objections.

GENERAL GUIDELINES IN DEALING WITH OBJECTIONS

Regardless of the method used when dealing with objections, it is rare that a salesperson ignores an objection. In dealing with objections, some general guidelines should be followed:

1) The salesperson should never respond to an objection quickly. Although the objection must be addressed, the salesperson should always pause and reflect, making sure the objection is clearly understood before responding. If a response is too quick, the prospect may feel pressured.

2) The salesperson should never provide too much information or too many answers. A salesperson can attach too much meaning to an objection and bury the prospect in information. This can create a negative state in which the prospect is overloaded with information. After handling an objection, the salesperson should move on to other positive elements in the sales call and not dwell on the objection. A salesperson should also remember that a

prospect buys because of the benefits of the product presented, not because of the skills displayed in handling objections.

3) A salesperson should never guess or present wrong information in response to an objection. If you do not know the answer to the objection, promise to get back with the correct information as soon as possible, and then do so.

4) The salesperson should not argue about a prospect's objection. More importantly, an endless discussion should be avoided. A salesperson should not set the stage for an argument by responding to an objection with "No." Also, the word objection should never be used in the discussion. Rather, the objection or comment should be referred to as an "interesting point" or a "question." Remember, however, that some objections are not answerable. Even the best possible product may not have all the advantages desired by the prospect, and even the best possible answer will not be enough. When this situation occurs, the salesperson should move on to another positive point about the product, saying, "I perfectly understand your point, Ms. Skyrmes, and I have tried to explain it the best I could. There is something else I have not had the opportunity to mention about the product..."

5) The salesperson should never display doubts about the response to an objection. Act as if you have completely answered it. At all costs, avoid saying, "Does that answer your objection completely?" This merely casts further doubt and may even elicit a "No" response or, even worse, more objections. If you have not completely satisfied a genuinely interested prospect, you will be told.

EVALUATE OBJECTIONS

Some salespeople make mistakes by not understanding the difference between an unfavorable comment and an objection. This most frequently occurs in the area of price and cost. For example, a prospect may ask: "But what is this going to cost?" The salesperson should not immediately think that this question indicates an objection and respond with all the value received from purchasing the product. Rather, the salesperson should, without any additional information, respond with the cost information requested. Information questions like this one should be responded to openly and honestly as quickly as possible. Sometimes the sales-person does not have the information and needs to schedule a new appointment once the information is obtained.

Comments by a prospect can be classified as an excuse or a real objection. While there are many excuses offered, there are only two real objections to purchasing the product—the prospect has no need for the product or the prospect does not have the money to purchase the product. And, even these objections can often be dealt with effectively. As a salesperson, you will encounter far more excuses than real objections so you need to distinguish between the two.

While there is no scientific formula for separating excuses from objections, the circumstances surrounding the comment by the prospect usually provides some insight. Often the prospect's tone of voice or the type of reasons given indicate whether the objection is a sincere one, as well as how strongly the prospect feels about the statement. Salespeople must rely on their knowl-edge of why people buy, their past experience, observation, and questions to determine the nature and validity of the reason stated for not buying.

Some possible excuses and objections may become apparent by observing how the prospect responds to the aspects of the sales presentation. For example, if a salesperson notes that a prospect's interest decreases after discussing a particular feature of the prod-uct, the salesperson should stop the presentation and either repeat the description of the feature, expand on it or, if at all possible, demonstrate the feature in question.

Another method for determining the significance of the objections is by asking questions. If a salesperson asks: "What do you think about the fabric being used?," the tone of the answer— "It looks all right"—will provide an indication of the degree of satisfaction. Usually, if the fabric is the real objection, asking the question will cause the buyers to state their real feelings. Other good questions to use to determine the validity and strength of an objection are open-ended ones such as: "What is that?," "Can we talk some more about that?," or "Could you explain that in a little more detail?"

THE USE OF QUESTIONS

The proper questioning of a prospect is imperative to successful selling, particularly in handling objections. By asking questions, a salesperson can obtain two-way communication, thereby increas-ing the prospect's participation. When using questions in handling objections, a salesperson should know the desired answer to the question. If you know the answer you want, you can develop the best question to ask. The salesperson should ask only those questions that help make the sale and that a prospect is willing and able to answer. Questions should be carefully worded and used sparingly. There are four basic categories of questions that can be used: Direct, open end, rephrasing, and redirect.

Direct (Close-End) Questions

The direct or close-end question can be answered with very few words, frequently a simple yes or no. This type of question is particularly useful in moving a prospect toward a specific area. Some examples of this area, "Mr. Kary, are you interested in making extra money on vacant floor space in your store?" or "Making additional revenues is very important today in a retail store, isn't it?" A yes answer can be anticipated from both these questions because they help the salesperson focus on the topic desired: Use of floor space to make additional revenues.

A salesperson must be careful not to use a *direct negative*— any question that completely cuts off the conversation. The classic negative is one question used far too often in retail selling: "May I help you?" The usual reply, "No, I'm just looking," cuts the salesperson completely off from easily and logically continuing the conversation.

Besides yes and no direct questions, other questions are "How many?" or "What kind?" These direct questions ask for a short, limited answer from the prospect: "How many 12-ounce packages does your store sell in an average week?" or "What kind of delivery schedule do you prefer?"

Since direct questions elicit very little feedback, the answers do not provide a great deal of information. In dealing with a prospect's objections or in determining the prospect's needs and problems, more information is usually needed. This can often be obtained through open-end questions.

Open-End Questions

More information and two-way communication can be achieved by open-end questions. These can take the form of one-word questions—"Oh?" or "Really?"—with the tone rising at the end of the word so that the prospect is prompted to continue talking. Other useful open-end questions can be created by beginning the question with one of six words: Who, what, where, when, why, and how:

Who usually purchases this product?

What features are you looking for in buying a product in this category?

Where will you display the product?

When will you need the product delivered?

Why don't you like to use promotional allowances?

How frequently will you purchase this product?

Through open-end questions, a salesperson can obtain more information, leave the situation open for more discussion of what is really on the prospect's mind when voicing objections, and give the prospect the sense of participating in the sales call.

Rephrasing Questions

Rephrasing questions is particularly helpful in understanding more clearly what the prospect means. They are particularly useful in handling objections. Care must be taken to ask rephrased questions in a sincere, nonaggressive way. When a prospect objects to the price of an item, a salesperson might say, "Ms. Dalton, are you saying that price is the only thing you are interested in?"

In another situation the salesperson could ask, "Then, Mr. Frick, what you are saying is, if I can provide an introductory promotional allowance, you would be interested in purchasing 10 cases of this product?"

Of course, if the prospect answers "yes" to this question, the salesperson can work out the specifics of the introductory promotional allowance and close the sale. If the prospect answers "no," the salesperson can ask further questions to try to determine the real reason for not purchasing the product.

Redirect Questions

The final type of question is used to redirect the prospect's attention to a previous area of agreement. By focusing attention on already established areas of mutual agreement, this approach helps to handle objections by focusing first on positive aspects. The objection can then be dealt with from a more favorable perspective.

For example, when the prospect says, "There is really no reason for us to further discuss my purchasing this product. We are very satisfied with our present supplier." A salesperson could use redirect questions by saying, "Ms. Szirmai, we agreed that it is important to you and your company to have suppliers that can help reduce your costs and increase your sales. Would you not agree that you continually need to find new ways to reduce your costs and increase your company's sales in this particular market?"

This redirect question moves the conversation from a negative dead-end position to a positive or neutral position and reestablishes the possibility for positive communication.

To successfully use a redirect or any of the other three types of questions, it is necessary for the salesperson to listen. Due in part to the nature of the profession, many salespeople are so used to talking and presenting they forget to listen to what the prospect says. Many salespeople do not know how to listen. Anyone, particularly a prospect, appreciates a good listener. A salesperson who is a good listener is viewed as interested in the prospect and is seen as an individual who truly wants to help.

METHODS FOR DEALING WITH OBJECTIONS

Even though objections can make selling more difficult, objections can also be viewed as a sign of interest. They are also an indirect way of asking for more information. To avoid the risk of making a mistake or reducing purchase dissonance, the prospect raises different objections. *Purchase dissonance,* the concern a prospect has about making the purchase, can be dealt with by providing more information and increasing the confidence level of the prospect. If the prospect says, "This package does not look very good. I bet it will not keep the freshness in and will probably leak, leave a mess, and cause consumer dissatisfaction and product returns," then the prospect is really looking for more information and assurance from the salesperson that the product's package is strong. The salesperson should be able to overcome this purchase dissonance by describing the strength, quality, and sealing capability of the package.

Very often an objection is a stalling device or a way for the prospect to get out of the situation. When prospects say that they want to talk it over with other individuals in the company or cannot afford to buy now, they may be giving valid reasons, but often they are having too much dissonance or purchase anxiety to make a purchase decision. When this is the case, the salesperson must offer risk-reducing benefits or lose the sale. *Risk-reducing benefits* are those aspects of the product that help assure the prospect that a right decision is to make the purchase.

There are several successful methods for handling objections: The boomerang method, the counterbalance method, the denial method, the indirect denial method, the failure-to-hear method, and the question method.

Boomerang Method

When using the boomerang method, the salesperson attempts to turn the objection into a reason for buying, being careful to avoid making the prospect look foolish or ignorant for raising the objection. If a prospect says, "It is not worth it to take some space from the aisle to have you set up your point-of-purchase display," the salesperson responds, "Mr. Kitchin, you said you were concerned about not obtaining enough sales and profits from your store. This is an opportunity for you to earn $24 just for displaying 12 cases of the product for three days, using only a two by four feet space. This will increase your profit per square foot and still leave ample room for shoppers." As in this example, prospects must never feel they are being condescended to or made to feel stupid when the boomerang method is used.

Counterbalance Method

In the counterbalance method, an objection that cannot be denied is countered by citing an even more important benefit of making the purchase. One of the most difficult problems for a salesperson is trying to overcome a valid objection. When an objection like this is raised, a salesperson must develop a positive benefit of the feature. If a prospect says, "This computer clone is very difficult to access for repair," the salesperson could comment, "You are right, Ms. Dalton, it is difficult to access. The company designed it that way to keep unauthorized and untrained personnel from tampering with the machine. Other companies such as yours have found that this feature significantly reduced repairs by making it difficult for unauthorized people to attempt to repair or modify the computer."

Denial Method

There are times when a prospect has misinformation about the company or its products that hinder the sale. When the salesperson is sure that the idea is completely wrong and that without this being stated no sale can be made, often there is no alternative but to deny the idea politely and firmly. Whenever possible, supportive data should be furnished then or at a later date to confirm the accuracy of the denial. If a prospect states, "I would consider buying something from your company, but I understand your company is near bankruptcy," the salesperson could respond by stating, "Yes, Mr. Donaldson, I have heard that rumor, too, and the company is trying to find out how it got started because it is definitely not true. Our company had one of its best years ever last year, and I would be glad to show you the company's year-end and last-quarter reports."

Indirect Denial Method

The indirect denial method is useful when the comment of the prospect cannot be refuted directly. In this indirect denial method, also called the "Yes, but" method, the salesperson agrees with the prospect's comments and then immediately follows with a disclaimer. When a prospect comments, "I understand your company's cars are known for having a high recall rate," the salesperson can respond using the indirect method: "Yes, Ms. McCarthy, we had that problem in earlier models, but in the last few years our company has spent over $500 million to correct the situation. The result has been that the company's cars have had virtually no recalls in the last two model years."

Failure-to-Hear Method

A salesperson should rarely ignore any objection by a prospect. However, if an objection is patently absurd and it is apparent that the prospect really does not believe it or it is such a low-priority objection that it will not hinder the sale, sometimes it is better just to pretend not to hear the objection, avoiding a direct confrontation. This method should rarely be employed and only by salespeople who carefully listen to everything a prospect mentions, including the prospect's voice tone and body language, because even a very minor objection that is not addressed can block a sale.

Question Method

As discussed earlier, asking a question is a useful method throughout a sales call, but it is particularly useful in clarifying or handling a prospect's objection. By using a question in response to an objection, a salesperson puts the ball back in the prospect's court and causes the prospect to restate—and it is hoped—rethink the objection. In the best of circumstances this questioning causes the prospect to rethink the objection and minimize its significance. At least, however, the question gives the salesperson more time to think about the response to an objection. Restatement of the objection usually takes a form different from the original statement, which can help to clarify it for the salesperson. If a prospect says, "I do not like the design of this keyboard," the salesperson can ask, "Ms. Donovan, what specifically don't you like about the design?"

ESTABLISHING A PROCEDURE

It is important that each salesperson establish a procedure for handling objections. While each individual sales call case will be handled differently, by establishing a general procedure, a salesperson will be better able to handle the objections briefly and perhaps even change a strong "no" response to a more positive one.

The first item in the procedure is to listen, listen, listen. The salesperson must be sure that the prospect continues to talk without any interruption. Second, whenever a prospect raises an objection, be sure to repeat the objection, making it clearly understood by both parties. In so doing, the salesperson should always acknowledge the soundness of the objection by agreeing as far as possible and asking questions for further clarification. During this time, the objection raised needs to be evaluated in terms of the strength of conviction and whether it is an excuse or a real objection.

Depending on the strength of the objection and the stage at which it is raised in the sales process, the salesperson should select the best technique or method for handling the objection. Once you feel the objection has been dealt with, ask the prospect if it has, because a sale will not result unless all objections have been dealt with completely. If the objection has been dealt with, continue on with the sales presentation. If it has not, then ask some more questions and repeat the process of trying to deal satisfactorily with the objection.

CHAPTER PERSPECTIVE

Handling objections in a professional manner is one of the most difficult aspects of the selling process. Questions have many uses in dealing with objections. Six basic methods of handling objections are the boomerang, the counterbalance, the denial, the indirect denial, the failure-to-hear, and the question. Guidelines are provided for dealing with objections. No matter what methods or guidelines you follow, a salesperson should deal with every objection raised, even if you say, "I will get you more information." The slightest unanswered objection may cause you to lose a sale.

Closing the Sale

INTRODUCTION AND MAIN POINTS

One of the most difficult tasks in the selling process is knowing when and how to ask for the order—*closing the sale*. A very successful salesperson commented, "I was making wonderful presentations for my previous company, but I was never able to ask for the order. In my new position, I learned how to close the sale, and it has made me the leading salesperson in the district." A successful salesperson develops a selling technique that aids in sensing when and how to *close*, or ask for an order, with each prospect.

After reading this chapter:

■ You will know the essential aspects involved in closing a sale.

■ You will understand how to determine when to ask for an order.

■ You will be able to use several basic closing techniques.

ASPECTS OF CLOSING

Unless a salesperson uses an effective and timely close, a sale rarely happens. Even so, few individuals in any sales force close effectively. Indeed, it is the close that separates the great salespeople from the merely good ones. A salesperson who is good at closing spends significant time in preparing a sales call, has a strong desire to make a sale, is a good listener, does not accept "no" right away, and knows when to stop talking.

Individuals who are good at closing understand the importance of preparing the sales call. (This is discussed in detail in Chapter 6.) They take time to understand the industry, the characteristics of the customers, and each customer's needs and benefits. With this understanding, and a thorough knowledge of how the company's products produce these benefits, a good salesperson carefully plans several strategies for making a sale and looks for opportunities to use these different closing alternatives.

Individuals who are good at closing have a *desire* to close each and every sale. They are not satisfied by merely giving a good presentation. They need the close to feel they have done the job well. Each customer becomes a challenge to be met. This salesperson also understands that there may be times when the situation calls for a sale in the future, not during the present sales call.

An individual good at closing is also good at *listening*. Perhaps one of the greatest problems in not being able to close well is not being able to listen. Unless a salesperson listens carefully and hears opposing views and the strengths of various objections, it is almost impossible to develop the best answers to the objections and to choose the best time to close.

An individual who is good at closing never accepts the first "no." When a customer says "no," he evaluates the objection behind the no, and provides more information relevant to the objection. The good salesperson uses a trial close to ascertain whether the prior objection(s) have been overcome and to determine if there are more objections. (The trial close is discussed in detail later in this chapter.) Each time a trial close is attempted, a salesperson is one step closer to a sale.

Finally, an individual who is good at closing knows the importance of asking for the sale and then being quiet until there is an answer. After asking for the order, a good salesperson says absolutely nothing, knowing that every spoken word decreases the probability of making a sale.

The prospect understands that he or she must make a decision and respond to the close before anything else will be said by the salesperson. This time may seem interminable when making a close, but rarely does the silence last more than 25 to 30 seconds.

During this silent period, a good salesperson says nothing, projects *positive nonverbal signs* to the prospect, and prepares responses to probable objections. Every salesperson has the urge to talk to relieve the uncomfortable situation, an urge that gets stronger the longer the silence. A good salesperson overcomes this urge, knowing that talking to the prospect destroys the closing moment and does not allow the prospect to make a decision. Similarly, do not talk too much after the buyer says "yes." A continuation of the presentation at this time might provide information that would change the prospect's decision. Once a yes is obtained, the details of the sale should be completed and the salesperson should leave.

Factors Necessary to Close a Sale

Some of the most important factors in closing a sale follow:

▬ Put yourself in the prospect's position.

▬ Listen and learn to read—understand the prospect and his or her comments.

▬ Make sure the presentation is clear and understandable and presents the complete picture.

▬ Establish high sales goals.

▬ Never accept the first no.

▬ Always maintain a positive, confident, and enthusiastic attitude.

STEPS IN CLOSING

In developing a good close, it is helpful to follow an individualized version of the following series of steps. Because a salesperson cannot be successful by completely adopting another salesperson's closing techniques, devise a customized procedure that can be modified based on the customer's reaction. This will help you construct your own procedure, resulting in a better closing technique. There are nine steps to the procedure:

1) Plan the sales call.
2) Understand and confirm a prospect's needs and desired benefits.
3) Make a clear presentation.
4) Listen and ascertain the underlying objection.
5) Attempt a trial close whenever warranted.
6) Ask for the order, and then say nothing.
7) Always leave the door open for a future sale.
8) Be positive and confident.
9) Always be professional.

By remembering these nine steps, a salesperson does not succumb to the temptation of thinking that closing is just one giant step and the mystical nature of closing is removed. Closing is not something tricky. It does not require the ability to use just the right, clever words. A closing results when a salesperson knows good techniques and understands the customer and the nature of the selling process.

By following these nine steps, the close becomes a part of the presentation. The result may be that the prospect actually provides the close by saying, "That sounds all right. I will try some of the product." Although it seems obvious, some salespeople forget that prospects know the reason the salesperson is there: To sell them something. Depending on a prospect's level of interest and knowledge, the prospect may be well beyond the stage of the presentation. The prospect may actually be ready to make a decision very early in the selling process.

TIMING THE CLOSE

Probably the questions most frequently asked by sales trainees are, "How do I know it is time to close?" and "When should I attempt to close a sale?" The reason that these questions are so difficult to answer is that a prospect can be ready to buy at any point in the selling process. One prospect can be ready to buy at the approach stage; another prospect will only be ready the day following the presentation. This wide variation requires that the salesperson listen carefully and be very attentive to visual and verbal clues given by the prospect. The salesperson should remember, though, that 80 percent of the time, the close logically follows the presentation as planned.

Buying Signals

As prospects become involved in the selling process, they frequently give a signal about where they are in their own mental processes. This *buying signal* refers to any visual or verbal cue given by the prospect indicating his or her readiness to buy. Many buying signals indicate a prospect is near the conviction stage of the buying process (see Table 9-1).

Table 9-1
Buying Signals Made by the Prospect

1. The prospect makes a positive statement about the product.
2. The prospect asks about the use, price, installation, or delivery of the product.
3. The prospect asks the names of others who use the product.
4. The prospect asks about any buying incentives.
5. The prospect plays with a pen and order form.
6. The prospect physically handles the product.
7. The prospect changes voice to a more positive tone.
8. The prospect's expression changes from worried and defensive to more happy, and relaxed.
9. The prospect tests or tries the product.

One of the best buying signals is when the prospect asks questions about price, installation, delivery, buying incentives, or others now using the product. For example, questions such as, "How much is it?" "What is the earliest date of delivery for the first order?" "What support service do you provide?" and "What is your company's return goods policy?" indicate that a trial close is in order.

To better understand a prospect's thoughts about the product, a salesperson can respond to a question with another question. If a prospect asks, "What is the price of the product?" the salesperson can respond, "In what quantity are you considering purchasing?" If a prospect asks, "How many would you suggest that I order?" the salesperson can respond, "What is your usual production run?" If a buyer asks, "When can you make delivery?" the salesperson can respond, "When is the earliest delivery needed?" By answering a question with a question, a salesperson obtains additional information and can measure the interest level of the prospect. The more positive the response of the prospect, the higher the prospect's interest level in purchasing the product.

Another frequent buying signal is when the prospect relaxes and becomes more friendly. Once a prospect makes the internal decision to purchase the product, the pressures involved in the decision are eliminated. This often becomes physically apparent before it is verbally expressed. The visible anxiety or concern on a prospect's face can change to a more happy, relaxed expression.

A third buying signal is when the prospect either asks who else is buying the product or asks another person's opinion. When a person calls someone else into the office and asks for an opinion about the purchase, the interest level is high enough to attempt a trial close.

A fourth buying signal is when the prospect starts to handle and carefully scrutinize the product. This indicates that the prospect has more than a passing interest in the product and is indirectly asking for more information and reasons for purchasing the product. This warrants attempting a trial close, such as asking the prospect, "What do you think about...?" After receiving a positive response to this question, the salesperson moves to close the sale.

TRIAL CLOSE

Verbal or nonverbal buying signals may be sent by the prospect anytime during the selling process. Once a buying signal is given, a salesperson should attempt a trial close. A trial close is an attempt to determine if the prospect is ready to buy and therefore ready to close the sale. The concept of a trial close, or several trial closes, is illustrated in Figure 9-1. In beginning a trial close, a salesperson should highlight the major selling points desired by the prospect. If a positive response to the trial close is received, then the salesperson can proceed directly to the close. If a negative response is received, then the salesperson must determine the objections, meet these objections, and try another trial close. This process is repeated until either a positive response is obtained and the salesperson can move on to the close, or it is obvious that more trial closes will not bring about a positive response. When this occurs, the salesperson should be professional and ask for an appointment in the future and call on another prospect. Whether or not a trial close is successful, at the very least a trial close provides the salesperson with an assessment of the selling situation.

FIGURE 9-1
ILLUSTRATION OF A TRIAL CLOSE

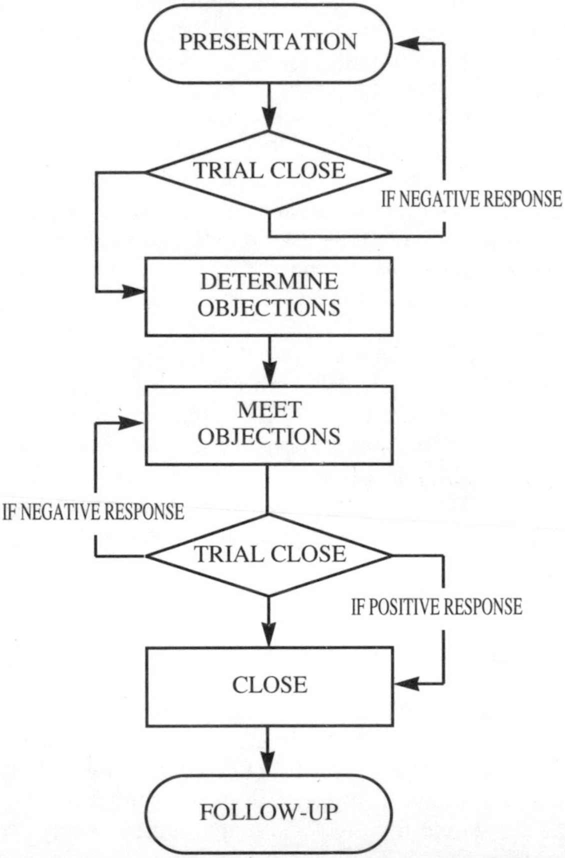

Forms of Trial Close

Trial closes have many verbal and nonverbal forms:

▬ Ask, "Would you be interested in comparing the lease versus buy options?"

▬ Ask, "Which model do you like best—Model 4000 or Model 8000?"

▬ Ask, Would you be interested in obtaining the maintenance contract that goes along with the purchase?"

▬ Allow the prospect to hold, touch, and evaluate the product using all senses.

▬ Ask the prospect whether the product will do the job.

▬ Ask, "In what quantities would you generally purchase the product?"

These and other trial closes elicit various responses from the prospect. Signs to proceed with caution that may emerge are the following:

▬ The prospect requests more information.

▬ The prospect refuses to communicate with the salesperson.

▬ No positive response occurs.

▬ An interruption occurs that affects the prospect's positive state of mind.

If a more positive response occurs during a trial close, the salesperson should then move to the closing part of the selling process using one of a variety of techniques.

CLOSING TECHNIQUES

A good salesperson knows that to close successfully it is essential to employ an appropriate closing technique. To do this the prospect's attitude must be observed as well as the response to the presentation and any trial closes. Instead of just asking prospects whether they want to purchase the product, a good salesperson selects the appropriate closing technique for the prospect from the many available methods.

In closing, one of the most important things a salesperson needs to keep in mind is that a sale is not necessarily lost just because the prospect says "no." A "no" may mean several different things such as, "I need more information," "I need more time to consider this purchase—don't hurry me," "Not now," or "I just do not understand the product and how it will benefit me." Whenever a "no" to the buying process is given, it should be challenged in a low-key positive manner with questions being raised by the salesperson so that the true meaning of "no" is understood.

Assumption Close

In the assumption close, the salesperson assumes that the prospect will purchase and indicates this feeling through comments and nonverbal actions. The salesperson could comment, "Do you want the order delivered this Wednesday or Friday?" or "Will that be cash or charge? We accept Discover, MasterCard, and Visa." Or "Do you need any more than the amount indicated on the sales plan?" Nonverbal actions can be getting out the credit card machine, handling the prospect a pen and order form, or starting to wrap the package.

Although useful in any selling situation, the assumption close is particularly good in repeat orders, when the salesperson has earned the confidence of the buyer to such an extent that the buyer almost always approves what the salesperson orders. In this situation a closing comment could be, "This is the amount I believe you need to order this month."

Compliment Close

The compliment close is particularly useful for a prospect who is a self-styled expert, has a big ego, or is in a bad mood. Such a prospect responds very favorably to compliments. Compliments help the prospect to listen and respond favorably.

All prospects like a sincere appreciation of their better points. A salesperson needs to find out what is important to prospects and then look for ways to compliment them in those areas as sales are being closed. Since almost every prospect can detect insincerity or an undeserved compliment, it is important that only genuine compliments be used.

Continuous-Yes Close

Similar to a summary close, the continuous-yes close uses benefit questions the prospect must answer, instead of summarizing product benefits. In this close, the salesperson identifies the benefits the customer indicates and poses these in question form before asking for the order. For example, if a prospect likes the quality, profit margin, and merchandising offer, a salesperson can develop the following scenario:

Salesperson:	"Ms. Kelly, you said you really like the quality of the product, correct?"
Ms. Kelly:	"Yes, that's true."
Salesperson:	"And you like the high profit margin on the product?"
Ms. Kelly:	"Yes, I do indeed."

Salesperson:	"You also said you like the merchandising allowance offer that is now in place?"
Ms. Kelly:	"That's right."
Salesperson:	"Ms. Kelly, as you like the quality of the product, the profit margin, and the merchandising allowance offer that will be in effect only for the next few weeks, you should be ordering...."

A series of questions about the product that the customer responds to favorably places the prospect in a positive frame of mind to say "yes" to the request to purchase the product.

Choice Close

In the choice close, the prospect is asked to choose between two versions of the product, not to decide whether to buy the product itself. The prospect is not given the choice of buying or not buying, but rather the choice of the product type or amount. Examples of a choice close are "Do you want the 4000 or 8000 version?" "Do you want three cases or four?" "Which do you prefer, the blue and yellow shirts or the blue pinstripe and red pinstripe shirts?"

If the prospect responds to this type of close with "I'm not sure," then the salesperson knows the prospect is in the desire, not the conviction, stage and more product benefits should be presented. If the prospect likes both options but cannot make a decision, the salesperson can ask, "Is there something you are not quite sure about, Mr. Hughes?"

The choice close is one of the most effective and yet one of the easiest closing techniques to use. It provides a choice between one thing and another, not a choice between something and nothing. When a choice is presented, the salesperson receives either an order or objections, which, if answered successfully, can result in an order.

Minor-Points Close

In the minor points technique the prospect makes progressively larger decisions by starting with minor points. For some buyers large decisions, such as purchasing the product, are difficult to make and it is much easier to concede and agree on lesser points. In the minor-points close, the prospect is asked to make a decision on minor areas concerning the product—features, size, color, delivery dates, warranty terms, payments terms, or size of order—before being asked for the order itself. This closing technique is especially useful for a prospect who has difficulty in making a decision or for a prospect not in the mood to buy.

Some minor-points closing questions are "Are you interested in the installment plan?" "Would you like your car to have a sun-roof?" "Would you prefer the deluxe or the regular model?" "Would you prefer delivery this week or next?" The approach can also be successfully used as a second close if the first failed. In this case, the salesperson can get the prospect to agree on minor points and then the purchase. This close is particularly good when the prospect said "no" to the first close because of difficulty in making a decision.

Summary of Benefits Close

The most frequently used close is when the salesperson concludes the presentation by summarizing the advantages of the major product features and the benefits to the prospect. The summary of benefits close is a useful technique when the salesperson needs a straightforward close that does not need to take into account any unique characteristics of the prospect. It is very useful for both consumer and industrial products.

For example, if a salesperson knows that the buyer likes the profit margin, 90-day payment terms, and two-day delivery schedule, the close could be, "Ms. Ellis, you have indicated that you like the profit margin, 90-day payment terms, and prompt delivery schedule of the product. These features have allowed other customers just like you to make a lot of money selling this product. I can have an initial order of ten cases here by next Monday so you can start making money for your store."

Supply Close

The supply close pressures the prospect to buy now, not to delay the purchase, by indicating that many people are buying the product and that it may not be available later or, if available, only in a smaller quantity than the prospect needs. Although this approach can be very honest, it can give rise to questionable feelings in the prospect—particularly if the salesperson appears insincere or if the supply problem mentioned was not made apparent previously. For the right product, situation, and prospect though, this can be a very effective closing technique. When extraneous factors such as strikes, bad weather, transportation problems, price increases, or government-imposed quotas are known to the prospect, this can be a particularly good closing technique. Some examples are as follows:

▬ "Mr. Donaldson, this machine will increase in price by 10 percent next week. Can I place the order today so you can avoid this announced price increase?"

▬ "This has really been a fast-moving item this month, and I'm not sure there are any left. I'll have to check availability once I have your order."

"Since it appears that a rail strike is going to occur next week, I suggest you order today to ensure you will receive your orders before the strike occurs."

"Unless something unusual happens, it looks as if the union will go on strike next week, causing severe problems in supply as well as delivery."

T-Account Close

The T-account close is based on the mental process each prospect goes through in making a purchasing decision. In this technique the advantages and disadvantages of buying the product are written on either side of a line in the center of the paper: a T-account. All the pros of buying the product are placed on one side of the line and all the cons on the other side. This simulates the process the prospect actually goes through in making a purchase decision—weighing the pros against the cons.

A salesperson can draw a large T on a sheet of paper, placing "To Buy" on the left-hand side and "Not to Buy" on the right-hand side. The salesperson then reviews the presentation, with the prospect listing the product features, advantages, and benefits on the left-hand side of the T and all the negative points on the right-hand side. This is a comfortable closing technique because prospects make their own lists and they can see that the benefits of purchasing the product outweigh the negatives and that they should purchase the product now.

For example, if during the presentation the prospect found that the quality of the product, the speed of delivery, and the profit margin were good and the terms of payment favorable, the T account during the review by the salesperson would be:

Buy	Not to Buy
Quality product	Poor payment terms
Fast delivery	
Good margins	

Some salespeople prefer to discuss the reasons not to buy

first and prefer that the Not to Buy column be on the left and the To Buy column on the right. This allows them to end the presentation on the positive side.

Other salespeople modify the T-account approach to one column only. Believing that it is better not to remind the prospect about reasons not to buy, they use only one column and list the reasons to buy. The T account or modified T account is a very good closing technique because it closes along the lines the prospect is thinking—weighing the positive and negative points of the purchase.

This technique can also be very useful as a backup close should a first technique, such as the summary, not end in a sale. There is nothing better than allowing the prospect to get the negatives, even on paper in the T account. An objection when seen in light of the benefits can then be placed in proper perspective by the prospect and sometimes may even disappear.

Closing Difficulties

Even though closing a sale should be one of the easiest steps in the selling process, it is the most difficult for many salespeople. Instead of viewing the close as a method for solidifying the details of the purchase agreement, these salespeople see the close as something the prospect views negatively. They forget that when a product meets the needs of the prospect, the close establishes the method by which the prospect can receive it. Of course, several difficulties may be encountered in closing the sale.

First, salespeople often make their own determinations, sometimes before the selling process even begins, that the prospect does not need the product being offered. Guided by this feeling, they just do not ask the prospect to make a purchase. These salespeople should remember that they are not in a position to make such a decision and it is the prospect's decision and responsibility to purchase or not to purchase the product.

Second, some salespeople fail to do their homework on the prospect's profile and benefits. This lack of effort usually results in a very poor sales presentation. When there is a poor presentation, the salesperson rarely has a good opportunity to close the sale easily by asking for a purchase.

Finally, some salespeople fail to close because of a lack of confidence in their abilities. Sometimes this reflects previous failures. This fear needs to be overcome so that a purchase can be requested, resulting in a successful close.

Number of Times to Close

A question that frequently arises when difficulties in closing are discussed is, "How many times should I try to close?" There is no magic number for the upper limit, and each salesperson should remember that he or she was hired to call on customers and prospects and sell the company's products. To accomplish this objective, multiple closes are in order. Courtesy and common sense should be used to determine the appropriate number of closes in a particular situation, but three to five well-executed closes should be used as a minimum. This number will not offend the buyer if professionally done.

Closing After "No"

Closing after being rejected on the first attempt is one of the most difficult aspects of closing, but it is very rare that a salesperson should stop closing after the first no. A salesperson must be able to ask a prospect to place an order even if the prospect has already said "no," is hostile, or is in a bad mood. The job of the salesperson is to sell the company's products to customers and prospects.

CHAPTER PERSPECTIVE

One of the most difficult stages in the selling process for many sales people is closing the sale. The nine steps for developing a good closing are: Planning the sales call, understanding the prospect's needs and benefits, making a clear presentation, ascertaining the real objections, attempting trial closes whenever warranted, asking for the order, leaving the door open for a possible future sale, being positive and confident, and always being professional. Successful closing requires the salesperson to understand the various buying signals of the prospect and then to confidently do a trial close or ask for the order. Regardless of the results of the sales call, it is important that the salesperson always be professional making it possible for future sales to occur.

The Follow up After the Sale

INTRODUCTION AND MAIN POINTS

After making any sale, a good salesperson always follows up to ensure that the customer is satisfied and to thank the customer for the business. The best customers in the future are satisfied customers now. Because many buyers have *postpurchase anxiety* (concern that they made the wrong decision in buying the product), a follow-up sales call not only can alleviate or at least minimize this dissonance, it may result in immediate additional sales. It can also help to develop a satisfied customer who will make purchases in the future.

After reading this chapter:

- You will know how to depart after making the close.
- You will be able to implement the appropriate follow-through steps.
- You will understand the importance and types of customer service.
- You will be able to use suggestion selling.
- You will be able to develop goodwill.
- You will be able to handle complaints.

DEPARTURE AFTER THE SELLING PROCESS

For many salespeople the period immediately following the close, when a sale is either made or not made, is very awkward. If the close has ended successfully, the time can be used for referrals or reorder periods. If the sale has been lost, even this negative event can be turned into a greater probability for a future sale.

Departure Following Success

When the sale is made, two predominant feelings emerge. A salesperson feels the excitement of victory and success, quickly followed by the second feeling—fear that the customer will change his mind and cancel the order. Both of these feelings should be controlled. The last stage of the sales call, the conclusion and departure, should lead to future sales. This is when the salesperson sincerely thanks the customer for the time and business. The words and attitudes of the salesperson can go a long way toward reducing the *cognitive dissonance* of the buyer, the buyer's feeling that perhaps the decision to purchase the product was not correct.

Dissonance can best be reduced when the salesperson, in a relaxed and natural manner, thanks the customer for the order and handles questions about delivery and payment. The salesperson assures the customer that he will answer future questions and will ensure that the order is delivered in a timely manner. The greatest error is to prolong the call and continue talking. The goal should be to leave as quickly and naturally as possible.

Departure Following Failure

A good departure after failure to obtain a sale, perhaps more than at any other time, is the mark of a true professional. A professional salesperson does not feel defeated or intimidated by the loss of a sale. Instead, the salesperson should ensure that the prospect believes the time has not been wasted and that the information was valuable, even if a sale did not occur. When the professional salesperson leaves, the prospect should have a favorable image of the individual and the company, which lays the groundwork for a future sale or a good referral. The salesperson must remember that no product meets the needs of every customer.

Even when the turndown is harsh and negative, a salesperson should remain courteous and friendly. The prospect, the secretary, and the receptionist should all remember the salesperson as confident and courteous regardless of the situation. The words and actions during a difficult departure can be the first step in achieving a sale the next time.

If future sales are possible, the prospect should understand the salesperson is interested in the individual as well as the organization in a continuing business relationship. The first step is to call or send a note of thanks for the prospect's time. Then, find out why the sale was not made by asking the individual for the real reasons the product was not purchased. Sincere, honest questions are usually answered honestly, and create the opportunity for a later call.

The final step can be the most painful: It requires the salesperson to analyze the entire selling process carefully to determine what went wrong. This critical self-analysis usually uncovers problems that, when corrected, can lead to a future, successful sales call. Questions that should be asked include the following: Did I prepare for the sales call properly? Was I awkward in approaching and greeting the prospect? Did I quickly arouse and hold the prospect's interest? Did I give all the key points in my presentation? Did I use all the sales aids available effectively? Was I successful in getting at all the objections and handling them effectively? Did I use the prepared trial close? Did I use the proper closing techniques? Did I have the proper attitude throughout the selling process? Did I leave pleasantly?

The answers to these and other self-evaluation questions will improve your ability to make successful sales presentations. No salesperson can close every sale, but through self-evaluation and application of sound principles and techniques the percentage of closes will increase.

ASPECTS OF FOLLOW-THROUGH

To ensure satisfied customers, always follow up after making a sale. Some salespeople may overlook this, and instead, pursue different customers or obtain new customers. If there is no proper follow-up, a once-satisfied customer may very well become disgruntled. While the exact nature of the follow through depends on the product and market situation, there are general steps a salesperson can follow to ensure complete customer satisfaction.

■ First, a formal letter on company stationery, an informal note, or even a postcard ensures that your appreciation is clear. This follow-up expression of appreciation in addition to the thank-you note after a successful closing, is done about two days after the sale.

■ Second, check delivery. On the scheduled day for delivery, a quick telephone call to the customer not only informs you that delivery was made, but that the buyer knows that you care and are mindful of service. If there are problems—the delivery was not made or the products were damaged—you can take prompt and appropriate action.

■ Next, ensure that the employees of the buying organization are knowledgeable about the product and its operation or use. Proper knowledge and training in the buying organization often eliminates complaints before a problem can occur.

■ Finally, for products that require installation, visit the buying organization soon after delivery to ensure that the product is properly installed. Even if there are no problems, this call affirms that you and your firm are conscientious and sincerely interested in building a long-term relationship.

By providing good follow-up, a salesperson ensures that the customer is completely satisfied. It is usually much easier to sell a satisfied customer more of the same or a new product than to locate and sell to an entirely new prospect. It can be difficult for buyers to find a salesperson willing to give prompt, efficient service. The trust and confidence established between a buyer and a salesperson almost always stems from the follow-up service. This leads to repeat business and further cementing of the relationship.

Good follow-up service also provides referrals to new customers because satisfied customers are usually the best source for referrals. One way a satisfied buyer can repay the salesperson's courtesy for follow-up interest and service is to provide the names of others who may be interested in a product or service. This relaxed atmosphere of the follow-up is much more productive for leads and referrals, or even an introductory letter or telephone call than the pre-sale environment. The testimony of a satisfied customer is the best support of the claims you make in a sales presentation.

FOLLOW-UP PROCEDURE

Because good follow-up is so important for building customer rapport, the professional salesperson develops and implements a follow-up procedure for the territory. Several initiatives are undertaken on a regular basis:

■ A company system ensures that all requests for information, complaints, or problems from customers or prospects are handled promptly and efficiently.

■ A company system regularly checks customers views of the products and salespeople.

■ Meetings are scheduled regularly (depending on the potential sales) with key people in both the selling and buying firms. Each of these individuals is on the seller's mailing list and receives all announcements and advertising and promotional material.

■ You must be informed of customer complaints and problems, and try to handle personally as many as possible.

■ Make yourself available to each customer, leaving evening and weekend telephone numbers. These numbers will seldom be used, and then only in extreme emergency.

■ Make your customers feel a part of your network, sharing with them names and contacting them on a regular basis.

By establishing and implementing a sound follow-up procedure, you develop a relationship with the customer that results in repeat sales.

OVERALL CUSTOMER SERVICE

Although not directly indicated in the stages of the selling process, personal selling also involves *servicing* the sale. Each area of marketing should be concerned about servicing the customer, because a satisfied customer is the key to sales in a profitable business. Good customer service keeps current accounts satisfied and helps attract new accounts by direct referrals and company reputation.

Each customer has two dimensions that makes a well-planned customer service program essential for the customer's comfortable feelings after the purchase. To understand what a customer feels after the purchase, reflect on your last major purchase. What went through your mind several days after the purchase? Did you think the purchase decision was correct? Were you concerned that a better product might be available at a better price? Did you feel good while making the purchase? Did the salesperson contribute to this good feeling? What factors other than the product and the price affected your purchase decision? Most buyers have these questions and reactions during and after a sale.

Creating a comfortable feeling during the sale requires that the salesperson focus on the buyer's need for compliments and recognition. Everyone responds positively to sincere affirmation and recognition and negatively to insincerity and indifference. A salesperson's handwritten note thanking the buyer for the order or a follow-up telephone call inquiring about the customer's satisfaction indicates that the customer is important and the business is valued.

The feeling of comfort after the sale focuses on insecurity after a decision. Whether this insecurity is based on late delivery or faulty installation or is just a vague feeling, it is still very real to the individual. The salesperson and company who minimize or even eliminate this feeling by providing good customer service are far ahead of major competitors in developing customer loyalty and repeat purchasing. It makes the customers feel that they are in the good, caring hands of the salesperson and the selling company.

COMMON PROBLEMS AFTER SALES

A good customer service program must address the most common problems occurring for the company after sales. While there are problems specific to each company, some common problems are price, changes, late delivery, poor installation, credit denial, lack of promotional information, and insufficient training.

Price Changes

Price changes, particularly price increases, can be a problem if they are not handled correctly. Any price changes should be immediately recorded on the company's existing price list if a new list is not issued. There is nothing that generates more distrust and irritation on the part of the customer than the price of the product or service not being correctly stated the first time. When prices have changed or are about to increase, customers should be notified so that appropriate action can be taken.

Late Delivery

No post-sale problem occurs more frequently and causes more buyer negativity than late deliveries. A late delivery can affect the buyer's plan and eliminate sales when an item is out of stock. Although a late delivery may be out of the salesperson's control, each salesperson should quote accurate delivery dates and keep the customer informed of delays and the reasons for the delay. The salesperson can help prevent some delays by making sure the submitted order is accurate, contains all the needed information, and is processed correctly by the company.

Poor Installation

For certain products, the satisfaction of the buyer is related to whether the product is properly installed. Often the installation of the product is not the responsibility of the salesperson, but it is usually to the salesperson's advantage to do everything possible to ensure proper installation. This can be done by lobbying for the best installers. The salesperson should at least contact the customer to be sure no installation problems have occurred.

Lack of Promotional Information

A salesperson must also be sure that each customer is aware of available promotional monies and allowances. Most companies periodically make available to customers promotional allowances in the form of money or products that can be beneficial to the customer. These allowances may be in the form of cooperative advertising, product purchase quantity, promotional display, or new product trial. Whatever the form, the salesperson should make each customer aware of the allowance and how the customer can use it.

Credit Denial

One problem that directly affects a customer's good feeling is being denied credit or being given limited credit. Each salesperson should become acquainted with company credit personnel and ensure that the responsible person(s) handling the account maintain a good business relationship with his or her customers. Potential credit problems with a particular customer should be anticipated and a careful explanation be given by the salesperson at the time of sale to avoid hurt feelings.

Insufficient Training

For certain products, it is important that personnel are well trained in how to use the product. In some instances, the technology is so complex that training is an integral part of followup. When the training is not sufficient, the product is not used properly and customer dissatisfaction results.

HANDLING COMPLAINTS

There is no area of post-sale service more important to the salesperson than the proper handling of all customer complaints. It is ridiculous for a firm to spend millions of dollars on advertising and promotion to make a sale and build customer loyalty and then be tardy or unresponsive to legitimate customer complaints. Always remember when handling complaints that even better sales and profits can be obtained from the repeat purchases of a satisfied customer than from the initial sale. It is well established that the cost of making the first sale to a customer is far higher than the cost of repeat sales. Correct handling of complaints actually provides the salesperson with the opportunity to resell the company and its products to the customer. Since very few people are chronic complainers, when a customer makes a complaint the company should make every effort to handle it to the satisfaction of the customer. An excellent way to handle customer complaints is through a personal visit by the salesperson. Several methods are usually successful in dealing with complaints in selling situations.

Encourage Customers to Explain the Problem

Individual customers feel much better after having the opportunity to disclose their irritation or anger. Whether the complaint is real or imaginary, they appreciate the opportunity to relieve bottled-up feelings. It is important to allow customers to explain the problem fully without interruption.

Interruptions add to existing buyer anger and hostility, making handling the complaint even more difficult. When anger and hostility are present, reason rarely prevails, making it almost impossible to arrive at an equitable settlement. The salesperson must be equally open in dealing with less emotional customers, who may give little evidence of their irritation, although they may have the same hostility. These customers are just not in the habit of voicing their complaints.

The ease in handling complaints is significantly affected by the atmosphere created by the salesperson at the beginning of the discussion. A customer wants a salesperson to be sympathetic and friendly without any indication of irritation or concern that the buyer is trying to cheat the company. After listening very carefully and attentively, without interrupting, to everything the buyer has to say, the salesperson should then express concern and regret for any inconvenience experienced by the buyer. Based on all the accurate information obtained, you should then attempt to discuss any points made on which there is mutual agreement. Agreeing with the customer whenever possible gets the process off to a good start.

Determine the Facts

Because it is easy to be influenced by a customer who is sincerely trying to make the case for a claim as strong as possible, you must be careful to determine the facts in the case. It is human nature for the buyer to emphasize the facts that strengthen the position. You have a responsibility to the company to ensure that a satisfactory solution is obtained based on the actual facts.

It is important to have the customer explain and show exactly what is wrong. You and the customer should physically examine the product together, unless the defect or problem is apparent without this. If physical examination is not possible or necessary, then make certain that the complaint is fully understood.

It is important that you learn as quickly as possible any reasons that a product appears defective when it is not. In many cases, the product was not used properly. Leather may become defective if placed on a radiator, food can be of lesser quality if frozen, or a duplicating machine may become jammed if improper paper is used. The facts may indicate that the customer is at fault. On some occasions neither the company nor the buyer may be at fault, such as when the product is damaged in shipping.

The most difficult situation arises when the facts do not indicate the reason for the problem or when both the customer and the company are at fault. When such difficult situations arise, the customer should be made aware of the difficulty in obtaining an equitable solution, making sure to avoid the impression that you are stalling. The customer must always understand that the object is to obtain a fair, equitable solution.

Provide a Solution

After listening to the customer and examining everything available at the customer's place of business, it is the salesperson's responsibility to take action and eventually come up with a solution. Some companies assign the responsibility for settling problems to the salesperson; other companies have the salesperson investigate the problem and make recommendations, with the actual settlement being made by the claims department at the home office. Companies that allow the salesperson to make the settlement believe that the salesperson is closest to the customer and best suited to make fair, satisfactory adjustments in a prompt manner. Companies using the opposite approach believe that the customer is more likely to accept the settlement offered if it comes from a higher level of management than the salesperson.

Regardless of company policy, remember that the customer is interested only in quick action. Avoid the temptation to blame the shipping department, installation crew, or someone else in the company. Passing the buck is not favorably regarded by a disgruntled customer. You have the responsibility to resolve the problem, and this should not include negative remarks about the company. Because nothing is so perplexing to a customer as having an action postponed for a long period of time or indefinitely, it is important to do everything possible to expedite response from the company. If the time taken to act is too great, there may be little opportunity to resell to the customer.

Most customers are reasonable people and are satisfied when they receive fair treatment. Be sure the customer understands that the settlement proposed is fair. In some cases this requires some convincing. Settlements fair to both the company and the customer do more to bring about goodwill than any other action on the part of the company. Persuading the customer of the fairness of the settlement sometimes requires a detailed explanation, reviewing the terms of the warranty or guarantee with the customer, or discussing the company's settlement process and the reasons for it. Under no circumstances should you take the customer's side setting up a customer-management confrontation. Agreeing with the customer does not develop a friendship, and it can cause the customer to lose faith in the company and the salesperson. Any problems involved in the settlement should be taken care of between the company and the salesperson without the direct involvement of the customer. The action should be related to the customer in a decisive, convincing manner by the salesperson.

REACHING A FAIR SETTLEMENT

To help the company provide a fair settlement, the following information must be obtained, in addition to the facts regarding the claim itself. This information includes the dollar amount of claim, frequency of customer claims, size of customer account, importance of customer, the extent to which any action taken will affect customer and other accounts, and the experience of the salesperson in dealing with other claims. On the basis of this information, the company's settlement can take one of many forms:

- Full product replacement without cost.
- Full product replacement, charging only for labor and transportation.
- Full product replacement and joint customer and company cost sharing.
- Full product replacement, with customer paying a reduced price.
- Product repaired at customer cost.
- Product sent to company factory for a decision.
- Customer proceeds with claim against a third party.

It is rare that a customer willfully tries to file a false claim, but if you are convinced that neither the company nor a third-party, such as the transportation agent, is at fault, you can give the buyer an opportunity to save face by suggesting a third party is to blame. You might say, "Perhaps the maintenance crew failed to..." Customers making unfair claims, who know this had been discovered, usually leap at the chance to save face and blame others. If this occurs, note this on the customer's profile and attempt to keep this account.

Another approach is far more risky. Call the customer on the fraudulent calls and attempt to appeal to the individual's sense of fair play. This action more than likely will lose the customer, which in some cases is not bad for the company. Great care should be taken when using this approach as the company does not want ill will spread by a disgruntled customer.

Follow-up After Complaint

A fair settlement provides the salesperson with an excellent opportunity to resell the company's products and services. Because the customer has just experienced that the company is very interested in keeping customers satisfied, he or she should be receptive to purchase other products from the company.

Take care to ensure that, whenever possible, "The customer is always right." In this regard, when making a settlement, be sure to act as a public relations representative, ensuring to the extent possible that the customer is satisfied. Good service and complaint handling lead to good customer relations and satisfied, loyal customers.

SUGGESTION SELLING

A form of customer service that is often overlooked is *suggestion selling*, the process of suggesting other products or services related to the main product(s) purchased. Suggestion selling is done only when you believe the additional items will significantly enhance the satisfaction level of the customer. Some salespeople believe suggestion selling is not a service but a bother to the customer, but when handled properly it helps improve relations with most customers. For these customers, a good salesperson can help solve problems by suggesting related items, larger quantities, or better quality items.

Suggest Related Items

Frequently, a salesperson represents a broad line of complementary products. At times, related products or services enhance the customer's satisfaction with the item already chosen and the complete package better meets the customer's needs. This is analogous to the experience many have after buying a new suit, when the salesperson suggests a new tie or shirt to go with the suit.

A related item that adds to the purchased product's versatility is especially good for suggestion selling. For the company just buying a new Xerox machine, an automatic sorting option might be appropriate. For an individual just purchasing a new, quality camera, an additional lens could significantly increase the camera's versatility. A service contract might be an important option for a customer to reduce the worry and costs of downtime.

Suggest Large Quantities

A salesperson must always be ready to suggest larger quantities of an item if this would be beneficial to the customer. The most common benefit is economy, as most companies offer a discount on larger orders. If the customer buys a few more items, the price per item of all the purchases can be reduced significantly.

Another common benefit of a larger order is to beat a forth-coming company price increase. If a salesperson is almost certain prices will rise in the not-too-distant future, customers should be informed so that they can take advantage of the lower prices. A good salesperson takes great care to ensure that if larger quantities are suggested it is to the benefit of the customer, not to make a sales quota or to win a sales contest.

Suggest Better Items

Because most companies offer a range of products in a given category varying in quality and price, the salesperson must assist the customer in carefully selecting the most appropriate price and quality of product. This allows a customer a choice in the purchase decision.

Sometimes a customer needs a higher-priced product than the one selected. This process of moving a customer to a better grade of merchandise, *trading up,* should only be used when there are benefits to the customer. Sometimes the better-quality product has a better warranty, trade value, comfort, durability, or additional options. Whether you show the higher-priced product first or last in the presentation is a contested issue among salespeople. You should do what is best in the particular product-customer context, remembering that the highest-quality product, whenever presented, becomes the benchmark for evaluating all other products by the customer.

This, as well as other forms of suggestion selling, should be viewed as one more way to provide service to the customer. When used correctly in the context of benefiting the customer, suggestion selling can build sales and increase customer rapport.

DEVELOPING GOODWILL

The entire thrust of the selling process, particularly the service after sales, should be oriented toward developing goodwill, the positive feelings or attitudes an individual has about a company and its products. For customers who are satisfied and who have confidence in the company and its products, there is a strong feeling of goodwill. When customers lose confidence, any previous goodwill created may be wiped out.

Goodwill not only helps to make the first sale but also secures repeat sales. It helps a customer choose the company's products over several competitive products of like grade and quality. It can help attract new customers and lead to referrals.

This positive word-of-mouth advertising is the best advertising a company can have.

CHAPTER PERSPECTIVE

An often overlooked and yet very important area in successful selling is the service after sales. Service after the sale covers a wide variety of areas, from proper departure after the presentation to developing goodwill. A salesperson must make sure professionalism is evident in leaving the sales call, even if a sale was not made, because this can help build the bridge to future sales. Awareness of the most common sales problems, as well as effectively handling complaints, is very important after the sale. When appropriate, suggestion selling can increase the benefits to the customer and, in turn, the customer's satisfaction. This, together with other types of customer service, leads to the establishment of goodwill and a strong relationship that will result in increased sales and referrals to potential new customers.

The Job of the Sales Manager

INTRODUCTION AND MAIN POINTS

Any career transition requires a degree of reorientation in both thought and action. This can be major, requiring extensive changes in behavior and approaches to the job, or it can be relatively minor. For some, the career transition is extremely difficult and for others, relatively easy. The transition from salesperson to sales manager is easy in the sense that many of the skills a salesperson uses to succeed are needed for the sales manager. It is difficult in that the responsibilities of a sales manager are very different in many respects. Although additional skills are needed for the sales manager, the transition, by and large, does not require new skills as much as the transformation of existing skills. This is often a more difficult process than learning new skills.

The sales manager, more so than the salesperson, plays the part of a "go-between" for different groups. The salesperson is a go-between for the company and the customers. The sales manager is a bridge between three groups—the company, the sales force, and the customer. This role as a bridge requires that the person understand the needs and desires of all three groups, know how to accommodate each party, within reason, and have the skill to satisfy the various parties.

One of the reasons the job of sales manager is attractive is that it represents an opportunity to build a lasting legacy. The job is also challenging because it is multifaceted. For these reasons, the job requires a unique set of characteristics.

After reading the material in this chapter:

▬ You will understand the characteristics of the successful sales manager.

▬ You will recognize the part the sales manager plays both inside and outside the organization.

▬ You will appreciate what it takes to make the transition from salesperson to sales manager and how to help others to do so.

THE NATURE OF SALES MANAGEMENT

One of the attractions of the sales manager's job is also what makes it unattractive to many salespeople—the increase in responsibility. A high achiever is attracted to greater challenges, precisely what the sales manager's job offers. Challenges tend to increase and vary the farther the person moves up on the management ladder. (Figure 11-1 depicts the ladder as an inverted pyramid because lower levels of management require specific but limited decisions, whereas upper management decisions are not as specific yet the managers have wider scope and wield more power.)

FIGURE 11-1
The Sales Management Ladder

As the person moves up the ladder, he or she must make a fundamental change in outlook. The first-line manager's decisions are more *tactical* in nature and deal with operational issues. The job requires more in the way of person-to-person interaction with salespeople. Moving up from a first-line manager to regional manager, the person must have a somewhat more holistic view and learn how to "manage managers"—a unique talent.

The decisions the regional managers make are much less tactical in nature, and more *strategic*. As the persons move into the upper reaches of sales management, they are required to shift focus again. At this upper level, the persons must be able to view the operation from a strategic standpoint and allow the operational decisions to be made by those under them.

Regardless of level in the sales management ladder, there are six basic functions the manager performs:

1) Plan
2) Organize
3) Guide
4) Monitor

5) Administer
6) Staff

These six functions are interrelated, interdependent and need to be treated as part of a system.

REWARDS OF SALES MANAGEMENT

Sales management is one of those interesting jobs that offer "mixed blessings." Although there are many aspects of sales management that are extremely rewarding, there are also some drawbacks for the salesperson moving into sales management. First, we will consider those aspects of the sales manager's job that make it worthwhile.

Expanding Horizons

Although the sales job has, in and of itself, a number of challenges and rewards for a person motivated to excel, the job of sales manager opens a whole new spectrum of opportunities. The person who moves into sales management no longer deals with one small part of the firm's operations but rather, begins to see the company from a different perspective—one that is wider and encompasses a much larger array of decisions and responsibilities. Good salespeople like challenges, and perhaps the biggest one is learning the various aspects of the sales manager's job, how the various functional areas of the firm interact, and how to adapt their strengths as salespeople to the requirements of sales management.

Cultivating People

An especially rewarding aspect of sales management is the chance to develop people. This seems to be attractive to salespeople who have been successful in selling (generally they are the ones considered for a promotion to sales management), and who have come to the point in their careers where they want to "share their success." For these people, management allows them to develop people with high potential and affords them the chance to share their success.

Guiding the Company

Sales management affords the opportunity to have a long-term impact on the success of the company. Strategic planning becomes part of the person's responsibilities and allows the person to "make his mark" on the company. The sales manager is called upon to develop a network to garner information for decision-making, facilitating planning. This means being put in the mode of constantly learning, and this is often very attractive for those who aspire to management.

Financial Rewards

Although salespeople potentially can make more money than managers, there seems to be a trend away from this with changes in methods of compensation. The sales manager will not only have a larger base salary, but will also have a larger expense account and will often have a bonus package tied to the performance of the sales force.

The Drawbacks

Although many consider the rewards that come with a sales management position to be greater than those of the sales job, there are a number of salespeople content to stay in the sales position who will turn down offers to enter management. Often their hesitancy to move into management is based on a perceived loss of autonomy. Salespeople enjoy their freedom and see a position in management as interfering with that.

Additionally, some salespeople shun management because of the increased responsibility that goes with it. Finally, in some organizations salespeople are in the position of earning a higher overall salary than their managers and do not wish to take the potential cut in salary.

The choice to move into sales management is one that the individual must make on their own. Generally, whether the person decides to pursue a management career is predicated on a variety of factors including individual variables, company factors, economic conditions and the person's age. There are rewards to be had, but with rewards go commensurate responsibilities.

CHARACTERISTICS OF THE SUCCESSFUL SALES MANAGER

As mentioned earlier, many of the characteristics necessary for the successful sales manager are simply extensions and transformations of the job of the salesperson, but some are unique to the position of sales manager.

Attributes

Successful salespeople share certain common attributes that set them apart from average and poor performers. In the same way, successful sales managers also have common traits. As mentioned previously, much of what it takes to be a successful salesperson is similar to the requirements for a successful sales manager.

Empathy is a major characteristic of successful salespeople because it enables them to understand the customer's problems. For the sales manager, empathy is critical because of the necessity of dealing with people as individuals. Each has a unique set of needs, desires, and goals. Given the hectic nature of the sales manager's job, the temptation is to attempt to "streamline" the process of dealing with individuals. Problems need to be solved quickly, and sales managers are often tempted to use "pat answers" to solve problems. Sales managers sometimes fall prey to viewing all salespeople as essentially the same—and to treating them that way.

Another characteristic of the successful salesperson is *resilience,* the ability to "bounce back" after a letdown. Although the sales manager does not face the same kind of letdown as the person selling, he or she needs to rebound from defeats, such as the failure of a salesperson in whom the manager has invested time. This is extremely discouraging, but failures happen despite one's best efforts. There is simply no way to foresee and address all the complications that face an individual who has difficulty. A lack of resilience in a sales manager results in that manager becoming discouraged when one of the staff fails. The manager may "write off" salespeople in the future who also show signs of failure.

Flexibility is another of the attributes of good salespeople and sales managers. A sales manager must have tremendous *flexibility* in dealing with staff. Because of the multifaceted nature of the sales manager's job, flexibility permits the manager to take care of unforeseen problems that arise daily.

The attribute of *integrity,* necessary for the development of trust in the buyer-seller relationship, is doubly critical for sales managers and their sales staff. "Don't do as I do, do as I say!" is the basis for the downfall of many a salesperson and manager. The sales manager must decide early in his or her tenure the limits of acceptability. A reputation for integrity grows out of personal ethics. It is earned and, if ever lost, is almost impossible to reclaim. In the words of Omar Khayyam, "The moving finger writes and having writ, moves on; Nor all your piety nor wit shall lure it back to cancel half a line; Nor all your tears wash away one word of it."

Although we might systematically discuss all the attributes necessary for the successful salesperson and sales manager, it is likely that you can go over the list yourself and develop specific applications.

Skills

As with attributes, the skills required of a successful sales manager are often the same skills required of a salesperson. Skills can be learned and tend to improve with practice. Sales management skills, like others, are usually complex combinations of actions. Generally, learning a skill involves practicing each component independently of the others and then joining them together. To prepare for a football game, the players must practice the "fundamentals": Blocking, tackling, ball handling, catching, and so forth. A running back who is great at catching the ball but does poorly at ball handling or who is afraid to block is not of much use. So, he practices each of these components. However, the components are not "the game." No matter how well the running back catches, the game of catch is not football. He must do all the things required of a running back if he is to be successful.

Listening may be the premier skill in selling in that it provides information and creates the basis for developing trust. Listening is also critical for the sales manager. It often provides a depth of information that otherwise is not readily available. It allows the development of rapport and trust between the sales manager and the subordinates. Often people who are having difficulties have a rudimentary understanding of the root cause of the problem. Active listening on the part of the sales manager allows persons to come to such an understanding on their own. When the person goes through this process, he "owns" the solution and is more likely to act on it.

On the other hand, the sales manager who is more ready to speak and tell the salesperson what to do often finds this effort thwarted, even when the problem has been correctly diagnosed. In this case, the sales manager is frustrated because the answer is "as plain as the nose on your face" and often concludes that the salesperson either does not care enough or is too lazy or stubborn to take corrective action. In reality, something in human nature makes us respond when we arrive at a conclusion ourselves instead of hearing someone else tell us the correct solution.

Effective speaking is necessary not only in sales but also in sales management. By *speaking effectively,* we mean accurately saying what is meant, not delivering a speech. Saying what one means is not as easy as it sounds. The speaker must speak in a way that will be understood by the other person. This involves having at least a rudimentary knowledge of that person. For the sales manager, knowing the salesperson should be the easy part.

The process also involves avoiding words with double meanings or negative connotations.

Furthermore, *how* a thing is said is at least as important as what is said. Often people confuse their objectives when they begin talking. When people are upset, they may state some truism, not for the purpose of giving correct information and providing feedback, but simply to "vent steam." This interaction may appear to give direction, but its purpose is very different. The results will be different than if the sales manager truly were speaking to benefit the salesperson. People often revert to patterns of communication that involve making generalized, sometimes derogatory statements about the behavior of others. For instance, a person might say, "You are always wasting time at the office instead of being out selling!" A better approach might be to say, "I've noticed you've been spending more time in the office lately." Both statements say the same thing. The former condemns and conveys anger; the latter is an observation that invites dialogue.

Organization is another skill that is important for both the salesperson and the sales manager. For the salesperson, it is critical that he or she be able to organize time, presentations, people from different departments and companies, and accounts. Poor organization is one of the great time wasters in sales, and it contributes to poor overall performance. As with a number of other attributes and skills, organizational skills need to be reoriented and enhanced for the sales manager who must not only be able to organize management's work, but also be able to assist salespeople in organizing theirs.

Organizing sales as a unit means that the sales manager coordinates the company's sales force and also any manufacturer's representatives the company uses. This requires strategic thinking about mission, objectives, strategies, and tactics. Given that sales managers generally travel more than when they were selling, it is essential that efficiency be paramount when making travel plans. Time is the one commodity that cannot be replaced.

Some sales management skills are probably not necessary to the salesperson. Among these are leadership skills, the ability to think strategically, "political" skills, and diagnostic skills. Leadership skills are discussed in Chapter 19. *Strategic thinking* skills involve being able to step back and look at the "big picture": To move beyond the immediate situation and understand the sequential nature of decision making. The specific objectives of the sales force must follow from the overall mission and objectives of the organization.

The objectives of the sales force lead to creating a *strategy,* the general plan to accomplish these goals. *Tactics,* short-term operational actions, flow from the sales force strategy. Sales managers often make the mistake of including tactics in strategy and then are confused about why the two do not mesh well. The sales force strategy is the "grand plan." If it is well thought out, the tactics are reasonably easy to develop. The discipline of planning is difficult, and sales managers who are action-oriented often tend to get ahead of themselves in the process. This leads to a poor planning effort.

By *political skills* we mean the ability to operate within the organization, by garnering necessary support and working with other functional areas. Sometimes this even means being able to "smooth the ruffled feathers" of a customer. This skill comes more naturally to the *pragmatist,* a person oriented toward practical solutions. Political skills also involve the ability to analyze situations and organizations and from this analysis develop effective courses of action. In the purest sense, the political nature of organizations may not be commendable or desirable: It is a fact of life and to prosper within the organization, a person must adapt. Political skills also involve the ability to "read people" and the flexibility to work with a variety of people. Additionally, political skill involves the ability to focus on important factors, not be sidetracked by minutia.

Diagnostic skills involve the ability to break down a problem into its component parts and to develop a plan of attack to address these components. The effective sales manager must be able to look beyond the "easy answer." Too often, easy answers address the symptoms rather than the root problem. This skill also involves *patience,* the ability to search long enough to find the right answer. The ability to diagnose problems properly involves having a good understanding of all the issues and components in the problem and bringing these to bear on the solution.

The Importance of Setting Goals

It is generally given that establishing goals is critical to success: "If you aim at nothing, you will hit it." Certainly, goals provide a sense of direction and help establish a set of priorities. Goals are also important when we attempt to determine the best allocation of resources. Additionally, they provide a benchmark for comparison and a "rallying point." Aside from these justifications for goals, they do have an impact on physiological mechanisms.

According to a number of studies, when a person has a well-defined goal, the brain tends to focus the senses on stimuli that help the person achieve a certain goal. For example, when a person buys a new car, that individual often begins to notice similar models on the street. In effect, the goal is to lower "buyer's remorse," or those feelings of uncertainty that accompany a major purchase. By focusing on all those other cars similar to ours on the street, we reduce those negative feelings. This process generally takes place subconsciously, but is nonetheless effective in reducing anxiety. That anxiety reduction is a goal we hold when we make a major purchase. Goals, then, are important on a number of levels, and the more well-defined they are, the more effective we tend to be in achieving them.

THE ROLE OF THE SALES MANAGER

If salespeople were willing and able to follow all the directives of upper management and if upper management were genuinely concerned about the needs of each salesperson, the sales manager's role would be relatively minor. However, given that this is not the case, the role of the sales manager is critical. A number of factors, both outside and inside the organization, have an impact on the sales force. These factors act to constrain behavior as well as enable certain behaviors. They establish parameters of action and have a major effect on employee behavior. Figure 11-2 depicts the role of the sales manager in relation to these factors.

The External Environment

Factors outside the organization create the environment in which the organization operates. The seven environmental forces depicted in Figure 11-2 interact to create both threats and opportunities for the organization. They have a direct impact on the strategic planning of the organization. However, the effect on the sales force is indirect. A major part of the planning process consists of analyzing this external environment. From this analysis, the organization is able to examine its mission statement, objectives, strategies, and tactics. The process of examining this external environment is known as *environmental scanning.* True environmental scanning consists of a continuing, systematic gathering of information from relevant sources, summarizing this information by a collection center, and dispensing the information to the appropriate functional areas in the organization.

One reason environmental scanning is so useful is that it does not require large initial investment. Most companies

FIGURE 11-2

Factors Affecting the Sales force and Sales Manager.

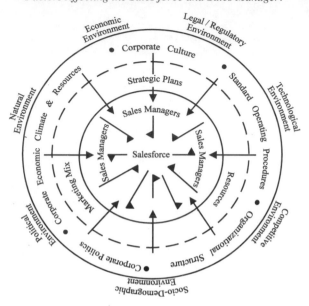

appoint a person to be coordinator of the system. The person solicits volunteers in the company, who receive magazines, trade journals, and other periodicals. These volunteers scan these publications for articles and information pertinent to the organization. The article is then clipped and attached to a single sheet on which the volunteer briefly summarizes the contents. This is sent to the coordinator, who forwards it to the appropriate parties. The payoff is that the company systematically obtains information from the environment that may give it an edge over the competition.

The Internal Environment

Within any organization there is an *environment,* a set of interactive forces that influence the operation of the organization. As shown in Figure 11-2, this internal environment is composed of the following:

Corporate culture

Corporate economic climate   Corporate politics

Standard operating procedures   Organizational structure

These forces affect the dynamics within the organization, the magnitude and use of resources, the strategic planning process, and specific strategies.

The Sales Manager as a Filter

As also noted in Figure 11-2, the sales manager acts as a *filter* between the sales force and these environmental factors. The sales manager is called on to play the role of interpreter and refiner of plans, and must decide the priorities that will be conveyed to the sales force. Additionally, the sales manager receives feedback from salespeople. This information not only affects the decisions but is also transmitted to upper management. The role of filter is critical in carrying out upper management's plans by taking into account the pertinent factors within the organization and adapting those plans for each unique application. Both the internal and external forces are dynamic, which calls for the sales manager to be flexible and creative.

The Sales Force as a System

It is instructive to examine the sales manager's job from the standpoint of how it fits in with carrying out the corporate strategic marketing plan. Figure 11-3 illustrates how the sales force can be viewed as a system.

Corporate input represents elements of the strategic plan. These elements, in turn, represent the resources made available to the sales manager who has the responsibility of manipulating these elements to get maximum results. *Sales manager controllables* are those factors over which the sales manager exercises control. Each of these factors affects the others, and they must be treated as a whole. The sales manager must recognize that the realm of control does not extend beyond this set of controllables: The sales manager has the ability to directly affect only these controllables. The relative success of the sales force results from how well the sales manager deals with these elements.

This is perhaps one of the most difficult truths to accept, because many sales managers believe, "If I were there, I could make that sale." Often, the sales manager is tempted to take over a sales call when riding with a subordinate. This tends to have a negative impact on the salesperson's self-confidence and can harm future credibility with the buyer. Riding with the salesperson, except when needed for support on a major order, should be dedicated primarily to providing curbside training and giving feedback.

FIGURE 11-3
The Salesforce As A System

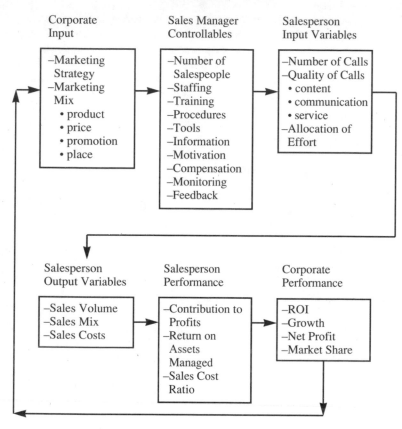

Adapted from: Henry, Porter (1975), "Manage Your Salesforce As A System," *Harvard Business Review*, (March-April), 85–95.

Salesperson input variables are those areas over which the salesperson exercises direct control. In premise selling, the salesperson must be depended on to make the right number of high-quality calls and to allocate efforts correctly. In other words, the salesperson needs to work "smart" as well as hard. The *Salesperson output variables* flow from the inputs. Sales volume is critical; however, many companies recognize that the sales mix and the sales cost have almost as much importance as sheer volume and, in some cases, are more critical. With the rising costs of selling, a balance between these output variables is essential. *Sales force performance* results directly from the output variables. Granted, there are times when the performance of salespeople is subject to unusual environmental pressures that affect it detrimentally. However, in situations in which a salesperson's output variables are reasonably healthy but performance measures are low, the cause can often be traced to a salesperson input variable or to a sales manager's controllable variable.

Corporate output is the net result of all the other elements in the system, the bottom line. It is the way we measure success, obtain feedback about the quality of the overall program, and how to fuel the machinery for future business. Corporate performance, although it is in large part dependent on the performance of the sales force, is affected by a number of environmental and corporate factors. Although upper management should examine these elements in the sales force system, it should also consider environmental and corporate factors. Too often, companies look for scapegoats, and this usually turns out to be the sales manager. This, however, is similar to firing the coach after a losing season. It might have been that the coach was lousy and needed firing; however, if he were good enough to hire, it may be that he did not receive enough support or did not have access to the right equipment to do the job. Upper management needs to look beyond the bottom line and examine whether the problem lay elsewhere, such as with the marketing strategy or the marketing mix.

CHAPTER PERSPECTIVE

In this chapter we have explored the job of the sales manager. Specifically, we examined the attributes and skills that the successful sales manager needs and how those differ from what is required of the salesperson. In reality, many of the attributes are the same ones required for salespeople, but their application must be adapted to the particular requirements of the sales manager's position. The role of the sales manager in the organization is to span boundaries because the manager must be able to function within the "no-man's-land" that exists between upper management and the sales force, and between the company and the customer. It is a difficult tightrope the sales manager must walk; balance becomes vital.

The sales manager cannot directly control the actions of the field sales force but rather controls such things as hiring, training, compensation, and the tools used by the sales force. The extent to which the sales manager is effective in doing that affects how well the sales force performs, and consequently, the effectiveness of the manager.

The Sales Organization

INTRODUCTION AND MAIN POINTS

Organizational design is critical because it has implications for how individuals within a firm relate to each other. Especially in terms of the sales force, where the dynamics of the job and the interaction of sales managers with their subordinates is different from any other area in the company, organizational structure has a major impact. Organizational design decisions are often made without giving enough thought to assumptions about the individuals within the organization or to the role of communication.

While good organizational structure does not ensure success, poor structure certainly impedes progress. It is essential that organizational design decisions be made after consideration is given to management's goals, the nature of the industry, the needs of the customers, and the characteristics of the company. Given that businesses evolve, change is an inherent part of any organization, but for some organizations the degree and speed of change is much more dramatic than in others. Consequently, the structure must be suitable to the dynamics of change in a given firm.

The sales manager is faced with the issue of how best to use the resources at hand. Customers vary considerably in terms of needs, approaches to purchasing, and demands they place on supplier firms. The sales manager must consider these issues when there are changes to the system. For some situations, the geographic organization of the sales force is the most appropriate; for others the sales force may best be divided along product lines. The structure has a direct impact not only on customer service but also on sales costs, which are the two sides of the coin of sales force success.

After reading the material in this chapter:

■ You will understand the major organizational issues that relate to the sales force.

■ You will have some insight into what has made certain organizational designs successful for other companies.

■■ You will recognize the role of the environment and the marketplace in developing an appropriate organizational design.

■■ You will be able better to consider the factors that relate to specific design issues.

■■ You will have some understanding of the change process in the organization.

ISSUES IN ORGANIZATIONAL DESIGN

Managers often think their particular organization is striving to be the "most effective and efficient" firm in the marketplace. This certainly sounds like a reasonable and perhaps even noble goal for any organization, but it is something of a contradiction.

Efficiency is generally thought of as performing a function in a way that reduces costs to the lowest possible level. Effectiveness, on the other hand, is generally thought of as providing more precisely what the customer wants—better meeting customer needs. A firm cannot be perfectly effective and perfectly efficient at the same time. It is a matter of trading a degree of efficiency for an added degree of effectiveness, and vice versa.

For a salesperson, efficiency means holding down sales costs to the lowest level, which might involve calling on customers in only a small geographic area in a given day. Effectiveness, however, means meeting as many of customer needs as possible. If the salesperson receives an emergency call from a customer in an area other than where he or she is working, effectiveness dictates taking care of the needs of that customer despite what this does to efficiency. The sales manager must recognize that this is the trade-off faced in designing the sales organization.

Bureaucracy and Professionalism

Sales is becoming more professional. Sales managers are attempting to legitimize selling as a profession and as a viable career choice for new college graduates, a career track that in and of itself has all the challenges and rewards necessary to make it attractive, a way to the "fast track" in the corporate world. Also, given the meteoric rise in the costs per sales call, sales managers recognize that they can no longer afford to have salespeople who act in an unprofessional manner. Additionally, pressures are being brought to bear from upper management to have the sales force yield long-term, profit-oriented results instead of short-term, sales volume-oriented results.

With the growing professionalism in purchasing, buyers are

less willing to work with a salesperson who does not act in a professional manner. A major problem is that many sales managers have not yet adjusted their approach to *managing* salespeople as professionals. The implicit assumption on the part of many sales managers seems to be that there is really no difference in managing professionals and nonprofessionals. The sales manager often establishes an organizational structure more appropriate to managing bureaucrats than managing professionals.

Although bureaucratic and professional orientations are similar in a number of ways, they are fundamentally different in the way they assign responsibility, manage people, make decisions, and relate to the client group. The sales manager needs to evaluate the sales force organization and approach to management in light of the comparisons in Table 12-1.

TABLE 12-1
The Professional and the Bureaucratic Orientation

Professional	Bureaucratic
Similarities	
The trained professional is a specialized expert who enjoys no given authority outside the area of expertise.	The bureaucrat has specialized knowledge restricted to an area of expertise; that is, circumscribed authority.
The relationship with clients is characterized by effective neutrality. Professional codes forbid emotional involvement with the client.	The relationship with clients is marked by impersonal detachment.
Differences	
Decisions are based on the judgment of the professional, predicated on training and the standards of the profession.	Decisions are based on the rules and procedures of the organization, not subject to the judgment of the individual.
Decisions are governed by universal standards and objective criteria, independent of the particular case.	Decisions are governed by abstract principles applied to particular cases.

Self-control is practiced through voluntary associations; the norms are established by the colleague group.	Control is imposed through the directives of the organization.
Performance is judged by the standards of the profession, independent of the individual organization.	Performance is judged by compliance with the rules of the organization.
A practitioner's decisions are predicated on furthering the good of the client.	Decisions are predicated on furthering the good of the organization.

Compiled from: Blau, Peter M., and W. Richard Scott (1962), *Formal Organization,* San Francisco: Chandler Publishing Company.

Principles of Organizational Structure

Whenever one examines the structure of an organization, certain characteristics seem to stand out as facilitating a smoothly run operation. Although there is tremendous variation in organizations, some principles can be applied to any organization.[1]

The following is a list of the major organizational principles:

The scalar principle. From the bottom of the organization, each position or level in the organization is subordinate to another position above it.

Unity of command. No person in the organization should be responsible to more than one superior. The *matrix organization,* in which specialists are accountable to both a superior from their area of expertise (e.g., engineering or production) and a coordinating manager (e.g., project manager), is an exception to this rule but can only be applied in certain circumstances.

Span of control: The number of subordinates reporting to one superior should be limited. The number is determined by the complexity of the job and the market and the ability of the supervisor, as well as a number of other factors.

Distinction between line and staff: The line performs the major functions of the organization; the staff provides support, advice, and service to the line. These two are separated so duties can be more efficiently assigned and the main thrust of the organization is not bogged down in paperwork.

[1] (for a more in-depth discussion, see Organ and Hamner, 1982).

Specialization. Jobs are designed so that there is little or no overlap in work. The idea behind the concept is that as people perform a particular job, they become more proficient in carrying it out. This approach increases the overall operating efficiency of the organization.

THE EXCELLENT ORGANIZATION

In just about any discussion of business today, the themes of excellence and quality prevail. Quality assurance programs and the concept of quality circles are rapidly becoming central to the operation of organizations. Quality and excellence represent ideals for an organization and, as such, are difficult concepts to grasp. Implementation is, therefore, not an easy process.

It is clear that how a firm is organized has a direct impact on implementation. At one time, the ideal organization was centrally organized and stressed efficiency of operation. Henry Ford's concept of the Model T and the assembly line approach is an example that demonstrates that such an approach can be extremely successful. However, the same Mr. Ford and Model T are equally good examples of how such an organization can have disastrous consequences.

The Peters and Waterman Approach

The importance of the organizational structure to the successful operation of a firm was demonstrated by Peters and Waterman (1982) in their classic, *In Search of Excellence.* This book was the result of examining the dynamics of a set of *excellent* companies, companies that seemed to demonstrate a successful approach to meeting the needs of the marketplace while coordinating the efforts of a large organization. Peters and Waterman found that each of their excellent companies had eight distinguishing traits in common:

1. *A bias for action:* The atmosphere promotes decisive action, avoiding "paralysis through analysis."
2. *Closeness to the customer:* The individual customer is of utmost importance. That concept is constantly stressed at all levels.
3. *Atmosphere of autonomy and entrepreneurship:* Companies sponsor leaders and innovators. Their reward system encourages individual initiative.
4. *Productivity through people:* Trust of the employee and the importance of the employee's contribution are stressed.

5. *Hands-on, value-driven management:* Management is involved with operations and is a role model. "Management by walking around" is practiced.

6. *Stick to the knitting:* Companies stay reasonably close to the business they know. They look for ways to lead their industries.

7. *Simple form, Lean staff:* Organizations are not overly complex and stress structural flexibility. This allows them to move with their markets.

8. *Simultaneously loose and tight properties:* The organization grants autonomy to the workers while maintaining its core values. Upper management sets the tone and does not try to make all the operational decisions.

Since its publication, *In Search of Excellence* has come under fire from a number of quarters. The crux of the criticism is that Peters and Waterman were too simplistic in their reasons why these companies did well. It has been pointed out that some of the excellent companies have fallen on hard times since the book's publication, which calls into question the long-term viability of the Peters & Waterman formula. Also, some have suggested that these companies were in industries with similar dynamics and that the formula may not be applicable to other situations. Others have indicated that the Peters & Waterman approach would not apply to organizations outside the United States.

While some of this criticism may have merit, the Peters and Waterman approach can provide valuable insight for the sales manager. Certainly, their suggestions would need to be adapted for each situation, but the basic principles would hold. Concerning the criticism that the approach would not work in other countries, Goldsmith and Clutterbuck (1984) conducted a similar study in England and arrived at similar conclusions.

Sales managers should consider the Peters and Waterman concept of excellence and ask themselves how the eight principles might be applied. Basically, the Peters and Waterman approach places a premium on customer satisfaction, being adaptive to the environment, and on making employees a part of the team of high performers.

ISSUES IN THE DESIGN OF THE SALES ORGANIZATION

It is often expedient for the producer to use *manufacturer's representatives* in place of a company sales force. A primary advantage of a manufacturer's rep is that the rep operates on a straight-commission basis and so represents a minimum of overhead costs. A major disadvantage of the rep is that the company exercises less control over how the rep operates than it could over a company salesperson. This means that the company can exercise less control over the allocation of effort and the resulting sales mix. Additionally, the manufacturer's rep may not provide the level of customer service the company wants. The sales manager must ensure that the salespeople employed by the manufacturer's rep are kept up to date and fit the image the company wants to convey. For the customer, the rep is the company.

Particularly when the company is entering a new territory, the rep may provide advantages. A rep is generally already familiar with the territory and has established contacts. The company is not forced to go to the expense of opening an office in the region, with all its associated overhead costs. In a similar vein, if a territory has gotten to the point of no longer being able to support a company sales office, the company can contract with a representative to continue coverage in the area after it has withdrawn its own salespeople.

For the small company, the manufacturer's rep provides the chance to have a sales force present in the field, which costs money when the product is sold. This reduction in overhead makes it possible for the smaller company to operate in areas that would otherwise be impossible to cover. For the small company also, the rep can be a major source of market intelligence that would otherwise be difficult to access.

A major decision faces companies using manufacturer's reps when sales climb to the point of making it profitable to have coverage by a company salesperson. In Figure 12-1, we see the decision from an economic point of view. Although the company sales force begins with a much higher set of fixed costs than the manufacturer's rep, the variable cost of the company sales force is lower. Before some point x on the graph, using a manufacturer's rep has a lower marginal cost than using a company sales force; however beyond point x, the marginal cost of using a manufacturer's rep exceeds that of the company sales force. Theoretically at least, point x on the graph is where the company should substitute the company sales force for the rep.

Although we tend to agree with the adage, "There is nothing quite so useful as a good theory," we recognize that there are not that many good theories. The graph depicts a situation that ignores many considerations pertinent to the decision to disengage a rep and institute a company salesperson in an area. For instance, companies with a reputation for "pulling the plug" on

FIGURE 12-1

The use of manufacturer representatives (double line)
versus company sales force (dashed line).

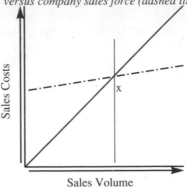

reps once they have reached a sales milestone soon find it difficult to obtain the best reps when they seek to enter new territories. Also, if the reps perceive that the milestone is being
reached, they may curtail selling efforts a bit to forestall being
"cut off."

Although reps may understand the logic "some MBA" is
using to make the decision, this does not negate the ill feelings
such a decision will cause. Those ill feelings often result in reps
informing buyers in their territory that, after all their hard work,
they are being cut off. However, they often pick up a new line to
substitute for the old, and the buyer, having developed a good
working relationship with the rep, may be willing to switch.

Additionally, when the new company salesperson enters the
territory, a certain amount of learning must take place. This
means a loss in sales momentum, so that point *x* on the graph may
move significantly.

In the final analysis, the decision to switch from a rep to a
company salesperson is difficult. It is never as clear-cut as the
graph leads us to believe. The company must recognize this and
be open about it with any rep they consider hiring. Furthermore,
the company might consider a "phase in-phase out" approach: As
the sales volume begins to near point *x,* the salesperson can be
introduced to the territory by the rep. As an incentive, the company might agree to give the rep a percentage of the rep's former
commission even after the company salesperson has taken over
the territory.

Whenever a firm is contracting with a rep, an escape clause should be included. The clause would specify that either party has the right to end the relationship after a certain period (often sixty days) with written notice. This protects both parties in the agreement and provides leverage in negotiations.

The Place of Telemarketing

With the ever-increasing cost of personally contacting a customer, sales managers are looking to the telephone as a way to increase the efficiency of the overall selling effort. In reality, the telephone has been used for selling ever since its invention. The term "telemarketing" generally applies to more recent efforts by sales forces to incorporate the phone as a strategic weapon in sales. Buyers have found that telemarketing is actually more efficient for them as well and have readily accepted it as a business practice (See "Rebirth of a Salesman: Willy Loman Goes Electronic." *Business Week* {Feb. 27, 1984}, 104).

As with manufacturer's reps, the sales manager must take a different approach with telephone salespeople (Moncrief et al., 1986). For example, the sales manager should recruit people with other types of skills than are necessary for outside sales personnel. Also, inside salespeople must undergo a separate kind of training. Inside salespeople are more likely to use a formula-based selling approach (e.g., a sales presentation script), whereas outside salespeople use more of a problem-solving, consultative selling approach.

Servicing Key Accounts

In selling, the *80:20 principle* applies to the customers of a firm: 80 percent of the business comes from 20 percent of the customers of the firm. Because this is true, many sales managers recognize the need for special attention to the needs of the few major customers that constitute the majority of the business. There are several viable approaches to the handling of these key accounts:

Separate key accounts division: This entails an entire division of the company devoted specifically to the needs of the major accounts. The justification is that they are important and different enough to warrant a division-level approach. However, this entails a great deal of added expense for the company.

Separate sales force: This involves using a dedicated sales force to service the key accounts. It has the advantage of being able to meet the sales and service needs of these accounts without incurring the expense of a separate division. It also has the benefit of providing a track for better salespeople if they do not want to enter management.

Assign to sales managers. This has the advantage of giving special attention to the key accounts and being able to use the manager's power to take action when needed. It also lets the accounts know that they warrant special attention. This can place an added burden on sales managers, however.

Use the regular sales force: The benefit here is principally for the company and the sales force. It saves the company money and lets the salespeople keep the most lucrative accounts. However, it usually results in these accounts not receiving the attention they need.

APPROACHES TO ORGANIZING THE SALES FORCE

There are four major approaches to dividing the sales force into territories. The complexity of the market and the product line are perhaps the most critical factors in deciding which to employ, but others, such as the location of customers and the tasks involved in the particular sales job, are also important.

Geographic Organization

Dividing the sales force by geographic region is the most commonly used approach. Even when another approach is employed, it is used in conjunction with a geographic division. About the only time geographic organization is not used is either when the company serves only one area of a country or when the customer base is very limited.

The benefits of using this approach are as follows:

■ The salesperson is able to become an "expert" on a given region.

■ It generally means lower travel costs and fewer nights away from home for the salesperson.

■ Customers know exactly who they need to speak with about a question or problem.

■ This approach is generally easier to administer.

■ A company can better ensure that a region is being adequately covered.

■ This approach lends itself to conducting a limited test market.

The drawbacks of the geographic organization are as follows:

■ If the company has a wide spectrum of products, it is very difficult for one person to know the full line.

■ If there are very different types of customers, a salesperson may not be able to provide proper service for each.

■ It may difficult to get the necessary "push" needed or desired for a given product.

■ Salespeople may not be willing to relocate when they are assigned a new territory because they have put down "roots."

■ Salespeople must be generalists instead of specialists, and this can create difficulties in certain circumstances.

Product Organization

For companies with a wide variety of product lines or for those that have several very different and complex lines, the product organization can provide the most effective approach to selling the products.

The advantages of using this approach are as follows:

■ The salesperson can become a specialist on a particular product or product line.

■ The salesperson can better serve the more specific and complex needs of customers.

■ The marketing of a particular product can be better controlled and monitored.

The disadvantages of this approach are as follows:

■ There is a duplication of effort: more than one salesperson covers a given geographic area, which leads to an increase in costs.

■ It can be confusing to customers.

■ Travel time and travel costs for salespeople increase.

■ The administration involved with this approach is more difficult.

■ Sometimes this approach can lead to parochialism in that each product group tends to protect its own turf.

Customer Organization

With an increasing emphasis on developing closer alliances with customers, firms are looking for more effective ways to serve their specific needs. Purchasing departments, production processes, and the corporate cultures of a firm's customers are sometimes different enough that salespeople need to be specialized along customer lines.

The advantages of a customer organization are as follows:

■ The specific needs of the different customer segments are served.

■ Because salespeople are closer to the customer, they know what is happening in the industry and how it is changing.

■ Resources can be better allocated to the different segments vying for them.

■ Salespeople can work more closely with salespeople to develop new technologies and products.

The disadvantages of this type organization are as follows:

■ Efficiency is decreased because more than one salesperson covers a geographic area.

■ There may be provincialism among salespeople covering the different types of customers.

■ Salespeople must know the entire product line.

■ Administering and coordinating the efforts of the different groups are more difficult.

Functional Organization

The sales job includes a variety of different skills and tasks. These are often in conflict in that performing one well means not doing an inadequate job on another. Also, individual salespeople often do not have the time to perform all their tasks. Dividing the sales force by function is sometimes the best approach.

The advantages of this approach are as follows:

■ The strengths of individual salespeople in the company can be coordinated for effective use.

■ The firm can concentrate on certain critical tasks.

■ A more defined allocation of resources is possible.

The drawbacks of the functional organization are as follows:

■ Costs increase because more salespeople are needed to perform specialized functions.

■ There may be customer confusion.

■ It is difficult to find the "right" salespeople to be the specialists.

■ The system is difficult to administer.

CHAPTER PERSPECTIVE

Organizing and coordinating selling efforts is a complex process. Decisions are often made based on less-than-adequate consideration of the implications. For example, a decision that might result in increased efficiency in the organization could also lead to decreased effectiveness. The manager must decide which is more important. Sales managers often complain that their salespeople are "unprofessional," and yet the organization they have developed is more bureaucratic than professional in nature and therefore salespeople are not really allowed to be professionals. In designing for excellence, the appropriate design depends on the environment and the market of the company. The work of the sales force can be divided differently, depending on a number of factors, each of which can affect the firm.

REFERENCES

Blau, Peter M., and W. Richard Scott (1962), *Formal Organizations,* San Francisco, CA: Chandler Publishing Company.

Goldsmith, William, and David Clutterbuck (1984), *The Winning Streak,* London: Weidenfeld and Nicholson.

Lucas, George H. Jr., and Larry G. Gresham (1985), "Power, Conflict, Control and the Application of Contingency Theory in Marketing Channels," *Journal of Academy of Marketing Science,* 13 (Summer), 25-38.

Levitt, Theodore (1974), *Marketing for Business Growth,* New York: McGraw-Hill Book Company.

Moncrief, William C., Charles W. Lamb, Jr. and Terry Dielman (1986), "Developing Telemarketing Support Systems," *Journal of Personal Selling and Sales Management* (August), 43-49.

Organ, Dennis W., and W. Clay Hamner (1982), *Organizational Behavior,* Plano, TX: Business Publications, Inc.

Peters, Thomas J., and Robert H. Waterman (1982), *In Search of Excellence,* New York: Harper & Row.

Designing Sales Territories

INTRODUCTION AND MAIN POINTS

One aspect of organizational design that helps achieve the goals and objectives of both the organization and the sales force is the definition of the territory and the assignment of salespeople in that territory. The territorial design affects the accounts to be called upon and the frequency of the calls. The call frequency has become increasingly important because of the increasing costs of a sales call and the increasing competition.

After reading this chapter:

▬ You will understand the importance of territory and time management in achieving sales objectives and minimizing sales costs.

▬ You will be able to establish sales territories by understanding the rationale and basic methods.

▬ You will be able to revise sales territories.

▬ You will understand the impact of new technologies on territory management.

ADVANTAGES OF USING TERRITORIES

A sales territory is a group of present and potential customers assigned to a specific salesperson or branch. Territories provide for systematic market coverage as the responsibility for each customer or prospect is clearly assigned. By having been assigned responsibility, a salesperson is likely to invest more time and effort in an account that will directly benefit from activity. This sole responsibility for a specific territory increases salesperson's involvement and pride in the job. Sales people can help establish the objectives and therefore, have benchmarks to evaluate their own success.

Customers benefit as well from the use of territories. Because a salesperson has sole responsibility and makes repetitive calls, a customer becomes better known. This can result in each customer having individual needs met. This better service will occur with less investment of time and effort.

Sales territories are also beneficial to the company as they help reduce marketing costs. Call schedules can be established for customers or prospects in proportion to their potential sales or profit contribution. Travel time can be minimized by careful routing and more time can be given by each salesperson to the selling effort. Also, duplication of sales calls can be eliminated. Salespeople in well-designed territories incur lower costs as a percentage of sales.

Finally, assigned territories assist in hiring, training, evaluation, and control. Sales personnel can be hired and assigned to fit the characteristics of a territory and its customers. Any training needed can be tailored to the specific needs of each territory. Also, the performance of each salesperson can be more easily controlled and evaluated. Because salespeople operate in a specific territory, performance can be compared against quotas and potential, across territories, and over time. These comparisons provide information for much better control.

Are sales territories always beneficial? Although sales territories have many benefits, there are times when a company does not need territories. This occurs particularly when salespeople contact customers infrequently or when a company sells directly to customers, as in the case of real estate brokers, stockbrokers, and insurance agents. Even in these instances, sales territories are sometimes used to avoid duplication and confusion and to increase sales performance and customer satisfaction.

BASIS FOR SALES TERRITORIES

For good sales performance, it is important to have a sound basis for establishing sales territories. A sales territory is usually a geographic area containing customer accounts. The number of accounts is such that a salesperson can economically and efficiently make the optimal frequency of calls on each account. Since customers are a mixture of past, present, and potential customers, good territorial division and allocation matches sales efforts with the sales opportunities of each account. This is frequently accomplished using various computer models that allow a company to effectively use time, decrease costs, and maintain account call frequency. A good sales territory and call procedure groups customers and prospects in a manner that allows each to be called on as conveniently and economically as possible for maximum effectiveness.

Designing good sales territories aids sales management as well. Because the market of most companies is too large to manage efficiently, sales territories facilitate the sales manager's task of directing and evaluating the personal selling effort. Even though most territorial design is done on a geographic basis, the emphasis should be on the customers and prospects. The *market*—the matching of supply and demand so that a transaction can occur—is composed of present and potential buyers regardless of geographic area. While the overall reason for designing sales territories is to make the selling function optimal, there are also specific reasons for the design as well.

Minimize Selling Costs

Given the significant rise in the cost of food, lodging, and transportation, as well as other costs involved in personal selling, the costs of a sales call have increased markedly over the past several years. This increase has caused companies to find ways to minimize the costs of overnight stays and other travel-related expenses in designing sales territories.

One method of reducing selling costs that has received increasing use in recent years is *telemarketing,* the use of the telephone to augment more traditional marketing techniques, such as personal selling. Telemarketing is increasingly being used to sell existing accounts, qualify sales leads, maintain customer rapport, and establish appointments, thereby helping to reduce the high personal selling costs and increase territorial efficiency. Through telemarketing, a salesperson can contact a large number of customers and potential customers and prioritize those that should receive a personal sales call. By identifying customers who are most likely to buy, telemarketing can significantly reduce the time and money spent in identifying good sales leads.

Increase Market Coverage

A well-designed sales territory can be covered correctly, with the appropriate number of calls being made to existing and potential customers. A sales territory should be designed so that a salesperson does not spend all the time traveling. Instead, the focus should be on making the needed number of calls on each customer based on the size of the customer's firm and potential business. It is as costly to call on a customer too often (calling more frequently than deserved given the potential business) as not frequently enough. Each sales territory should be sized so that good work effort and planning are needed to cover the territory adequately, but not so large that the correct amount of attention cannot be paid to present and potential customers.

Develop Strong Customer Relations

A well-designed sales territory allows a salesperson to make best use of his time with present and potential customers and minimize travel time. The more interaction between the salesperson and customer that can be facilitated by a good sales territorial design, the stronger the relationships will be. This greater familiarity facilitates better understanding of the needs and problems of the customer on the part of the salesperson, which, in turn, helps to determine the most effective way the company's products can meet those needs. A well-designed sales territory allows each customer to be called upon on as regular basis as is warranted by the size and potential sales volume of the customer's firm. While it might be nice to call on a large supermarket or industrial company every two weeks, for a small "Mom and Pop" store or industrial account, regular visits might be made every eight weeks. This allows a salesperson to establish rapport, take orders from busy customers by telephone, and quickly transmit information on forthcoming price increases or product unavailability. The better the customer relationships, the better will be the resulting sales from a particular territory.

Improve Sales Force Effectiveness

A well-designed sales territory can increase the morale of the sales force, motivate each salesperson, and allow better evaluation. A good sales territory design gives each salesperson a reasonable work load relative to other sales personnel and defines each job and its responsibilities. With a good territorial design, a salesperson becomes the manager of a territory and works accordingly to ensure maximum results. By taking pride in effectively managing a territory, a salesperson becomes a "mini corporate president," or what is now commonly labeled an *intrapreneur,* who wants to manage the territory in the most effective way possible. When this occurs, the best in territorial design has been achieved. Minimum conflict between salespeople occurs and each salesperson thoroughly understands the accounts in the territory and the results expected.

Good territorial design also provides an effective means for evaluating each salesperson's performance. Also, an examination of the performance in each territory provides a view of changing market conditions and any adjustments that may be needed.

Coordinates Sales with Other Marketing Functions

Well-designed sale territories facilitate the performance of other marketing functions. It is easier to perform accurate market research and cost and sales analysis on a territorial basis than on an entire market area. The territorial estimates can then be consolidated into total market estimates and used to establish quotas, sales estimates, and expense budgets. Better customer service and assistance can also be accomplished.

Helping customers to use cooperative advertising, setting up point-of-purchase displays, and implementing company sales promotion programs are more easily accomplished on a territorial basis when the work is done by a salesperson who is familiar with the customer's needs. Through a well-designed sales territory, the responsible salesperson can better respond in a timely manner to any new customer leads and can identify new customer needs.

INAPPROPRIATE SALES TERRITORIES

Despite all the advantages, in some situations a sales territory is not needed. Designing sales territories and allocating salespeople to them is necessary only when a company has a large sale force geographically dispersed across a wide region. A small company with only a few salespeople may not require a sales territory design.

Sales territories are also not as necessary when the market is so large and/or growing so fast that the sales coverage provided by the company is well below the sales potential of the market area. In this situation, every available salesperson assists in identifying and selling as many accounts as possible to reach the maximum sales potential and to avoid neglecting potential market. Even in these cases, however, a well-designed sales territory enables a company to focus its sales efforts.

ESTABLISH SALES TERRITORIES

Given all the benefits of a well-designed territory, it is important to understand the procedures by which one can be established. One procedure that is easy to implement and provides good results has several steps: First, establish the base unit; perform account analysis; perform a salesperson work load analysis; develop the sales territories; and assign salespeople to the established territories.

Establish the Base Unit

The first step in establishing sales territories is to select the base unit. Some frequently used base units include zip code areas, standard metropolitan statistical areas, regions of the county, and countries. As small a unit as possible should be used at the start as this allows the location of sales potential to be more easily identified and territorial adjustments to be more easily made. For example, a sales territory based on zip codes can be more easily adjusted to add a salesperson than one based on states. Base units are most commonly states, counties, or cities. These are the same geographic breakdowns used for census data and other government and business information. Within these, smaller units such as trading areas can be designated to aid in understanding buyers' needs and expectations as well as in collecting sales and other relevant data.

The state is a frequently used geographic control unit in establishing sales territories because of its ease of implementation. It is especially good as a basis for establishing the sales territories of a company just starting to create a nationwide distribution system or a company with a small sales force attempting to cover the market selectively. Sometimes in each of these instances a salesperson is assigned to more than one state until the market develops enough to warrant more intensive coverage. Even though sales territories based on states are simple, convenient, and relatively inexpensive, states are not used as the base unit for developing territories, for several reasons.

First, many customers cross state boundaries to purchase a multitude of products, making it difficult to match sales with inhabitants. Also, some states are not large enough to warrant a territory, but others, such as New York and California, usually need more than one salesperson for adequate coverage.

A smaller and, in some ways, better focal point for dividing territories is the county. There are only 50 states in the United States, but there are more than 3,100 counties. Given their smaller size, counties are easier to use to develop sales territories or equal sales potential. In addition counties are usually the smallest unit base for government data and other sources of market data, such as disposable personal income, effective buying income, population, retail sales, employment, and production data. The small size of counties also allows territorial problems to be more easily identified and rectified and appropriate changes to be made to the existing territorial allocation.

As with states, counties are not similar in size and potential sales. In some cases even counties are too large to be a good base unit. Some counties such as Cook County, Chicago, need more than one salesperson, and an even smaller base unit is needed for territory allocation.

When a small base unit is needed or when increased territorial coverage is planned, zip codes offer the best geographic base unit for territory design and allocation. The section of the county is delineated by the first three of the first five digits of the zip code. The last two digits of the first five denote a more specific geographic area within the section. In nine-digit zip codes, the last four digits break down the geographic area even further. When using zip codes, data on sales, sales potential, industry and population characteristics can be easily obtained because most data are collected and stored on a zip code basis.

Another useful small base unit is the trading area. Because the trading area is based on the natural flow of goods and services, not an arbitrary political or economic boundary, it is a good base unit for sales territory design, particularly for those firms selling through wholesalers or retailers. A trading area usually consists of a geographic region containing a city and its surrounding area that is the dominant wholesale and retail center for that area. Although trading areas can overlap, customers in one trading area usually do not conduct business in another. As such, a trading area represents customer buying habits and patterns of trade in the particular area, allowing specific plans for the area to be developed. This results in much better planning and control.

There is a major drawback to using trading areas—after-market information is published on a county, not a trading area basis. The less the county data can be correlated with the trading area, the more difficult it becomes to develop market plans and to determine market penetration.

Perform Account Analysis

Once the base unit is determined, an audit of all the accounts in the area must be done to identify customers and potential customers and to determine the sales potential of each. To accurately estimate the sales potential, each account must be specifically identified by name and address. Company records can be used to identify present and past accounts, but identification of new (potential accounts) poses a more serious problem. Various sources of information on the potential accounts in an area include the following: The yellow pages, mailing lists, list brokers, trade directories, associations, the local chamber of commerce, the state department of commerce, and the Instant Yellow Pages Service (a computerized data base of business listings).

Once identified, the sales potential must be estimated by the sales manager. Estimates drawn from past and present accounts and based on company data allows far more accurate projections for prospective accounts than estimates based on judgments. Summarizing the estimate for each account provides an estimate of the sales potential for each territory. This should be modified as needed to reflect: The company's future marketing plans in the territory, the level of competition, the company's comparative advantage, and the strength of the competitive company having the existing accounts.

Each account must then be classified according to the sales potential, which is ultimately reflected in its assigned call frequency. An approach frequently used by consumer packaged goods companies is an ABC classification. Accounts with the largest sales potential expressed in dollar sales are classified as A accounts, the accounts with the next greatest potential, B accounts, and the lowest potential again, C accounts. For most consumer packaged goods companies, an A account is called on by a salesperson at least once every two weeks, a B account at least once every four weeks, and a C account at least once every eight weeks. By using this call frequency, a salesperson spends the most effort calling on accounts with the greatest potential.

Salesperson Work Load

The number of accounts in a territory, the geographic size of the territory, and the call frequency of the accounts provides the initial basis for estimating the time and effort required for adequately covering the territory.

Additional factors considered in the salesperson work load analysis include the following:

▬ Typical length of each call
▬ Amount of nonselling time needed
▬ Travel time required

All of these factors are used to determine the best sales call frequency and size of territory. Many computer programs are available to assist in this analysis and to determine the best route and call pattern to maximize sales or minimize costs. The area most difficult to determine and, therefore, most frequently underestimated in this work-load determination is the amount of nonselling time needed in an account. Nonselling activities include waiting time, preparing for the sales call, order processing, account reporting, and account support activity.

Developing Sales Territories

The previous methods defined the best geographic building blocks used as the basis for developing appropriate sales territories. The sales manager can then combine adjacent units into territories or can attempt to achieve territories of equal sales potential. In the past this process was a laborious effort, but a number of computer software packages are now available that assign units into territories quickly and evenly. Even when using a territorial mapping program, the territories may need adjustment because of differences in difficulty of coverage. These revisions accounting for coverage can then result in territories that are different in sales potential.

Territories that are unequal in sales potential are not necessarily bad, as salespeople are also not equal, with some having greater experience and ability than others. More qualified salespeople can be given territories with greater potential and a larger work load. Although assigning the best salespeople to the territories with the greatest potential usually produces good results, sometimes adjustments in sales quotas and/or commissions are necessary for fairness.

Assign Sales Personnel

Once the best territorial alignment has been devised, the sales manager is ready for the final step, assigning salespeople to each territory. Because salespeople vary in ability, initiative, and experience, care must be taken to ensure that the territory work load is commensurate with the ability of the salesperson and that the customers, prospects, and social and cultural aspects of a territory are appropriate for the salesperson. A salesperson who performs poorly in one territory may perform well in another because of the compatibility of the social and cultural composition of the territory and the salesperson.

A salesperson should be assigned to a territory based on his or her sales effectiveness in the territory. The potential sales effectiveness depends to a large extent on the degree that the cultural, social, and physical characteristics of the territory are matched to those of the salesperson. An individual growing up in a large metropolitan area, such as Boston, is likely to be more effective in a larger metropolitan area on the East Coast than in a rural setting in Kentucky. Salespeople tend to do better where they feel comfortable with the territory and the customers. Given the amount of secondary data available on a geographic basis in the United States, most of which is computerized, this matching can be accomplished relatively easily.

OTHER METHODS FOR DETERMINING NUMBER OF TERRITORIES

Besides the workload method, there are two other basic methods for determining the optional number of territories: Sales potential method and breakdown method.

Sales Potential Method

A very popular approach for determining the number of territories is to estimate the sales potential in an area. A simplified version of this method used by some pharmaceutical companies is to first estimate the sales potential of drugstores, hospitals, and physicians. Then the amount of sales potential that warrants a salesperson is established and the number of salespeople needed is determined by dividing the total sales potential by the size of the sales potential that warrants a salesperson.

A more refined version of the method can be used in an established organization having territories of unequal potential. Since territories with smaller sales potential generally have higher proportional sales than larger sales potential territories, in applying this method, the sales manager must first determine the relationship between sales potential and sales penetration. The next step is to calculate what would occur if all the territories were reallocated resulting in all territories having equal potential.

Finally, the sales manager needs to determine if the sales increase resulting from a larger number of territories is greater than the corresponding increase in sales costs to cover the new set of territories.

Breakdown Method

The third method for determining the number of territories—the breakdown method—involves only two calculations. First, the amount of sales volume required per salesperson is determined. The sales volume per salesperson needs to be large enough to cover the salesperson's direct costs. This breakdown volume is determined by dividing the direct costs per salesperson by the gross margin percentage. Then, this sales volume is divided into the total sales potential (or forecast) to determine the number of salespeople needed. The sales forecast of the company divided by the breakeven volume yields the number of territories that the sales forecast can support.

The breakdown method, like the workload method, is based on the assumption that sales force volume determines sales force size. The method yields a breakeven number of sales territories, not the number of territories that contributes to a profit or sales goal. To incorporate profit into the breakeven method, a target profit amount should be added to the nonselling costs in calculating the gross margin percentage.

ROUTING IN THE TERRITORY

There is no more essential task in effectively and efficiently covering a territory than planning efficient routes in calling on customers and prospects. Routing is the process of establishing a pattern for the salesperson to use when calling on customers and prospects in the territory. Routing can be very time consuming, and a computer can be used to take into account a variety of factors in finding the most efficient route. Routing can be as simple as locating each account on a map and determining the best order for calling on each, along with the best roads.

Although a suggested route is frequently given to each salesperson, the salesperson is ultimately responsible for determining the best plan for efficient and effective operation in the territory. Once the salesperson becomes familiar with the territory, this is usually not difficult and is a task best handled by the individual in the field, who knows the territory better than anyone else.

A properly designed route provides good territory coverage and communication and reduces travel time and selling costs. With detailed information on the numbers and locations of customers and their respective call frequency, an orderly and thorough coverage of the market is possible. The sales manager can better monitor the activities of salespeople when each is on a planned-call schedule. The resulting improved territorial coverage and communication help to reduce the time and selling costs, allowing the salesperson to spend more time with customers. Even with a carefully planned route, a salesperson still spends a significant amount of nonselling time in travel, backtracking, and waiting. These can take up to one third of the daily work time. Imagine the increase in lost time and nonselling activities that would occur without a well-planned route.

This increased efficiency resulting from using a routing plan far outweighs some of the disadvantages frequently cited. These include the fact that routing reduces the salesperson's initiative and flexibility in handling the territory. Given that the salesperson is involved in the initial territory design and knows that he or she can make changes in the established route when warranted by market conditions, this disadvantage is not significant. A salesperson should also feel free to modify the call sequence if customers are better served and sales are increased.

Flexibility is necessary in every routing plan and procedure, and some situations call for even greater flexibility. A firm entering a new market that does not know the nature and location of customers and potential customers needs to allow the salesperson significant flexibility until customers are identified by location and relative call frequencies are established. A company in an established market is more likely to have an in-place routing system. Also, very accomplished salespeople (as well as manufacturer's representatives) need much more flexibility in handling a territory. These quality, individualistic salespeople resent a strict schedule that implies they are not capable of making optimal use of their time and call pattern.

The degree of flexibility in routing also reflects the nature of the product and the amount of servicing involved in the particular sales jobs. The more the product warrants regular calls and frequent servicing, the more necessary it is to route properly so that the appropriate number of calls are made in a timely fashion. Similarly, the more routing, the less creative is the selling.

Establish a Routing System

Establishing a good territorial routing procedure involves obtaining information on the location of each customer, the distance from account to account, the method of transportation, the call frequency per account, and the number of calls to be made each day by the salesperson. This information can then be entered into the computer or used on a map to develop the best route. This route minimizes backtracking and crisscrossing, allowing the salesperson to reduce the amount of nonselling time involved in covering the territory.

Several basic routing patterns are frequently used. In a *straight-line route,* the salesperson leaves the office, making calls in one direction until the end of the territory is reached. In a *circular pattern route,* the salesperson leaves the office, making calls in a circle until the office is reached again. A *cloverleaf route* is similar to a circle route in that a circle is followed that covers part, but not all of the territory. The next day an adjacent circle is followed. This pattern continues until the entire territory is covered. In the fourth routing pattern, the *hopscotch route,* the salesperson starts at the farthest point in the territory from the office and makes calls back to the office. The next day a different distant point is selected and the same procedure is followed. If a large distance is involved, the salesperson flies to this farthest point and drives back, making sales calls along the way.

Another routing pattern—the skip-stop route—can be used with the other four patterns. When call frequencies are different among customers in a particular routing pattern, the salesperson calls on all customers in the route on some trips and skips those in the route with lower call frequencies on other trips.

Routing Models

There is probably no other area in marketing that has received as much attention in developing computerized mathematical models as routing. Given the complexity that can occur in routing, this is not surprising. The number of possible routes varies greatly depending on the number of geographic areas and can easily reach thousands of different routes when multiple geographic areas are considered simultaneously. Most mathematical routing models have the basic objective of maximizing selling time or minimizing travel time or cost.

Among the many mathematical models, the two most frequently used are CALL PLAN and ALLOCATE. In CALL PLAN, not only must the customers and their locations be identified, but an estimate must be made on the response to various call frequencies. With this information, CALL PLAN develops equal sales territories and routes salespeople through each territory based on customer call frequency, customer potential, length of sales calls, and travel time. Also, the ability to match the effectiveness, experience, and general characteristics (education, personality, traits, and work experience) of the salesperson with the demographic and business characteristics of the territory can be evaluated.

Another frequently used mathematical routing plan, ALLOCATE, also provides estimates of the amount of selling effort that should be spent on each customer based on the potential sales and current share of the customer's purchases.

REVISING SALES TERRITORIES AND ROUTING

It is important for a company to monitor sales territory allocations and established routing procedures and to modify them as necessary. Revisions are almost always necessary in a market area because it is very difficult to accurately estimate the territory's potential and work load due to myriad problems that arise. Over time revisions are also necessary to reflect changing market conditions and the abilities of salespeople.

Causes for Revisions

Sales territories are probably most frequently revised because market size has been underestimated. When the company does not hire additional sales personnel, the sales results can be misleading because the territory cannot be covered adequately. In this situation, a 100 percent increase in sales in the territory may be the result of a poor territorial estimate, not a good selling effort.

The opposite situation occurs when the sales territory has been overestimated. Environmental changes or bad allocation can cause the sales potential in a territory to be so overestimated that no salesperson can perform effectively.

Another frequent reason for revising sales territories is that they overlap. This can cause friction in the sales force and loss of good customer relations. Overlapping sales territories also means higher selling costs and less selling time. Overlapping territories need to be immediately corrected so that sales representatives are satisfied to the extent possible.

CHAPTER PERSPECTIVE

Proper organizational design requires territorial assignments to obtain optimal sales performance. A sound basis for establishing sales territories is required. Because customers are always a mixture of past, present, and potential customers, territories significantly aid the sales manager in achieving good sales results.

Territorial design in sales helps minimize selling costs. These territories allow an adequate budget for selling costs without under- or overbudgeting. This design also increases market coverage, which in turn develops stronger customer relations. Because of regional differences, territories allow a more homogeneous work force, minimizing salesperson-customer conflict. These sales territories make the best of all the important sales features and minimize bureaucratic chaos at the base unit, thereby benefitting the organization.

Training the Sales Force

INTRODUCTION AND MAIN POINTS

Hiring good people is critical to the success of the sales force. However, hiring is only the first step in the building of a successful sales team. There are really two processes involved in a person's becoming a part of the sales organization: Socialization and training. Generally speaking, we think of socialization as an informal process; on the other hand, training is viewed as the formalized way of introducing the person to the aims and expectations of the firm. This idea has some merit, but it is more instructive to view training as a specialized form of socialization. Socialization has specific, overt goals and tends to be specific in the approach it takes. Informal socialization extends beyond the initial training of new salespeople: It is an ongoing process of acculturating the person into the organization.

Training involves more than the dispensing of information. If this were not so, we could simply give each newly hired person a manual and have it memorized. In addition to providing important information, training helps the person make the transition to the new environment, establishes a forum for the person to develop the skills necessary for success in selling, and imparts the corporate culture.

Training is the process of facilitating directed learning. Through training, salespeople are introduced to the overall goals of the organization, the procedures used to accomplish specific tasks, and the skills and knowledge necessary to succeed in selling the company's products. Newly hired salespeople not only must be shown what they need to learn but also must be approached in such a way as to maximize the learning process. Veteran salespeople must be motivated to involve themselves in the training process so that they can learn new information and update their skills.

After reading the material in this chapter:

■■■ You will understand the role of training in the organization.

■■■ You will appreciate that learning is a process that involves not only transferring information but also facilitating skills development.

■■■ You will be better able to organize your training to cover the appropriate topics using the correct approach.

THE SOCIALIZATION PROCESS

Whenever an individual joins a new organization, that person is called upon to assimilate the beliefs and practices of the organization. This assimilation is called *socialization*. At this point it may be tempting to dismiss the concept of socialization as relatively unimportant given a strong training program. However, the moment a person walks in the front door of a firm, the individual is subjected to a host of influences and messages about what is acceptable and what is unacceptable. Some of these messages are formalized company policy, and some are part of the informal culture. Both can be powerful influences on the person.

Often the first words heard by the new salesperson after the initial training program is complete and the party arrives in the field are, "Okay, now forget all that stuff you learned in training—this is how it's really done!" This person often initially rejects such advice until he or she meets with failure and/or discovers that what was taught in training does not correspond to what life is really like in the field. In either case, the person will reevaluate what has been learned and may reject it, and the training will have been for naught. The sales manager must be aware of the "informal culture" operating in the company, admit to newly hired salespeople that it exists, and address this in training.

Second, the sales manager must ensure that what is taught in training is in line with reality. An approach to training that dismisses reality and proposes a "sure fire approach to selling" is a waste of time and resources.

ESTABLISH TRAINING OBJECTIVES

At the outset of designing a training program, sales managers must develop a set of objectives in line with what they are trying to accomplish. These objectives are directly related to the nature of the group being trained. For example, if a company is training newly hired salespeople recruited from colleges, a number of topics must be covered:

1) Selling skills
2) Customer knowledge

3) Product knowledge
4) Company knowledge
5) Industry knowledge
6) Competitor knowledge

When training veteran salespeople, whether they are newly hired or have been with the company for some time, the training must aim at sharpening skills and knowledge. The training should present new material, perhaps with the introduction of a new product or marketing program. Training the veteran is very different from training new recruits.

In establishing objectives, the sales manager must ask the fundamental question: What does this group not know or what is it not able to do well? Sometimes the manager must develop different objectives for different groups because of variations in their skills. Obviously, it is impossible to customize training to fit every individual's needs. However, to use this as an excuse for offering a training program in which "one size fits all" is not justifiable. The optimal approach may involve using a modular system in which different topics are arranged in groups or modules. The manager can then select the module(s) that best fits the needs.

PRINCIPLES OF TRAINING

For a training program to be effective, several principles of training must be taken into consideration when designing the program. When a training program is less than effective it is often because one of these principles has been violated. The principles that are particularly pertinent to sales training are discussed here.

Purpose: The trainer must understand the objectives of the training program and should include training material and exercises that are relevant to accomplishing these objectives. Additionally, during the course of the training, the relevance of these materials should be explained to trainees.

Motivation: Many managers operate under the assumption that salespeople should be willing to become involved enough in a training program for it to be effective. This might be so in an ideal world, but the world is always less than ideal. For newly-hired salespeople, particularly those just beginning their careers, the motivation level is generally high. However, training that is perceived as irrelevant or boring can quickly sap this motivation. For veteran salespeople, training is often viewed as something of an intrusion. They often possess an intuitive assumption that training does not yield results in proportion to the effort expended. Also, for them the time spent training means time they are not selling, and hence training takes money out of their pockets. Sales managers should make provision for continuance of income during training for veteran salespeople and should be able to show that the training will yield positive results for the veteran.

Reinforcement: The law of relative effect states that people tend to repeat those behaviors for which they are rewarded. In training, when a person learns material or performs well on an exercise, there should be a reward by affirmation. By the same token, if the person fails to perform a particular skill or to learn some material well, there should be feedback about the problem. Feedback in this case serves as a type of reinforcement in that it lets the person know that the problem can be corrected and affirms that the individual is able to do the job.

Participation: Learning is a two-way process. Trainees should not be viewed as passive recipients of the trainer's wisdom. Rather, they need to be involved in the program. First, they can experience the concept first hand, and second, participation tends to alleviate boredom.

Practice: Similar to the idea of participation, practice involves the trainee in the training experience. Particularly when we talk about learning skills, the more often a person has the chance to perform these skills repetitively, the more the skills become ingrained. Listening, for instance, is a skill that improves with practice.

Repetition: As new material is introduced, the trainer should attempt to tie it to past material. In this way, the material is reinforced. Also, reviewing material tends to drive it home.

Plateaus: Learning is not a process that takes place consistently over time. Particularly when learning a new skill, a person often absorbs the basics very quickly but then seems to reach a point at which the person apparently does not learn at the earlier rate. This is similar to the way a tree grows. Trees tend to grow in spurts, and then growth subsides for a time. During this time of no-growth, the recent growth matures and gains strength. In training people, the trainer must be aware of these plateaus and also must let the trainee know it is normal to plateau. Otherwise the trainee, when he or she hits such a period, will become frustrated.

Productivity: People learn better at different times of the day and for a limited amount of time each day—usually, around midmorning and midafternoon. Given that a training program cannot possibly be contained to within these times, the trainer can use different approaches to break up the monotony and to involve people in the process during the "off-times." In this way, effective learning can be facilitated for a longer period of the day. The second half of this principle has to do with the amount of time a person should be in training each day. Perhaps this is the most violated aspect of these principles. Especially when training new salespeople, managers want to impart as much information as is possible. As a result, they often schedule more than eight classroom hours each day (six to seven is probably optimal) and then have trainees study workbooks or view tapes at night, interspersed with meetings of various kinds. We appreciate the desire to provide employees with as much ammunition as possible, but it is probably more critical that a person learn the important things well than many things poorly. The trainer should keep in mind: "We teach people, not things!"

Realism: Sales training, perhaps more than any other type, must reflect reality. Often, trainees go through training only to find that they have been given unrealistic expectations. This tends to negate the effectiveness of the entire program. Sales managers must themselves be realistic about what can be accomplished through training and include those areas that best result in achieving this goal. Additionally, training should accurately reflect the corporate credo. For example, if the person is told in training that "the customer is first" and then, upon arriving in the field, is told by the manager that sales volume is first, the trainee tends to discard the training program as "pie in the sky." In doing so, perhaps the person may reject some very solid concepts conveyed during the program. (If the corporate credo is something that the company is ashamed to convey in training, then probably the credo should be changed.) Again, whether the sales manager likes it or not, the person goes through a process of socialization and is confronted with any number of "truths." If in training the persons are given a realistic picture of what it is like in the field, they can better sort through these influences.

TOPICS IN SALES TRAINING

A number of topics can be covered in a sales training program. The composition of a given program depends on the objectives of the program as well as the nature of the people being trained.

Selling Skills

Particularly with new salespeople, training in the area of selling skills is important. As part of a recent study of sales managers, managers were asked to rate the importance of various sales training topics. (The study was conducted by Conrad N. Jackson and Ralph W. Jackson with sales managers from a variety of types of firms.) Interestingly, the two highest-rated topics had to do with selling skills. In the study, the topic of sales follow up and customer service was rated the highest of the various topics presented to these managers.

The next highest-rated topic in the study was listening skills. These two topics are related to the concept of *relationship marketing,* the idea that selling is involved not so much in bringing about a transaction as in building an ongoing relationship with the customer. Selling skills, like any other skill, can best be learned through the interactive process. The more the person is given the chance to employ the concept in the training setting, the better able that person will be to employ it in the field. Among the areas covered under the topic of selling skills are the following:

Listening skills
Presentation skills
Time management
Probing and fact finding
Customer service
Prospecting and qualifying
Handling objections
Organization skills
Closing the sale

Product Knowledge

Perhaps the most common topic in sales training is product knowledge. Especially for products that are highly technical or in industries that are very dynamic, product knowledge training is generally an ongoing process. Another reason for the proliferation of training on product knowledge is its importance in helping the customer to solve problems. Often this type of training lends itself to a self-paced, computer-aided program, given the need for the person to be able to absorb the information adequately.

Customer Knowledge

This topic deals not so much with reading the customer as it does with the nature of the market the company serves. Given the wide diversity in organizations, the salesperson must be equipped with a well-rounded grasp of the customers. For instance, the salesperson needs to know how the customer uses the product and how the product fits the customer's overall operation.

Product differentiation is often difficult to achieve, and a company is often forced to differentiate itself through customer service. Our customers' main problems in life are not where and how to buy the kind of products we sell but rather how and where to sell the products they make. The salesperson who understands the customer's market can better assist the customer in solving that main problem and is viewed as an ally of the buyer.

Competitor and Industry Knowledge

It is probably almost as important to know of your competitor's products as it is to have a thorough knowledge of your own. Sometimes the actual difference between product offerings is insignificant. This is not all bad because the salesperson is then forced to figure out what can be done to better the competitors' salespeople. This can create a competitive advantage that cannot be readily copied. In the words of Peter Drucker, "The essence of competition is doing those things well that are the most difficult to emulate." Salespeople need to understand their own company's competitive advantages, not so they can put down the competition, but rather so that they can highlight the benefits and advantages unique to their products.

Company Knowledge

A final topic in sales training has to do with the person's company. Especially for newly hired people, this is critical information. The new salesperson not only needs to know about the operations of the company and how the sales force fits in, but also must be introduced to the corporate culture. Subsumed under the concept of corporate culture are the *corporate credo,* the set of values that guide decision making in the company, corporate ethical standards, interdepartmental relations, and the company outlook regarding the place of the customer in the scheme of things, among others.

APPROACHES TO TRAINING

The most widely used approach to training is probably *on-the-job training* (OJT). OJT has the advantage of introducing trainees to "real-world" experiences. Additionally, it provides the trainer with the chance to critique the trainee's performance in an actual setting. OJT also provides the candidate a "reality check" before being turned out on his or her own in the field. The trainer must establish a forum for OJT to be an effective learning experience. There are several actions a trainer or sales manager can take:

1) Discuss each sales call with the person before entering the business place to help the trainee organize the call and to point out any difficulties the person might face.

2) Go on the call with the person, but do not become directly involved in trying to make the sale. Instead, observe and mentally critique the sales presentation. This distance from the sales is very difficult for a sales manager; however, the trainee will generally learn as much from failure as from success.

3) After the call is completed, give feedback to the trainee, pointing out specific things that were done correctly as well as problems with the presentation.

OJT usually works best in conjunction with other approaches to training. All too often, sales managers justify their reliance on OJT alone by saying that "Experience is the best teacher," or "The best place to learn to sell is in the school of hard knocks." We respond to those old saws with two new ones:

"Experience is indeed the best teacher, but it is a fool who learns by no other."

"The school of hard knocks has a tuition higher than most can afford to pay."

Classroom Training

Classroom training lends itself well to presenting certain types of information and conveying information in an efficient manner. It enables the company to frame what it wants to convey in a precise manner. The classroom lends itself to the use of videotapes, which can be extremely useful in helping trainees model behavior. Obviously, classroom training has its drawbacks, such as boredom, because trainees tend to grow weary of this approach more quickly than the others. Additionally, trainees retain little of what they hear and just a bit more of what they see. Confucius is purported to have said, "I hear and I forget; I see and I remember; I do and I understand."

This certainly applies to the training situation. Finally, classroom training requires presenters who are interesting and well prepared to be effective, and such people are expensive.

Electronic Training

In recent years, training with computers and interactive videos has been growing at a rapid rate (Urbanski, 1988). Interactive programs, through which the student receives instant feedback, especially provide the opportunity for the student to be more involved in the process. The additional benefit of this approach is that it helps familiarize the trainee with what the computer can do and may also remove some of the phobia surrounding the use of computers in selling.

Training by Experience

Although the structured, lecture format of the classroom is appealing to sales managers who fear that their salespeople will miss information with another approach, it is limited in what and how effectively information can be conveyed. Trainees often learn best when they are allowed to attempt to apply concepts and, sometimes, when they fail in the attempt. One way to allow this to take place without risking sales and with minimal risk to the trainee's ego is through experiential learning exercises. Among those that have been successfully applied are the following:

1) Role playing
2) Case studies
3) Experiential exercises
4) Group projects

Although training should not consist exclusively of these methodologies, they can be included in the training process at appropriate times. Experiential training can cut down on boredom by being interwoven in a classroom lecture setting. The exercises allow the trainee to learn by doing and to receive instant feedback. The trainer must be able to draw truths from the experience and to help the trainees understand the dynamics of what took place.

Mentoring

Another approach to training that seems to be growing in stature can be referred to as mentoring (Bragg, 1989). Mentoring gives a new salesperson assistance in areas where there are problems, and provides a role model in the company. Generally, in mentoring programs, new salespeople are assigned to a veteran who works with them on selling or on a special marketing project. The trainee has access to the accumulated expertise of the veteran, and the veteran enjoys intrinsic rewards from working with new people, often at a time in one's career when these intrinsic rewards are particularly important.

Curbside Training

In this final approach to training, the sales manager acts in the capacity of a coach. This type of training is ongoing. It allows the sales manager to monitor the progress of the salespeople and to provide feedback in a timely manner. Additionally, it helps sales managers to evaluate the individuals who report to them.

When designing a training program, the sales manager uses a combination of the various approaches. One should keep in mind these principles of learning as the training program is planned. Alternating the approaches alleviates some of the difficulties that arise from any violation of these training principles.

Who Does the Training?

The sales manager is faced with the question of who should conduct training sessions. The choices are as follows:

1) Use outside consultants.
2) Use inside training specialists.
3) Use company salespeople.
4) Sales manager conducts the training.

The use of outside consultants has the advantage of supplying people who are experts in training salespeople (and who specialize in sales training). Additionally, outside trainers may be perceived as having more credibility than inside people. The drawback, of course, is the high cost of good outside training. Although there are inexpensive training programs, usually there is a fairly strong price-quality relationship in training.

Using inside training specialists has the advantage of calling on someone who is an expert at training and who is often lower in cost than an outside person. However, these people generally do not specialize in sales training and therefore may not be able to meet the particular needs of salespeople.

Using veteran company salespeople guarantees that a person experienced in selling a particular type of product in a given industry does the training. This person is familiar with the specific issues and problems in selling the company's products. Also, this choice can provide intrinsic rewards to these salespeople. Obviously, the salespeople chosen to conduct training sessions should be volunteers and should be among the best-performing salespeople. A major drawback to this approach is the problem of taking veteran salespeople out of the field. In addition, these salespeople are not training specialists and may be tempted to "grandstand," and they may not be perceived as having credibility as trainers.

Training by the sales manager is an advantage because this person knows the weaknesses of the salespeople and knows the industry and products well. However, new salespeople may be intimidated by the prospect of "the boss" doing the training. Additionally, sales managers are not professional trainers and often have enough to do without trying to conduct training sessions.

Where Should the Training Be Done?

The sales manager is faced with the prospect of conducting training either in the various regions or at a central location. Conducting training in the sales regions enables the salespeople to learn in a comfortable environment. Also, if part of the training consists of familiarizing salespeople with their territories, regional training is particularly useful. Obviously, regional training saves the company the expense of sending its regional salespeople to the central location and of providing housing. A major drawback is that the salesperson has the distractions that are part of training in the home environment.

Centralized training enables the company to more closely monitor the progress of the training and ensures a greater degree of standardization in the training. It may also enable the company to use approaches that might be too expensive to use in several locations but that are reasonably efficient when used in one place with a larger number of people. Centralized training makes the training seem more "special" to salespeople, and perhaps because of this, they take it more seriously.

CHAPTER PERSPECTIVE

There are problems inherent in trying to help salespeople realize their potential and become good producers on a continuous basis. Selling involves a number of skills and a good deal of knowledge. Training is the best way to ensure that salespeople have the chance to obtain these. There are some that sales managers should consider principles of training when designing training programs. Generally speaking, a good training program begins with a concrete idea of what needs to accomplished, factors in the principles of learning, and has a content that adequately addresses the problems that salespeople will face.

REFERENCES

Bragg, Arthur (1989), "Is a Mentor Program in Your Future?," *Sales & Marketing Management* (September), 54-63.

Urbanski, Al (1988), "Electronic Training May Be in Your Future," *Sales & Marketing Management* (March), 46, 48.

Sales-Forecasting Techniques

INTRODUCTION AND MAIN POINTS

Everyone is fascinated by tomorrow, by what will happen in the future. Accurate forecasts are essential to the sales planning process.

After reading this chapter:

■ You will understand the relationship between planning and forecasting.

■ You will be able to estimate market potentials for consumer and industrial products.

■ You will be able to select the most appropriate qualitative and quantitative sales technique.

SALES FORECASTING AND PLANNING

The central focus of future planning in a company is the sales forecast. Regardless of the size of the company or the sales force, the sales forecast influences all aspects of planning, budgeting, and establishing quotas. Developing a good sales forecast is not simple. Before determining the appropriate sales-forecasting method, it is important that all factors affecting the forecast be examined. These can be classified into two groups: Controllable and uncontrollable.

Controllable factors are those that are under the control of the firm, such as pricing policies, distribution channels, promotion activities, new products, product characteristics, accounts-receivable policies, and the firm's own financial capability. Controllable factors are elements of the internal business environment that affect future sales that can be controlled by the firm.

Uncontrollable factors are environmental elements over which the firm has little, if any, control. These include the state of world and national economy, inflation, interest rates, shifts in population, changing consumer tastes and other demographic data, competitive conditions, and industry trends. Uncontrollable factors affect the sales and performance of the firm to varying extents. It is important that factors having the greatest impact be carefully monitored and taken into account when developing the sales forecast. Of course, one factor influencing sales, regardless of the market, is the general economic situation.

A company should determine the indices of general economic conditions most relevant to its product category. The three general categories of indicators are indicated in Table 15-1. *Leading indicators,* indices that lead general business activity, are closely examined because the movement of these indices (upward or downward) precedes the sales of the product. (Unfortunately, this movement does not consistently mean an upswing or downturn in product sales.)

TABLE 15-1
Principal Business Indicators for Use in Sales Forecasting

Leading indicators
> Average work week of production workers
> Value of manufacturer's new orders (durable goods industries)
> Construction contracts awarded to commercial and industrial
> buildings
> Contracts and orders for plants and equipment
> Newly approved capital appropriations
> Net change in the business population (new businesses incorporated
> and failures)
> Corporate profits after taxes
> Index of stock prices
> Change in business inventories
> Value of manufacturers' new orders

Simultaneous (coincident) indicators
> Unemployment rate
> Index of help-wanted advertising in newspaper
> Index of industrial production
> Gross national product
> Personal income
> Sales of retail stores
> Index of wholesale prices

Lagging indicators
> Business expenditures on new plants and equipment
> Book value of manufacturers' inventories
> Consumer installment debt
> Index of labor cost per unit of output

Simultaneous (coincident) and lagging indicators are less important in making the sales forecast. *Coincident indicators* are those that are in harmony with fluctuations in product sales and are useful in establishing marketing strategies in various stages of the product life cycle. For example, a firm that must borrow funds should be aware that interest rates usually go up some time after a coincident series peak has been reached. Finally, lagging indicators are those that lag behind fluctuations in the market. If a trough occurs, interest rates often reach their lowest levels a few weeks later, an ideal time to obtain financing.

Forecasting Concepts

Each sales manager is concerned with four concepts when developing a forecast: *Market size,* market potential, sales potential, and sale forecast. Market size is the total number of units a particular market could consume in a given year without taking into account such marketing activities as price and competitive activity. The part of market size represents the highest possible total industry sales of a product in a given time period is *market potential. Sales potential* is a subset of market potential that represents the maximum market share a company could obtain in the specific time period. Finally, the *sales forecast,* a subset of sales potential, is the amount of sales in the specific market that the company may obtain in a particular period of time.

Estimating Consumer Demand

For companies marketing consumer goods, some excellent basic economic data is found in the "Survey of Buying Power" of *Sales and Marketing Management* magazine. Particularly helpful to the sales manager in estimating future sales is the buying power index (BPI), which uses a weighted combination of population, income, and retail sales expressed as a percentage of national potential to forecast purchasing ability in a particular market. BPIs are listed in the magazine for the standard metropolitan statistical areas of major cities. The sales manager can compare the percentage in a particular city with the percentage of total company sales in that market to evaluate whether present company sales results are adequate. If there appears to be *untapped potential* in the market, the sales manager can obtain more information about the market and the amount of competition. The analysis may indicate that an increase in sales efforts and/or selling expenditures is warranted.

Estimating Industrial Demand

An approach unique to estimating industrial sales is the *Standard Industrial Classification (SIC)* code approach. The SIC code is a uniform numbering system that classifies all companies according to the nature of the product produced or the operation performed. All companies are assigned to a category, with each major industrial group identified by a two-digit number (see Table 15-2). Within each two-digit SIC code, there are specific product classifications. Within SIC code 20-39, indicating a manufacturing company, for example, SIC code 34 indicates a manufacturer of fabricated metal products and SIC code of 3441121 a manufacturer of fabricated structural iron and steel for buildings. The SIC code numbers can help the sales manager locate potential customers, determine market potential for an area, and assist in making accurate sales forecasts.

TABLE 15-2
The Standard Industrial Classification (SIC) System

Two-Digit SIC Number	Major Industry Classification
01-09	Agriculture, forestry, fishing
10-14	Mining
15-17	Construction
20-39	Manufacturing
40-49	Transportation and other public utilities
50-51	Wholesale trade
52-59	Retail trade
60-67	Finance, insurance, and real estate
70-89	Services
91-97	Government
99	Nonclassifiable establishments

To complete a list of potential customers in a market area in a particular SIC code, the sales manager can use the state's industrial directory or another directory, such as *The Thomas Register of American Manufacturers, Moody's Industrial Manual,* or *Standard & Poor's Register.* Each of these references provides current information on corporate officers, company name, address and telephone numbers, products or services offered, annual sales, and number of employees. These data can also be purchased by SIC code classification from a variety of firms, such as Dun and Bradstreet. The SIC code also guides the sales manager in obtaining other relevant information in such reference sources as the *U.S. Census of Manufacturers, U.S. Industrial Outlook, County Business Patterns,* and *Sales and Marketing Management,* "Survey of Industrial Purchasing Power."

SALES FORECASTING AND SALES BUDGET

To effectively achieve a specific sales objective, a budget must be established to fund the necessary programs to reach these objectives. A sales budget consists of planned expenses developed on an annual basis. The sales budgeting process starts when the company's management develops a marketing and advertising plan and makes a sales forecast. The sales forecast then becomes a guide for determining how many salespeople are needed and how many travel and other expenses will be incurred by the sales force to reach this forecast figure.

A question is often raised: Which comes first, the availability of the resources (the budget) or the forecast of sales? While a sales budget cannot be established until expected revenues are known, in turn, expected sales revenues cannot be accurately determined until a budget has been established. Although they are clearly interdependent, usually the sales forecast precedes establishing the budget.

NONQUANTITATIVE FORECASTING METHODS

Because no single method results in accurate sales forecasting, it is usually better to use several methods simultaneously. The results from one method act as a check on the results from another. One of the most important determinants in selecting a forecasting method is the amount of data available. Nonquantitative methods most commonly used in sales forecasting include:

1) The jury of executive opinion
2) Sales force composite
3) Buyer's expectations
4) The Delphi technique
5) The scenario technique

Jury of Executive Opinion

The *jury of executive opinion,* one of the oldest and simplest techniques, asks top executives of the firm to forecast future sales. By averaging these views, a broad-based forecast is obtained, which is usually more accurate than one obtained using only a single estimate from one executive. Estimates of sales are generally obtained from executives in such areas as marketing, finance, production, and purchasing.

The advantage of the jury of executive opinion is that it is quick and easy. The major disadvantage is that it relies on the opinions of executives who may not be associated with the company's products and may inaccurately predict its sales.

Sales Force Composite

The sales force composite method compiles sales force estimates of future sales. Sometimes salespeople make these estimates alone, and sometimes the estimates are made in consultation with the sales manager.

The results from the salespeople are then totaled for the district or region. The district or regional managers evaluate the estimate by comparing it with the accuracy of past estimates of sales. The resulting deviation factor and their own experience is then used in developing the final district estimate, which is forwarded to the home office, where a total sales estimate is made.

A common bias in this method is that the forecasted sales are usually lower than the actual sales that occur. These lower forecasts can be compensated for by establishing an index of pessimism for each salesperson. The index is derived by comparing each previous sales estimate with the actual sales for each salesperson. The difference, when divided by the estimate, become the salesperson's index. In one company the estimates for about 90 percent of the salespeople were within 10 percent of actual sales when indices of pessimism were applied.

Even though the sales force composite method allows sales to be estimated by knowledgeable people closest to the market, there are two problems in the method for producing an accurate forecast. First, the structure of the market affects the ability of the sales force to accurately forecast sales. When salespeople sell to relatively few accounts or if relatively few accounts compose the predominant proportion of their business, the forecasts are usually more accurate. The second problem with the sales force composite is that salespeople's evaluation, compensation, and promotion are based on sales, not on forecasting accuracy. Therefore, they spend as little time as possible in making sales forecasts.

Buyer Expectation Method

Many companies ask present, past, and potential customers about purchase intentions. This approach, the *buyer's expectation method,* works most effectively when there are relatively few important customers. These potential customers can be queried about purchasing plans by mail, telephone, or in person. Queries in person provide more accurate and detailed estimates. A problem can occur in using this method if potential buyers overstate their buying intentions. One way to correct this is to reduce artificial demand by creating an index of optimism similar to the pessimism index established in the sales force composite method. This index is based on past purchases versus forecasts for each industrial buyer.

Delphi Technique

The *Delphi method* can be used to forecast product sales and to predict the future direction of an entire industry. The method is often a controlled succession of brainstorming sessions among a panel of experts. Responses to the first round of questions are summarized and form the basis of the next round of questions. The judgments, insights, and expectations of the experts are evaluated by the entire group, resulting in a shared, more structured, and less biased estimate of future sales.

A Delphi sales forecast involves forming a panel. This panel is composed of 10 to 1,000 persons possessing knowledge of the field and comprises those of various backgrounds and training and organizational positions. A letter is mailed to participants, asking them to provide estimates of general industry sales and product sales. Panel members are also asked to indicate their knowledge of the field. The answers are edited, and a list of items or statements drawn up. This list is mailed to all panel members and participants are asked to provide their opinions about when any change will occur, as well as the probability of various sales estimates. The answers are tabulated and further steps implemented as needed.

The quality of the sales forecast resulting from the Delphi method is dependent on the expertise of panel members. This makes it very important to choose an expert and panel to combine their answers carefully.

Scenario Technique

The *scenario technique* provides a broad picture of future product sales based on alternative sets of assumptions. By outlining internally consistent, qualitative, alternative future courses of action, including a discussion of all the important events and their end points, the sequence of events from the present situation to future sales is developed.

The first step in using the scenario technique is to choose a number of sectors and to describe all plausible variations and alternatives within each sector. The factors and sectors are then combined in schematic configurations of patterns that may exist in the future. The relevant reference scenarios are then selected using the criterion of internal consistency. Finally, the scenarios are outlined so they are coherent when viewed one at a time.

QUANTITATIVE FORECASTING TECHNIQUES

Quantitative statistical techniques are also used to forecast future sales: Correlation and regression analyses, time series analysis, the moving-average method, and the Box-Jenkins method.

Correlation and Regression Analyses

Correlation and regression analyses are probably the most widely used quantitative procedures for forecasting sales. These procedures establish the mathematical relationship between sales of the product and at least one other variable. Correlation analysis is frequently used to determine the relationships between sales and the appropriate leading indicators in the external environment. From these relationships, regression analysis can be used to predict the future value of the dependent variable—-the sales of the product.

Time Series Analysis

Similar to correlation and regression analysis, time series analysis predicts future sales based on past sales. While correlation and regression analysis focuses on relationships among variables, time series analysis focuses only on historical sales data. In forecasting sales, four types of movements are evaluated:

Cyclic (C) movements are wavelike movements of sales, irregular in occurrence, that are longer than one year.

Erratic (E) movements are one-time, specifically identifiable events affecting sales.

Periodic (P) movements, also called seasonal variations, are a consistent pattern of sales movements within the year.

Trends (T) are upward or downward sales movements resulting from basic developments in capital, population, or technology.

Moving Averages

This method of time series analysis eliminates extremes by averaging several time periods of sales (usually weeks or months). As the actual sales data from the new period are added to the data, the sales from the last period are eliminated. The number of periods is decided by the sales manager. The moving average method not only reduces seasonal variations but also minimizes the impact of the most recent sales figures, leading to a more conservative sales estimate in times of increasing sales.

Exponential Smoothing

When the sales manager is performing a short-range forecast—less than six months—exponential smoothing is frequently used as this method is very responsive to the most recent sales. The method systematically stresses most recent sales while reducing the emphasis on the oldest sales data. The most critical factor in the accuracy of this method for forecasting future sales is the value chosen by the sales manager for the smoothing constant or weights. For short-run forecasts for a company in a mature or stable market, exponential smoothing is an excellent method for the sales manager to accurately estimate future sales.

Box-Jenkins

The Box-Jenkins method employs a computerized mathematical technique to select the model that best fits the past sales data and therefore provides the most accurate forecast. The technique requires a large number of sales data points and a fairly high degree of expertise. It can be used as a very good sales-forecasting method for the sales manager when a particular product or service has a long history of sales.

CHAPTER PERSPECTIVE

Forecasting sales is an important area of sales planning. Both controllable and uncontrollable factors need to be taken into account when making the forecast and the sales plan. Good information can be obtained for estimating consumer or industrial demand from a wide variety of reference material. Specific sales forecasting methods are: Jury of executive opinion, sales force composite, buyer expectation method, delphi technique, scenario technique correlation and regression analysis, time series analysis, moving averages, exponential smoothing and Box-Jenkins method.

Budgets and Sales Quotas

INTRODUCTION AND MAIN POINTS

Successful selling in the future will require well-thought-out plans. Budgets and sales quotas are an important part of this strategic planning: they assist in the planning, evaluation, and control of selling activities.

After reading this chapter:

▬ You will understand the relationship between planning and budgeting.

▬ You will understand the reasons for establishing sales quotas.

▬ You will be able to implement procedures for setting sales quotas.

SALES BUDGETS

One of the major responsibilities of the sales manager is to prepare sales budgets and monitor the actual versus the projected expenditures. A *sales budget* is a financial sales plan indicating the manner in which resources and selling efforts should be allocated to achieve the forecasted level of sales. The various levels of sales that can be obtained with a given budget should be evaluated given the expenditures required to reach the sales level forecast. The sales budget serves three primary purposes: Planning, coordination, and control of all selling activities.

Planning

To achieve a sales forecast, the selling tasks and support services should be specified. These tasks and their estimated costs must be determined by the sales manager for a particular period of time. This time period is usually one year, but it can be as short as three to six months.

Coordination

To predict sales and positively affect the profits of the company, the forecast must be closely integrated with most of the other budgets. All budgets, such as the promotional budget or the amount set aside for bad debts, must reflect the sales budget and selling activities projected to occur.

Control

Sales budgets also establish the financial benchmark by which the actual results are measured. A good sales manager constantly monitors the budget, looking for any significant variations—the difference between actual results and budgeted (projected) results.

PREPARING THE SALES BUDGET

The preparation of the sales budget, although considered an onerous task by most sales managers, presents an opportunity for careful resource allocation and profit planning. Several steps are typically followed in preparing most sales forecasts.

The first is to review the previous year's situation, beginning with the previous selling period. All variations occurring most frequently center on such line items as salaries, direct selling expenses, commissions and bonuses, in-house support, benefit packages, promotional materials, and achievements.

Upon completing the review, sales goals and objectives should be established and communicated to all managers. Everyone relevant should be included in the budgetary process. This helps commit individuals to the budget, which will assist in its implementation.

Third, any problems or specific market opportunities should be identified. Specific resources should be set aside in the budget to deal with these unique aspects.

Fourth, an initial budget should be prepared that allocates specific selling efforts and resources to particular activities, customers, product lines, and sales territories. This initial budget should be as accurate as possible, but it is revised several times before the final budget emerges.

Then, usually, a budget presentation is developed and presented to upper management. This presentation usually requires a sales job in itself, particularly if an increased allocation of funds is desired. As with any sales presentation, a successful budget presentation requires a succinct summary of the proposed budget with alternative scenarios.

The final step is to implement the budget and closely monitor the results. This allows resulting variations to be dealt with quickly so that budget goals can be met. It is the responsibility of each group to stay within its budget, but the sales manager is ultimately responsible for ensuring that the overall budget is met.

SALES QUOTA

After the sales force and sales budget have been prepared, the sales manager must establish specific goals for quotas for each selling activity and develop plans that will help these quotas be achieved. Quotas are usually established based on sales volume, but they can also be established for gross margins, selling expenses, or profits, or a combination of these. They are used as standards that indicate the desired level of performance of the individual salesperson, sales territory, district, or region. Quotas are very useful: They provide goals, control the activities of the sales force, control the selling expense, improve the compensation package, and evaluate performance.

Provide Goals

Given the competitive nature of salespeople, it is important that a benchmark figure be established for distinguishing success or failure. The quota provides a quantitative measure of selling ability and should be something for which the sales person strives. It is important that the quota be realistic and attainable. When attainable quotas are established, a salesperson feels responsible for attaining the quota.

Control Activity

Since salespeople are responsible for obtaining the established quotas, they in effect enable management to direct and control selling activities. By establishing a specific number of sales calls per day, a specific amount of a product to be sold, or a specific number of new customer calls to be made, the sales manager can clearly guide the activities of the sales force so that the objectives of the company are achieved within the budget.

Control Selling Expenses

Similarly, quotas can be used to control the amount of money spent on meals, lodging, and entertainment. This results in controlling the costs of selling and keeping selling costs at a minimum. If the quotas are not met or are exceeded, the increased expenses can be charged against the salesperson's compensation and can be noted in the next performance evaluation.

Improve Compensation

Sales quotas can play a role in the salesperson's overall compensation package. In some companies, the quota must be exceeded before a commission is paid. For example, a salesperson can be given a quota of $300,000 in sales for the year and would receive a 7 percent commission on every sale above the quota. On a sale of $400,000, the salesperson would receive a commission of 7 percent X ($400,000 − 300,000), or $7,000. This type of quota provides a strong incentive for significant sales performance because there is no cap on the commissions earned.

Another company may use a different approach to compensation through quotas. The quota is the basis for calculating the bonus and the quota is set quite high, with the bonus limited to a maximum amount for 10 percent quota attainment. If the salesperson does not make the quota, the percentage of the quota is calculated with the bonus set at the percentage of the maximum bonus amount. For example, if a salesperson can earn $4,000 for obtaining his or her quota of $300,000 in sales but achieves sales of only $250,000 (83 percent of the quota), the salesperson receives a bonus of 83 percent X $4,000, or $3,320.

Quotas can also be used for sales contests, which can be excellent short-term incentive tools. The quotas established for sales contests should be adjusted so that each salesperson has an equal opportunity of winning. A well-designed contest that everyone can win can positively affect sales performance.

Evaluate Performance

Probably the best known purpose of a sales quota is to measure the performance of the salesperson. Care must be taken in using a quota as a measure. If a sales quota is exceeded, this indicates either that the salesperson is working very hard or the quota was set too low. Similarly, a quota that is not met may indicate that the salesperson is not working hard enough, the territory has problems, or the quota was set too high.

TYPES OF QUOTAS

There are four types of quotas frequently used by companies: Sales volume, financial, sales activity, and combination quotas. The company can use one or more of these quotas depending on the product, industry, and specific company situation.

Sales Volume Quotas

By far the most commonly used quotas are those based on sales volume; this usually means dollar sales, not unit sales volume. Some sales volume quotas are based on sales of particular products, sales of new products, sales to new customers, and unit sales. These quotas are used in performance evaluation, providing the minimum-expected performance level for the specific period of time.

Sales volume quotas measured on either a dollar or unit basis are established for a specific period of time, usually for a product or product line, customer or prospect type, or geographic area. The smaller the marketing unit and the shorter the time period, the better. Using a small marketing unit provides better control and can be extended, when needed, across many units. Unless sales are seasonal, quotas should be established on a monthly or quarterly basis.

Dollars Versus Unit Sales Quotas

A question frequently arises about whether to use a dollar or unit basis for quotas. Both are used by companies in various industries, and each provides advantages to the sales manager. Sales volume quotas expressed in dollars are the usual measure for product activity and are easily understood by the salesperson and management. They are particularly useful when the salesperson is responsible for selling many products because a dollar sales volume figure can be established for groups of products. Dollar sales volume figures also make it easier to evaluate and calculate the comparative ratios, such as selling costs to quotas and selling expenses to sales.

When only a few products are sold, unit sales volume quotas are useful. The unit basis is particularly useful during rapid price increases or decreases. When there is extreme price volatility (for example the oil price fluctuations in the late 1980s and early 1990s) dollar sales volume quotas are extremely inappropriate and may lead to frustration on the part of the salesperson as well as a poor performance appraisal. The unit sales volume basis is more appropriate when products are expensive. A quota of $500,000 may appear more unattainable than a quota of 10 units at $50,000 per unit.

Basis for Sales Volume Quotas

The basis for establishing sales volume quotas can be past sales, sales potential, or market estimates, or a combination of these. By far the easiest (and most frequently used) method for setting sales volume quotas is to base them on past sales in the territory. The new quota is established by increasing last year's quota by the percentage amount the market should increase. If the market is expected to increase 5 percent next year, the quota for each salesperson is last year's quota plus 5 percent, or 105 percent of last year's quota.

The second basis for establishing a sales volume quota is to use the sales manager's estimate of market opportunity and the effort needed by the salesperson. This procedure uses the company's sales forecast, not the sales potential. The salesperson has input into the quota by providing an estimate of the territory's potential. The sales manager then adjusts this estimate upward or downward, taking into account such factors as the ability and characteristics of the salesperson. This new estimate is adjusted again based on the company's future marketing plans. The sales manager then converts these estimates into sales quotas, which are summed up including all salespeople to determine the company's total sales forecast.

Some companies that are very small or very new base their company's sales estimate on market estimates. In these companies, top management establishes the quotas, which are passed on to the salespeople using one of two different methods. In the first method, the total company sales forecast is divided into territorial estimates and adjusted accordingly. Recognizing that adjustments at the corporate level are different from adjustments at the territorial level, the second method first adjusts the company's forecasted sales based on future company marketing efforts. These adjusted estimates are then broken down into territories and adjusted accordingly.

Financial Quotas

Financial quotas are used when a company is interested in controlling gross margin or net profit. The quotas indicate to the salesperson that the company prefers to make profits rather than move large volumes. Financial quotas help modify the salesperson's natural drive to sell as many product units as possible regardless of the profit. A salesperson may be doing the company a disservice and costing it the opportunity to earn higher profits from higher margin items if too much time is spent on less profitable, easy-to-sell products.

Salespeople also tend to spend more time with customers with whom they feel more comfortable regardless of their profitability. By placing a quota on net profits, salespeople are encouraged to spend more selling time on more profitable products and with more profitable customers.

In emphasizing profit, these financial quotas have disadvantages. First, financial quotas are harder for salespeople to understand. Since the net profit goal is composed of a range of products and their respective margins, it is difficult for the salesperson, at any given time, to determine how well he or she is doing. This can cause frustration and even a lack of motivation.

Second, it takes more time to calculate the net profit, which leads to additional clerical and administrative costs. Finally, because the salesperson's salary, based on the net profit, is much more sensitive to various external and internal factors, financial quotas may be viewed as less fair.

Expense Quotas

Expense quotas are used to emphasize the selling costs to the salesperson and therefore to help control them. To try to contain the rapidly escalating costs of travel, food, and lodging, a sales manager can tie reimbursement for these expenses directly to the sales volume or compensation plan. For example, a salesperson may be allowed 4 percent of the sales volume as an expense. Another way is simply to determine maximum amounts that can be spent per day on food and accommodations. A third method is to use an expense-to-sales ratio in determining the amount of expenses allowed. Because a salesperson's job is to sell, when using expense quotas care must be taken that the sales performance is not hindered just to contain costs. Remember also that some territories are more expensive than others. Each salesperson's expense quota must be based on a realistic assessment of the territory.

Activity Quotas

Because salespeople are given latitude to plan and carry out their daily activities, some companies require each salesperson to follow and meet an established activity quota. Activity quotas may be particularly beneficial to younger, inexperienced salespeople. In establishing appropriate activity quotas, the first task is to determine the most important activities of the sales force. These can include making sales calls, establishing new accounts, obtaining better distribution for products, launching the new products, selling a merchandising or advertising program, and demonstrating products.

Each activity is evaluated to determine an average completion time. Finally, each activity is assigned a frequency that will become the target level of performance, as indicated in Table 16-1. By establishing activity quotas for the areas listed in the table, salespeople are better able to plan their daily activities and routing and make efficient use of time. This allows management to control and reward salespeople for performing tasks related to, but not involved in, a direct sale, such as rearranging a shelf in a supermarket or calling on customers who purchase very infrequently.

To ensure that attention and effort are given to achieving sales volume, activity quotas are frequently used in conjunction with sales volume quotas. This eliminates the problem of not focusing on the task of selling while rewarding salespeople for undertaking many nonselling functions.

TABLE 16-1
Commonly Used Activity Quotas

Number of calls made
Number of sales calls on present customers
Number of sales calls on new customers
Number of demonstrations
Number of service calls
Number of training sessions given
Number of store advertisements sold
Number of new accounts established

COMBINATION QUOTAS

Combination quotas, such as the activity and sales volume quotas just discussed, are used when the sales manager wants to control several aspects of the selling task. When a single index of measurement is desired, the measurement unit of each quota must be converted to points. This can be accomplished most easily by computing the percentage of each quota obtained and then multiplying this percentage (which now has no unit of measurement) by a weight indicating the importance of the quota to management.

Like net profit quotas, combination quotas are somewhat more difficult for salespeople to understand, thereby making it difficult for them to gauge their performance levels. Despite this disadvantage, combination quotas are an excellent way for the sales manager to direct and control the sales force on an activity or individual product basis.

ADMINISTERING QUOTAS

Regardless of the quota system employed, it will be ineffective unless it is properly and carefully administered. The sales manager must establish realistic and understandable quotas so that salespeople do not become anxious and nervous.

Establish Realistic Quotas

A salesperson is motivated by a quota that is attainable and by resulting rewards that are worthwhile. Quotas are established based on different theories of motivation and attainability. Some companies establish an average quota and reward salespeople based on the percentage of quota achieved, believing that salespeople should be motivated to continue to work hard. Other companies establish high quotas and reward salespeople for performance above these quotas, believing that salespeople should be rewarded only for excellent performance. This company has a higher base salary for the salesperson than the first company to help compensate for the potential difference in earnings. It is important that the quota system be seen by the sales force as fair, realistic, and attainable.

Establish Understandable Quotas

Part of the problem of quotas lies in perception. A clear understanding helps to gain the cooperation and acceptance of the sales force. The sales manager can help the sales force understand quotas by including each salesperson in the quote-setting procedure, and by ensuring that each is informed on a regular basis about the performance relative to quotas and any changes in the procedure. A clear understanding allows the quota system to be an effective method for motivating, evaluating, and controlling the sales force.

CHAPTER PERSPECTIVE

Sales budgets and quotas are important aspects of strategic planning that assist in the planning, evaluating and control of selling activities. Preparation of a sales budget involves review of the activities and results of the previous years, establishing sales goals and objectives, identifying any problems and market opportunities, preparing an initial budget, making a presentation to upper management, implementing the budget, and monitoring the results. Sales quotas are helpful in establishing objectives and monitoring the results of the budget established. The four basic types of quotas most frequently used are: Sales volume, financial, sales activity, and combination quotas.

For the most part, quotas are based on sales volume although they can also be based on gross margins, expenses in selling, and profits. The quota system employed needs to be carefully implemented for optimum results. As a result, it becomes important for the sales manager to establish practical quotas for the sales force.

Motivating and Leading the Sales Force

INTRODUCTION AND MAIN POINTS

A persistent challenge facing sales managers is to effectively motivate and lead the salespeople who work for them. These two topics are related and could be thought of as opposite sides of a coin. In essence, a good motivational program creates "followship," or, in other words, the desire to follow the leader wherever he or she wants to go. These topics have perhaps engendered more debate than any others in sales management. There are sales managers who believe that salespeople are only motivated by money. Others would argue that money, though important in retaining good salespeople, is not really an effective tool for motivation. There are those who hold that true leaders are born and that if a person does not possess certain characteristics, that person cannot succeed as a leader. Others would argue that it is the circumstance that forges the leader. It is likely that the truth about motivation and leadership, as in so many other cases, is to be found somewhere in the middle ground.

After reading this chapter:

▬ You will understand the basic theories of motivation and how they speak to the process of motivating people.

▬ You will be able to relate principles of motivation to programs that the sales manager can enact.

▬ You will have some understanding of the major theories of leadership.

▬ You will be able to distinguish the different types of power operating in an organization.

▬ You will understand the implications of different styles of leadership.

Although these two topics are related, they really require separate discussions. In this chapter we will begin with a presentation of principles of motivation and will then take up the discussion of leadership.

WHAT IS MOTIVATION?

In reality, no one can "motivate" another person. We can attempt to make a change in behavior attractive to another, but unless that other is willing to accept our influence then what we do is meaningless. We might coerce a person into altering their actions, but that is not really motivation. If it were, then we could conclude that the person who holds up a convenience store is an expert at motivation. Motivation results in a person voluntarily altering their action or opinion. In the words of French, motivation is:

> The desire and willingness of a person to expend effort to reach a particular goal or outcome. Individual motivation is a consequence of many forces operating simultaneously in the person and the person's environment (1990, pg. 122).

Motivation is a complex process involving a number of factors, both from inside and outside the person.

Concepts of Motivation

Without an understanding of some basic concepts a discussion of motivational programs becomes largely anecdotal without any way to predict what can be done to influence another. Perhaps the most basic concept in motivation is referred to as "the law of effect." According to this, people tend to repeat behavior for which they are rewarded, and conversely, they tend to avoid things for which they are likely to be punished. In other words, people's actions are largely a result of either seeking reward or avoiding punishment. There are two elements in the law of effect: A person must understand what it is that the supervisor wants the individual to do or not do, and the supervisor needs to use an appropriate set of rewards and punishments.

Attribution Theory

Attribution Theory has to do with what people mentally assign as the reasons for their success or failure. A person's performance can be categorized as either good or poor and the cause of that performance can be thought of as either personal or environmental. The reason for relative success or failure will either be viewed as being a function of what the individual did or did not do, or as a function of something outside the individual. Figure 17-1 depicts how a person might go about making these assignments.

When a person performs poorly, there will be a tendency to ascribe those results to something external, but when that person performs well, he or she will assign that to personal reasons. For example, students will almost always say: "Dr. Jones gave me a

FIGURE 17-1
ATTRIBUTION THEORY

ATTRIBUTION

		personal	environmental
PERFORMANCE	good	"I did well because of my efforts"	"I was just lucky"
	poor	"I did poorly because my work was not up to par"	"I did poorly because I have a lousy territory"

D, but I made an A in Professor Smith's class." Salespeople do the same thing when they blame a "lousy territory" for a failure to make quota or attribute a highly successful quarter to their own abilities, when in both instances there may be other reasons for the outcome.

Not only do people go through the process of attribution for their own performance, they do it for others. A major part of the sales manager's job is to evaluate salespeople and that involves the attribution process. The sales manager needs to examine whether the attributions made are accurate, and must be able to give accurate feedback to salespeople to help them make correct attributions.

Herzberg's Two-Factor Theory

One of the major debates in sales management has revolved around whether money is the only truly motivational incentive for salespeople. There are sales managers who believe that if their salespeople are not motivated by money, there is no way to really motivate them. Others would hold that salespeople are motivated by both money, which is an extrinsic reward, and by various intrinsic rewards, such as recognition.

Herzberg (1966) addressed the power of extrinsic and intrinsic rewards and found they both have their place in motivating people. According to his theory, there are certain factors associated with satisfaction and a separate set of factors that bring about dissatisfaction. The factors related to satisfaction and motivation consist of intrinsic rewards associated with the job such as recognition of achievement, experienced responsibility, advancement, and the challenging nature of the work itself. These factors tend to be associated with increased levels of satisfaction. These factors related to dissatisfaction and demotivation consist of extrinsic rewards such as salary, work conditions, and company policy. If these are positive, the person experiences lower levels of dissatisfaction. However, their presence alone does not ensure satisfaction or a high level of motivation.

An adequate salary will tend to cut down on dissatisfaction, but it will not necessarily lead to a high level of motivation. Most salespeople know, or think they know, about what other salespeople make, and they expect their salary to be in line with what others are making. Just because it is in line does not mean that they will have a higher level of motivation. If the sales manager wants to increase motivation levels, the manager needs to build in some intrinsic rewards. Keenan (1990) suggests using a variety of incentives in the motivational program to increase satisfaction and motivation.

Expectancy Theory

According to the Expectancy Theory, a person must believe that one is able to perform whatever it is that is asked and must believe that the promised outcome will take place. Finally, the person must feel that the net gain is worthwhile. These elements are essential if a person is to be motivated by a particular program. The Expectancy Theory can be illustrated this way:

In other words, whenever an individual is asked to perform a specific task, he or she mentally assesses the likelihood that a given level of effort will lead to a particular performance. That mental assessment is referred to as the person's "expectancy." Furthermore, the person assesses the likelihood that a given performance will lead to the desired outcome. This is the person's "instrumentality." Finally, the person weighs the net gain or value of the outcome, which is his or her "valence." To illustrate the concept we will use an example from sales.

A sales manager decides that her company needs to increase

sales volume in the next quarter. Currently, she has fifty salespeople working for her. She develops a sales contest whereby any salesperson who increases sales volume by fifty percent in the next quarter will win a one-week, all-expense-paid trip for two to Hawaii. However, in this company, salespeople are expected to render a high level of service to existing accounts and are currently averaging sixty hours per week to simply keep up with current volume.

Effort = the work necessary to increase volume
Performance = increasing volume by 50 percent
Outcome = trip to Hawaii (positive valence)
= feelings of accomplishment (positive)

In this case, the salesperson's instrumentality (link between performance and outcome) should be relatively high knowing that a fifty percent increase in sales volume in the territory over the next quarter, will result in a trip to Hawaii. The salesperson's valence (net value of the outcome) could be high or low. If we assume the salesperson really wants to go to Hawaii and would have a sense of accomplishment, this person should have a positive valence. In our example, the expectancy (the linkage between effort and performance) will likely be extremely low. This is because the salespeople are already stretched to the limit with existing levels of performance. In all likelihood, they will conclude that they cannot put forth enough effort to increase volume by 50 percent—it is viewed by them as simply impossible. In this instant, the person will not be motivated by the contest even if the individual has a very high valence (really wants to go to Hawaii) because of the low level of expectancy.

For the moment, let us change our example a bit. Say, for example, the sales manager designs the contest so that only the first person to increase sales volume by *ten percent* over the next quarter will win an all-expense-paid trip for two to Hawaii. In this case, the expectancy (linkage between effort and performance) will be much higher than in the first case because increasing volume by ten percent is much easier to accomplish. However, the instrumentality (linkage between performance and outcome) will be considerably lower because only one person will win and so the chance of going to Hawaii is significantly lessened. The valence should still be high because the person really wants to go to Hawaii.

Finally, if we assume for the moment that the sales manager designs the contest so that the first 15 salespeople who increase volume by 10 percent will win the trip. Again the expectancy will be reasonably high as will the instrumentality, given that roughly one-third of the sales force will go to Hawaii. However, suppose the vast majority of the sales force have families with small children and that they place extremely high value on spending time with their families. The increased workload will mean significantly more time away from home. Additionally, since the trip is only for two, the salespeople must either pay their childrens' way on the trip or find a place for them to stay. These represent negative valences and the net effect may be that the Hawaii trip is viewed as more trouble than it is worth. In this case, the contest will have little motivational power.

Thomas Quick (1989) discusses the power of expectancy theory in motivating salespeople. In his discussion, he provides some guidelines for its application:

1) Tell your subordinates what you expect of them.
2) Make the work valuable.
3) Make the work load reasonable.
4) Give them feedback.
5) Reward your salespeople when they've been successful.

Equity Theory

One motivational concept relevant to salespeople is referred to as the Equity Theory. According to it, people seek fair treatment in the way they are rewarded for job performance. According to Organ and Hamner: "We compare the ratio of our outcomes to inputs with the ratio of outcomes to inputs for some comparison person. The comparison person may be a co-worker or a group average (such as prevailing standards in a department, organization, community, or industry)" (1982, pg. 170). The manner in which we compare would take the form of:

$$\frac{\text{Our Outcomes}}{\text{Our Inputs}} \quad \text{versus} \quad \frac{\text{Others' Outcomes}}{\text{Others' Inputs}}$$

People expect to be treated fairly. The fact that they are treated equitably does not necessarily motivate them; however if the reward system is inequitable, this will likely demotivate them. So in a sense, equity theory is a theory of demotivation rather than one of motivation.

Issues in Motivation

It is generally accepted that individuals progress through various stages in their careers. Super (1957) proposed that a person passes six stages during a lifetime, four of which take place during the career. This career life cycle concept was applied to the sales force by Marvin Jolson (1974).

According to Jolson, salespeople progress through four stages during their careers: Exploration; establishment; maintenance; and disengagement. William Cron (1984) expanded the earlier work of Jolson and offered the following descriptions of these stages.

Exploration: In this stage, individuals (typically in their twenties) are concerned with finding an occupation in which they can feel comfortable and succeed. The fundamental question addressed during this period is: "What do I want to do for the rest of my life?" Personal commitment to an occupation usually is low and several changes in occupation are likely.

Establishment: Establishment-stage people (usually in their late twenties) seek to attain stability within an occupation and to secure a place in the working world. Concern focuses on adding structure and stability to one's career, often about the same time that other important life commitments (e.g., getting married, buying a home, establishing roots in a community) are being made. Achieving professional success is of utmost importance and frequently involves a desire for promotion.

Maintenance: This stage normally begins in a person's late thirties to mid-forties. Concern during this stage is with retaining one's present position, status and performance level, which are likely to be relatively high. Desire and opportunity for future job movement diminishes. Greater commitment to an organization is probable because people in this stage are less prone to switch organizations. However, they must adapt to changes, keep current with new developments, and acquire special knowledge and new skills to improve job performance.

Disengagement: In the early development of career stages theory, disengagement was associated with preparation for imminent retirement and sometimes loss of self-identity. Recent empirical research suggests that some people become frustrated long before retirement age and may psychologically disengage themselves from their work rather than search for a new job or occupation. Lower performance generally is associated with disengagement.

The sales manager needs to recognize that these stages exist and to address the special problems associated with each stage accordingly.

The Plateaued Salesperson

A persistent problem often related to career stage (although not necessarily so) is that of the plateaued salesperson. It has been estimated that as many as 15 percent of salespeople are plateaued (Keenan 1989). According to Keenan, plateauing can be the result of several factors. First, it may result from a lack of a clearcut career path; the person progresses satisfactorily only until the individual begins to feel that career growth is coming to an end. In this regard, salespeople should have the opportunity of advancing to the sales manager's position. Obviously, the sales manager in this case needs to work with the salespeople to assist them in developing new goals as current ones are met.

The second major reason for plateauing is inadequate management according to Keenan. Sales managers usually have so many things to occupy their time that, unless there is a major problem, they will simply not take any action. Also the sales manager may be tempted to view a down quarter for a salesperson as a temporary anomaly. Although that is often the case, it can be a signal that the person has plateaued and needs some guidance. The manager probably needs to discuss the issue with the salesperson early to determine if a plateau has been reached.

The other reasons mentioned by Keenan can be classed into two categories: Personal issues and career-related issues. In terms of personal issues, salespeople plateau because they may be bored, burned out, have met their economic needs, or because they lack ability. Career-related issues would include such things as being discouraged with the company, having been overlooked for promotion, avoiding the risk of moving into a management position, and the reluctance to be transferred. According to the Keenan article, there are some warning signals that can tip off the manager that a salesperson has plateaued. These include:

The salesperson does not prospect thoroughly enough.
The salesperson starts failing to follow through.
The salesperson begins to work fewer hours.
The person becomes resistant to management suggestion.
The salesperson lives in "the good old days."
The person does not keep up to date on new products.
The person's paperwork is late and/or poorly done.
The number of customer complaints begins to increase.
The person begins to manipulate commissions and quotas.

The rate of absenteeism increases.

In addition to giving increased attention to the individual, it was suggested that the manager give the salesperson a new assignment or get involvement in some leadership role.

Cultural Differences

Given the increasingly global character of competition and the pluralistic nature of our society, sales managers need to be more aware of the effect of cultural differences on motivating salespeople. In a recent article, Regina Eisman (1991) presented some of the difficulties experienced by Japanese managers in American plants. Trying to use the same approach to managing workers in U.S. plants as they did in Japan, they found that not only did workers not respond, but in some cases were hostile to the Japanese managers' efforts. Additionally, some Japanese workers were insulted when offered incentives for harder work because they felt that it was their duty to work as hard as possible anyway.

Although this article was based on a more blatant clash of cultures than a sales manager might have to face, it does highlight the fact that motivational programs that do not consider the cultural background of the employees will not be as effective and may actually result in a contrary reaction by salespeople. Cultural differences can often be found between different regions of the country. Approaches to motivating salespeople that work in the Northeast may not work in the Southwest. So, sales managers must be aware of and be somewhat adaptive to the cultural differences within the sales force.

Getting Involvement in Motivational Programs

Motivational programs are composed of both intrinsic and extrinsic rewards. The major form of motivation is salary, which will be discussed in the next chapter. Too often, when sales managers develop a program, they assume that salespeople will gladly participate in the program. Even if such programs do not violate the tenants of the major theories discussed earlier in this chapter, the sales manager cannot assume that salespeople will be interested in or motivated by a particular program. Urbanski (1987) points this out in his discussion of such programs, and suggests that the sales manager needs to investigate fresh approaches to gain involovement by the sales force. For sales contests, for example, Urbanski encourages the sales managers to get people involved along the way by using "teasers" or things to attract the attention and interest of the sales force. He uses the example of a company that used sales training as an incentive for its distributors' sales forces.

Elements of an Effective Motivation Program

When we pull together the basic concepts in motivation and the issues the sales manager faces, we recognize that there are several elements that must be a part of a motivational program. These include:

1) Any program needs to spell out explicitly the performance necessary to be rewarded.
2) The goals of the motivational program must be realistic and achievable in a reasonable time frame.
3) Good performance needs to be rewarded and bad performance should never be rewarded.
4) The rewards being offered need to be important to salespeople and not simply those that management prefers.
5) Any motivation program needs to contain both extrinsic and intrinsic rewards.
6) The motivation program needs to be designed to address the issues relevant for the sales force, and may at times need to be adjusted to cater to special groups within the sales force.
7) Salespeople need to perceive that the program is equitable.

WHAT IS LEADERSHIP?

Leadership could be defined as *giving a person or a group a sense of purpose by providing direction and guidance to achieve objectives considered worthwhile by the leader*. Although this definition is a bit broad, it can be applied to a number of situations. Leadership is a complex topic and should be broken down to gain a better understanding of it. Kotter defined four elements of effective leadership in his book *The Leadership Factor*.

Leadership consists of:

1) A vision of what should be, a vision that takes into account the legitimate interests of all the people involved;
2) A strategy for achieving that vision, a strategy that recognizes all the broadly relevant environmental forces and organizational factors;
3) A cooperative network of resources, a coalition powerful enough to implement the strategy; and
4) A highly motivated group of key people in that network, a group committed to making that vision a reality.

Theories of Leadership

At the outset of any discussion of leadership, one is tempted to try to isolate a set of characteristics that make good leaders and then go through the process of comparing oneself with the particular model that emerges.

A sales manager is often, in the back of the mind, plagued with the gnawing question of whether he or she is really a good leader, and for that reason, seeks a definitive answer. Often this approach to the question arises from the *trait theory* of leadership, i.e, the idea that leaders possess certain characteristics and non-leaders do not. In the name of trait theory, countless studies have been conducted to isolate those characteristics. The list of characteristics ranges from the sublime to the ridiculous. Everything from masculinity, height, weight and age to originality and fear of failure have been proposed and examined as being determinants of good leadership. Suffice it to say that a definitive answer as to which traits are necessary for a person to be a good leader has not been found, and will, in all likelihood, never be found. However, just because this is true does not mean that there is no way to understand the concept of leadership.

A more comprehensive view of leadership is provided by Fiedler (1964, 1967). He proposed that effective leadership is the result of a combination of personal and situational factors. He outlined three dimensions of effective leadership:

Leader-Follower Relations—the nature of the personal relationship between the leader and the members of the group.

Position Power—the extent to which legitimate power rests with the position the leader holds in the organization.

Task Structure—the extent to which the group's task is clearly defined.

Fiedler would probably argue that the leader-follower relations dimension is the most important in determining if a person will be an effective leader. His approach presents a much more realistic way of explaining effective leadership than does trait theory. Fiedler's approach recognizes that leadership is at least as much a function of the characteristics of the situation as of the individual playing the role of leader. This is the case particularly for the sales profession.

Another approach that takes into account the impact of the situation on leadership effectiveness was presented in an article by House (1971) as the *Path-Goal Theory*. Borrowing from Expectancy Theory of Motivation, House proposed that the leader's effectiveness rests in the ability to provide both intrinsic and extrinsic rewards as well as the ability to help subordinates complete tasks by providing guidance and direction in certain situations. House and Mitchell (1974) suggested that there are four categories of leadership, each of which is appropriate in various situations:

Supportive Leadership: Providing subordinates a supportive climate in which to work by showing concern for them personally.

Directive Leadership: Providing subordinates with specific guidelines for performance.

Participative Leadership: Allowing subordinates to have input into the decision-making process.

Achievement-Oriented Leadership: Setting challenging standards of performance and eliciting response by conveying high expectations of success.

In his model of leadership, Yukl (1981) proposed that the group as a whole takes on a certain set of characteristics that need to be considered as well as individual characteristics. He also included situational variables such as the task structure and the degree of role formalization as well as the nature of the leader-subordinate relationship. Yukl proposes that a leader's effectiveness is determined in large part by how skillfully that person is able to correct any weaknesses within the group, either of the individual members or of the group as a whole. A sales manager can enhance his own leadership by doing such things as initiating longterm development programs, changing the structure of the organization, and gaining more control over the amount and quality of resources used to support the sales effort.

Examining these theories of leadership removes some of the mystery of what it takes to make a good leader. Contrary to popular thought, the sales manager can understand leadership and develop those skills necessary to become a good leader. Summarizing the above theories, the following is a list of propositions useful for the sales manager in developing leadership skills or in deciding which salespeople would be good candidates for leadership positions in the organization.

1)   Being a good leader depends on several factors including:
▬ The nature of the product, the company and the industry in which the company competes.
▬ The dynamics of the relationship between the person and his/her subordinates and/or peers.
▬ The credibility and legitimacy the person has with his/her subordinates.

■■■ The approach the person uses in the decision-making process.

■■■ How effective the person is in addressing deficiencies within the group and problems facing the group.

2) There are several types of leadership, each of which is appropriate at different times—-the sales manager needs to be adaptive in his or her leadership style.

3) How a sales manager goes about leading is almost as important as where he or she leads the group.

4) Leaders develop within the organization either by watching those persons above them or by performing the leadership function.

Power and Influence in the Organization

The concept of power should not be limited to the legitimate authority that rests in a particular position within an organization. Although this does provide a source of power, to be effective, a leader must go beyond vested authority if one is to exert influence on subordinates. There are basically five sources of power in an organization:[1]

Legitimate Power: This type of power rests on the fact that the leader has the right to request/demand an action and the subordinate has an obligation to comply.

Reward Power: This rests in the ability to mete out rewards. Although this often corresponds to a legitimate position in the organization, the extent of this base of power will vary considerably.

Coercive Power: This is based in the person's capability of issuing punishment or negative sanctions. This may involve a loss of something tangible, such as money or position, or it could mean the loss of something more personal such as psychological support and friendship.

Expert Power: This is based in the knowledge possessed by the person and the willingness to share that knowledge.

Referent Power: This rests in the fact that a person is admired and others want to emulate or at least be identified with the person.

The sales manager who is truly a leader will rely on the latter two as the main bases of power. This is because field salespeople generally have a fair amount of autonomy in the execution of their jobs. They are constantly making decisions that have an

[1] See French and Raven (1959)

effect on their firms. For these decisions to be consistent with the policies and culture of the organization, the salesperson must have internalized the policies and that culture.

The salesperson who does a particular thing only because of the reward will ultimately require bigger and bigger rewards to do the right thing. The salesperson who complies with a request only because of the threat of punishment will ultimately lose the fear of punishment. The salesperson who takes a particular action because of being told that "I'm the Boss and that's all you need to know!" will soon lose respect for that boss.

Referent Power and Expert Power are powerful tools that can be cultivated. This cultivation process entails the following actions:

1) Treat subordinates with respect and as professionals.
2) Treat subordinates as people by showing concern for them as individuals.
3) Espouse and employ high ethical standards.
4) Involve one's self in the operations of the unit, or in other words, do not be afraid to "get one's hands dirty".
5) Keep up to date on information about the company, industry, competition, and the market.
6) Act as a coach more than as a critic.
7) Lead by example.

Autocratic vs. Democratic Leadership

A major decision facing the sales manager is how much input to seek from subordinates. Often there is the temptation to reduce the question to an all or nothing answer. In other words, some will say that either the leader is in charge or is not, and that any input from subordinates results in negation of the leader's power and influence. However, in reality, the degree to which subordinates can exercise some influence in the leader's decisions will vary a fair amount from one situation to another. There are at least four levels of subordinate input according to Yukl.

Autocratic Decision: The leader decides on courses of action without seeking input from subordinates.

Consultation: The leader seeks opinions and suggestions from subordinates but makes the decision him/herself.

Joint Decision: The leader meets with subordinates or a representative group and they make decisions together.

Delegation: The leader parcels out various decisions to subordinates who have the responsibility for making decisions regarding a particular aspect of the operation.

Yukl's approach is similar to the one suggested by Vroom (1986) who examined the extent to which leaders were people-oriented or task-oriented, and went on to suggest four leadership styles.

Tells: Emphasis is on the task performed rather than on the person performing it. The manager makes the decision.

Persuades: The heavy emphasis is on both the task and the person. The manager makes the decision and then "sells" the idea to subordinates.

Participates: Heavy emphasis is placed on the person and little emphasis is placed on the task. The decision is a joint one between the manager and the subordinate.

Delegates: A low emphasis is placed on both the task and the person. The decision is left to the subordinates who are responsible for carrying through with appropriate action.

Figure 17-2 combines these various approaches to leadership in a way that logically relates to them.

FIGURE 17-2

Autocratic versus Democratic Leadership

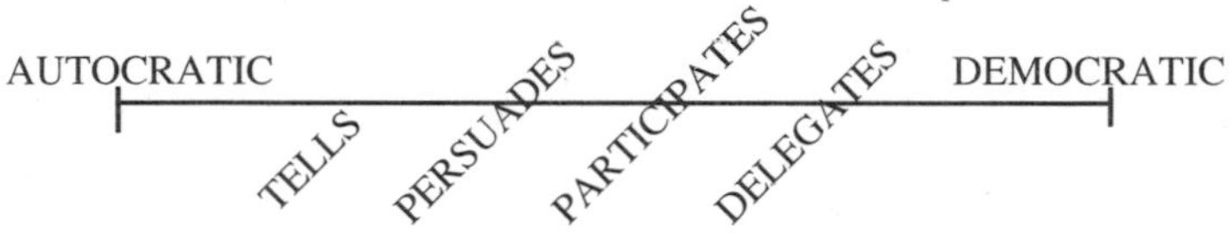

AUTOCRATIC				DEMOCRATIC
	TELLS	PERSUADES	PARTICIPATES	DELEGATES

high degree	*task orientation*	low degree
low degree	*people orientation*	high degree
nonexistent	*subordinate input*	extensive
minimized	*subordinate freedom*	maximized
minimized	*subordinate responsibility*	maximized
maximized	*specific guidance by manager*	minimized
extensive	*monitoring by manager*	limited

Several conclusions regarding sales can be drawn from these various writers:

1) Decision participation by subordinates is consistent with the personality characteristics of successful salespeople.

2) Participation in the decision leads to a greater acceptance of and commitment to sales goals, and more well-defined action plans for achieving them.

3) Participation will tend to increase understanding of the reward system and how rewards can be obtained.

4) Participation tends to increase cooperation in solving problems, which is an essential part of the sales job.

5) Participation can result in better decisions because both the salesperson and the sales manager is party to pertinent information that the other may not possess.

What Leaders Really Do

Now that we have discussed the bases of leadership, it is appropriate to examine what it is that leaders actually do, or what functions they perform in the organizations. There are eight major functions that leaders perform.[2]

Creating the Vision: The leader is the one who imparts to subordinates a sense of direction and vision. The sales manager helps salespeople to remember their main purpose and provides a set of goals for achieving that purpose.

Developing the Team: It is people who accomplish the task. No leader, regardless of how talented and driven, can bring about an effect without support. The sales manager not only hires the right salespeople for the job, but also forges them into a team that is greater than the sum of its parts.

Clarifying the Values: Any organization needs a set of values that clarify what it is that is important to that group. This set of values is drawn from the "corporate culture." They help the sales manager develop ethical standards as well as customer service levels.

Positioning: Regardless of how well the vision and system of values is delineated in the organization, without an effective strategy the organization will not perform up to par. The sales manager must present a strategic plan for approaching the various market segments and for attaining a unique place in the market.

[2] See Hitt (1988)

Communicating: The effective leader must be able to communicate well. The sales manager must be able to communicate not only with subordinates but also with upper management. In addition, the sales manager must establish an atmosphere of open communication with salespeople.

Empowering: Leaders are constantly involved in moving people toward goals. Sales managers in particular must be able to motivate salespeople to achieve their potential.

Coaching: Leadership is an ongoing process that involves providing guidance to those being led. For the sales manager, coaching is the forum for keeping salespeople current and for helping them sharpen their skills.

Measuring: The sales manager must establish an effective system for monitoring the progress of individual salespeople. This system must provide information adequate enough to assess sales performance and take appropriate corrective action when necessary.

CHAPTER PERSPECTIVE

In this chapter, we discussed the concepts of motivation and leadership. These are related but distinct concepts. They are related in that a good motivation program creates "followship"—the desire to follow where the leader wants to go. They are also similar in that what makes for positive motivation and effective leadership are determined by the situation at hand. They are distinct in that they represent two separate sets of tasks that the sales manager must perform.

The concepts are complicated by the popular misconceptions that seem to prevail about motivation and leadership. It is often difficult to separate what is useful from that which is not. They are also complicated by the fact that they are multifaceted.

The concept of power and influence was also discussed. Power is the tool of the leader and can derive from a number of sources. Effective leaders, especially those in sales management positions, will rely less on what is termed Legitimate Power and Coercive Power than on Referent Power and Expert Power. By the same token, the effective leader is not the person who feels one must exercise authority in an autocratic fashion. If the salespeople that work for us truly are professionals, they will chafe under such an approach.

REFERENCES
Cron, William L. (1984), "Industrial Salesperson Development: A Career Stages

Perspective," *Journal of Marketing,* 48 (Fall), 41-52.

Eisman, Regina (1991), "When Cultures Clash," *Incentive,* (May), 65-70.

French, J. R. P., Jr. and Bertram Raven (1959), "The Bases of Social Power," in *Studies in Social Power,* (ed.)D. Cartwright, Ann Arbor, MI: Institute for Social Research.

French, Wendell L. (1990), *Human Resources Management,* Boston, MA: Houghton Mifflin Company.

Herzberg, Frederick (1966), *Work and the Nature of Man,* Cleveland, OH: The World Publishing Company.

Hitt, William D. (1988), *The Leader-Manager,* Columbus, OH: Battelle Press.

House, Robert J. (1971), "A Path Goal Theory of Leader Effectiveness," *Administrative Science Quarterly,* 16,321-339.

House, Robert J. and T. R. Mitchell (1974), "Path-Goal Theory of Leadership," *Journal of Contemporary Business,* 3 (Autumn), 81-97.

Jolson, Marvin A. (1974), "The Salesman's Career Cycle," *Journal of Marketing,* 38 (July), 39-46.

Keenan, Willam, Jr. (1989), "The Nagging Problem of the Plateaued Salesperson," *Sales & Marketing Management,* (March), 36-41.

Keenan, William, Jr. (1990), "Shopping for Motivators?", *Sales and Marketing Management,* (April), 112-114.

Kotter, John P. (1988), *The Leadership Factor,* New York, NY: The Free Press.

Landy, Frank J. (1985), *Psychology of Work Behavior,* Homewood, IL: The Dorsey Press.

Organ, Dennis W. and W. Clay Hamner (1982), *Organizational Behavior,* Plano, TX: Business Publications, Inc.

Super, Donald (1957), *The Psychology of Careers,* New York, NY: Harper & Row, Inc.

Urbanski, Al (1987), "Motivational Masterpieces," *Sales & Marketing Management,* (September), 60-62.

Vroom, Victor H. and P. W. Yetton (1973), *Leadership and Decision-Making,* Pittsburgh, PA: University of Pittsburgh Press.

Vroom, Victor H. (1986), "Leadership," in *Handbook of Industrial and Organizational Psychology,* (ed.) Marvin D. Dunnette, Chicago, IL: Rand McNally College Publishing Company.

Yukl, Gary A. (1981), *Leadership in Organizations,* Englewood Cliffs, NJ: Prentice-Hall, Inc.

Compensating the Sales Force

INTRODUCTION AND MAIN POINTS

Besides the psychological motivations discussed in Chapter 17, motivation also occurs in the form of financial compensation. A top salesperson can be one of the highest-paid individuals in an organization, frequently earning more than the sales manager and upper level managers and sometimes even more than the president of the company. Given the importance of the salesperson and the potential for high earnings, an organization must design and administer an appropriate financial compensation plan. This chapter looks at compensation methods and their advantages and disadvantages, as well as other expenses in selling and their respective compensation and control.

After reading the material in this chapter:

▬ You will understand the various compensation programs.

▬ You will be able to decide the appropriate compensation method depending on the organizational circumstances.

▬ You will understand the various methods for controlling expenses.

▬ You will be able to implement alternatives to personal sales calls.

IMPORTANCE OF SALES COMPENSATION

The salesperson is the critical, and often the only link, with the customer. The well-being and happiness of the sales force is important to achieving forecasted sales and company profits. One of the key ingredients to the well-being and effort of the sales force is compensation. Not only does the compensation plan contribute to well-being, it can be related to the performance level achieved and direct the activities of salespeople. Since compensation is by far the largest share of all direct selling costs—about 79 percent—a good compensation plan is needed to maintain top returns for the investment.

The actual sales compensation plan varies depending on the selling tasks, the nature of the industry, and the structure and philosophy of the company. Sales force compensation costs are about 22 percent of total sales in direct marketing companies like Avon and Amway, but they are only four percent of sales costs in the retail food companies such as Pillsbury and General Mills. Despite this wide variation, there are three basic methods of sales compensation.

Straight-salary plan: The individual receives a fixed amount of money at fixed intervals (usually weekly or biweekly).

Straight-commission plan: The individual receives an amount that varies with results, which are usually measured in terms of sales or sales and profits.

Combination plan: The individual receives a fixed amount of money and then an additional amount based on performance in the form of a commission and/or bonus.

Depending on the industry, company, product, and market situation, one or more of these methods may be adopted. Given hypercompetition and broad international product lines, companies are finding that a single compensation method usually can no longer be universally applied throughout a company. Multiple methods are now used more frequently so that products can be sold, customers satisfied, and top salespeople appropriately rewarded and satisfied.

Customer satisfaction is an important aspect of implementing a compensation package and is negatively affected by a high level of salesperson turnover. To retain and motivate top-performing salespeople, a competitive compensation plan is necessary. More than any other employees in a company's organization, salespeople respond to monetary compensation. Salaries and compensation package vary greatly, with top salespeople earning up to $1.5 million a year. Salaries are surveyed yearly by *Sales and Marketing Management* magazine. Salespeople, like entrepreneurs, view compensation as a way of keeping score among their peers and are highly motivated by the opportunity to make good money.

Money is a more effective incentive for some individuals than others. Its usefulness also varies depending on the earnings level of a particular individual. Regardless of the differences in sales personnel, the compensation package must encourage sales efforts because the profits of a company are affected by the satisfaction of the sales force.

DESIGNING A SALES COMPENSATION PACKAGE

While there are different methods for designing the sales compensation program, one useful approach consists of five steps:

1) Prepare job descriptions.
2) Establish sales and other objectives.
3) Determine appropriate general categories of compensation.
4) Develop and pretest the compensation plan.
5) Implement and evaluate the plan.

Prepare Job Descriptions

Before any work can be done on establishing a compensation plan, detailed job descriptions for each category of salesperson and manager must be prepared. Each job description should specify the responsibilities and performance criteria of the position. Some sales jobs may involve little direct selling but may involve "missionary work," or "support services." Other sales jobs involve more direct customer contact and actual selling. The company must carefully analyze the tasks necessary and then write a job description for each salesperson. The job description is the basis for establishing the most appropriate compensation plan. Sales jobs of the same value to the organization should receive similar levels of compensation.

Establish Sales and Other Objectives

A principal purpose of a compensation plan is to achieve the organization's specific objectives. In addition to total sales volume, other specific objectives include:

The number of sales presentations made to customers.

The number of new products sold to established customers.

The sales of specific products.

The use by customers of company promotional material and displays.

The number of times the company's products are advertised by customers.

The level of *conversion ratio*—the number of orders as a percentage of sales presentations.

The number of new customers obtained.

The *operating efficiency* (the level of costs per sale) in a sales territory.

Because sales data is almost always readily available, the productivity of salespeople is easily measured against the established objectives (see Chapter 15).

The compensation plan of the sales force is important from both the company's vantage point and the salesperson's. For the company, a good compensation plan is simple to administer, offers maximum control over the sales effort, and provides a balance between sales results and sales costs. For the salesperson, a good compensation plan reflects ability and experience as well as other aspects of the sales jobs, provides a regular income, and provides substantial reward for good performance. These divergent objectives make it difficult for a single compensation plan to be implemented.

Categories of Compensation

Because a too-low level of compensation can create high turnover, it is necessary that the general level of sales compensation be high enough to attract and retain quality salespeople. Several factors affect the appropriate base level of pay for a sales force such as the education, experience, and skills required to sell successfully; the income level for comparable jobs in the company; and the income level for comparable sales jobs in the industry.

An initial approach to establishing categories of compensation is to assign numerical values to each job requirement that reflect the most significant factors in being successful in the selling task. The maximum value can be calculated and each sales job compared to this value. An example based on education, experience, and sales skills is indicated in Tables 18-1 and 18-2. This is a numerical rank order of the sales jobs and salary range. In this example, the company believes that sales skills are most important and are given a value of 10, followed by experience and education, the highest score possible being 23. Each of the other four positions are assessed by each of these factors, with the territory sales manager having the highest position total, 22. There is an overlap in each salary range assigned to a particular sales job, allowing growth and increased salary within each position depending on the individual's abilities and performance.

The level of compensation must also be adjusted for cost of living differences. Living costs for selected metropolitan areas are published annually in the "Survey of Selling Costs" in *Sales and Marketing Management* magazine.

Develop and Pretest the Compensation Plan

Most compensation plans are a mixture of regular salary, commission, and/or bonus. Companies have found this type of plan to

TABLE 18-1
Establishing General Levels of Sales Compensation

Job Requirement	Education	Experience	Sales Skills	Possible Total Score
Numerical value	5	8	10	23

TABLE 18-2
Minimum Score Required for a Sales Position

Sales Position	Education	Experience	Sales Skills	Position Total	Salary Range
Sales trainee	3	4	2	9	$20,000-26,000
Junior salesperson	4	6	6	16	$25,000-42,000
Senior salesperson	4	7	8	19	$32,000-65,000
Territory sales manager	4	8	10	22	$55,000-85,000

be most effective in accomplishing objectives and achieving good sales results. The key decision involves determining the appropriate blend of regular and incentive salary. Since a straight-salary plan is least expensive at higher levels of sales and a straight-commission plan least expensive at lower levels of sales, a good compensation plan usually shifts depending on the sales volume. The salary position of any plan should enable the salesperson to meet daily living expenses while encouraging and "compensating" for sales tasks that are not directly measured in the sales results. These tasks include customer service, shelf stocking, gathering comparative product price information, or gathering other needed market information. Even though these tasks are important, the fixed salary position of the sales compensation plan should not be so high that a salesperson can become complacent and not strive for increased sales. In many plans, about 70 percent of the total income of a salesperson is fixed.

Commissions and Bonuses

Incentives in the form of commissions and bonuses usually make up the remaining 30 percent of the total income of the salesperson. The amount of this compensation is based on the individual sales person surpassing an established *sales quota,* the minimum sales requirement. While the relationship between the amount of the compensation package that is incentives (not fixed) and the turnover rates of the sales force has not been definitively established, turnover rates for salespeople in the retail trade or those who sell technical products to first customers tend to increase in proportion to the percentage of the compensation package that is fixed salary. Conversely, turnover rates for a creative or new business sales force tend to increase as the percentage of the total package that is incentives increases.

Fixed commissions or bonuses are much easier to administer, but they do not offer the incentive needed for top salespeople in the company, who need to be challenged and rewarded for obtaining higher, more difficult levels of sales volume. To reward these high achievers, progressive commission rates are needed. With *progressive commission rates,* the commission percentage increases as the sales volume increases. Sometimes, particularly when there is a high probability that windfall sales (sales that are not due to the effort of the salesperson) will occur, *regressive rates* are used: Commission rates decrease as sales increase. A company may offer a 5 percent commission for all sales up to 2,000 units, a 4 percent commission for all sales from 2,000 to 3,000 units, and a 3 percent commission for all sales 3,000 units and over. The choice of commission plan (fixed, regressive, or progressive) should reflect the objectives of the company, the capability of the sales force, and the profit potential.

Even more difficult than establishing the original commission plan is establishing a system for splitting commissions when two or more sales representatives are involved in the sale. This problem frequently occurs when one sales representative calls on a customer's headquarters and other sales representatives call on divisions, local branches, or outlets of the same company. Care must be taken to split the commissions to reward each individual proportionately for the effort involved in the sale while continuing to provide motivation for all salespeople involved. If, for instance, the sales representative calling on a branch office got the manager to ask corporate headquarters to order the product, this individual might receive 90 percent of the commission for the products sold to the branch office and the sales representative

calling on the headquarters would receive 10 percent.

Stock Options

A problem most companies face in retaining top-quality sales people can sometimes be solved by offering stock options. With a *stock option,* a salesperson has the right to purchase stock in the company at a future date at a preset price that should be lower than the market value. If the price of the stock rises (which usually occurs in fast-growing, dynamic companies), the salesperson can buy the stock at the lower established price and then sell the stock (if desired) at the higher market value. When the company is growing and the stock price is increasing, a salesperson is more reluctant to leave the company because there will not be an opportunity to exercise the stock options and to realize the profit at a future date. This incentive is further increased when stock options are awarded based on performance or when the company allows top-performing salespeople to contribute to a special equity fund matched by the company when they achieved specified sales goals. If a salesperson leaves, the individual receives any contribution to the equity fund but forfeits the company's matching contribution.

When the stock of the company is not increasing in price and therefore has no future incentive value, an alternative to stock options should be implemented to retain top-performing salespeople. Alternatives used most frequently include performance unit plans and stock appreciation rights. Under a typical *performance unit plan,* the salesperson receives stock or cash when certain long-range goals or objectives are achieved. These goals can take the form of a specified level of sales, distribution, or profits. Under a *stock appreciation plan,* a salesperson actually receives cash or stock equal to the gain that would have been possible by exercising a stock option without being required to have the money to purchase the stock.

Other Incentives and Fringe Benefits

Other incentives in the form of *fringe benefits,* used to provide motivation and rewards, include: Club memberships, use of a company airplane, special vacations or trips for salespeople and spouses, financial counseling, loans, and leaves of absence. Most of the fringe benefits are used on a case-by-case basis to tailor a total compensation package that reflects the industry, company, and individual situation.

Pretest the Plan

Given the importance of the sales compensation plan, it should be pretested whenever possible before being implemented. Pretesting is not possible for start-up companies because it requires sales data for the preceding three years. When this data is available, it can be used to determine the effect of the plan on the company's sales and profits. In larger, multidivision or multiarea companies, the proposed plan can actually be implemented and evaluated in a few areas before it is implemented throughout the company.

Another pretesting method that can be used in every company, including new companies, involves presenting the proposed compensation plan to a committee of key salespeople for comments and reactions before it is implemented. The approval of this group allows a proposed plan to be implemented and accepted more easily.

Implement and Evaluate the Plan

Some key factors that allow a compensation plan to be more easily implemented provide that the plan be written clearly, easy to understand, easy to calculate, fair, and flexible. Whenever significant changes occur in market or company conditions, the compensation plan should be evaluated and altered as needed. Sometimes, particularly when a "hot product" is introduced or shortages occur for other reasons, a plan needs to be altered. Such modification indicates that a short-term company objective is to equitably allocate available products, which minimizes any possible ill will. The amount of nonselling activity, such as obtaining competitive product market information, should also be reflected in the compensation plan.

One concern in administering a sales compensation plan is the disclosure of other salaries. Usually, providing salary information causes friction and jealousy among the sales force, as well as creating greater demands for pay justifications and more objective performance measures. These demands are often accompanied by increased dissatisfaction with sales managers and others in positions of responsibility.

A well-administered plan requires periodic review and evaluation to determine its continued effectiveness in attracting, motivating, and maintaining a quality sales force. This review should be done on at least an annual basis.

RELATIVE BENEFITS OF ALTERNATIVE COMPENSATION PLANS

In designing an effective sales compensation plan, the advantages and disadvantages of alternative plans should be considered in light of various market and company conditions. The basic plans (straight commission, straight salary, or the combination) should be understood, as well as the issues surrounding expense accounts and fringe benefits.

Straight Commission

The straight-commission compensation plan maximizes incentives, minimizes security, and frequently results in very high productivity and earning levels for salespeople. This plan is usually employed in direct marketing, retail furniture, real estate, and group sales. Under this plan, unproductive salespeople eventually resign because commissions are paid based only on performance, measured in terms of sales. When establishing a straight-commission plan, a base or unit must be established that becomes the basis for paying commissions. This base is usually units of sale, dollar sales, or gross profits.

Second, the rate that will be paid per unit must be determined, which is often expressed as a percentage of gross profit or sales. Third, the starting point for the commissions must be set. This can be the first unit sold after obtaining a specific level of sales or an established sales quota.

Finally, the time period for payment of commissions, as well as the method for handling sales returns, cancelled orders, or nonpayment must be established. Commissions are usually paid when the order is received, goods are shipped, or payment is received. These commissions are usually adjusted in the next payment period for nonpayment, cancelled orders, or returned merchandise in the previous period.

To help ensure prompt delivery and build customer relations, companies often pay commissions once the order is shipped. Under this system salespeople work with production and shipping to ensure that they receive their commissions and that the order is not cancelled because of delay.

To help offset fluctuations in the salary of a salesperson under straight commission, some companies establish a draw on the commission plan established. A *draw* is a sum of money paid to the salesperson against future commissions. The money obtained from the draw is repaid to the company from commissions earned in the next payment period. The remaining commissions are then paid to the salesperson. A *guaranteed draw* extends the conditions of the draw and need not be repaid by the salesperson even if commissions earned are not enough.

The time period before commissions are paid varies and may cover more than one payment period. This is very similar to a salary plus commission plan and is used infrequently. A draw against future commissions provides some security for a salesperson while also providing incentive to perform and produce. With an upper limit placed on the size of the draw, a negative draw position, even one extending for several weeks, does not pose a problem. A draw is particularly effective when a salesperson is just getting started as it provides necessary income while a customer sales base is established. An example of cash flow for a salesperson with a $200 weekly draw and a 12 percent commission on sales is indicated in Table 18-3. In week one, there were no sales and a draw of $200. This left a negative balance of $200. In week two, sales of $1,500 at a 12 percent commission rate yielded earned commissions of $180. With a draw of $200, the salesperson was in a negative balance of $220. This negative balance continues until week five, when sales of $3,000 earned commissions of $360 and positive balance of $80.

TABLE 18-3
Sample Salesperson Commission Structure

Week	Sales Volume	Earned Commissions	Weekly Draw	Balance
1	$0	$0	$-200	$-200
2	1,500	180	200	-220
3	2,000	240	200	-180
4	2,500	300	200	-80
5	3,000	360	200	80
6	5,000	600	200	480
7	7,000	840	200	1,120
8	2,500	300	200	1,220
9	3,500	420	200	1,440
10	1,500	180	200	1,420
Totals	$28,500	$3,420	$2,000	$1,420

Based on a $200 weekly draw and a 12 percent commission based on Sales Volume.

With or without a guaranteed or unguaranteed draw, straight-commission plans are used in many industries, particularly when the company wants a strong incentive to sell. Some industries, such as the consumer packaged goods industry, tend not to use a straight-commission plan because of the difficulty of relating sales volume to the efforts of a particular salesperson. For example, the sale of a 96-ounce box of Ultra Tide at a Stop-n-Shop store in Holliston, Massachusetts, might have been the result of a coupon from Procter and Gamble, not the work of a salesperson. It may also have been a result of a call by the sales manager to Stop-n-Shop's headquarters, a display allowance given by Procter and Gamble to the Stop-n-Shop store for displaying the product, product advertisement, or the salesperson's call on the manager of the Braintree Stop-n-Shop store. In all likelihood, a combination of these affected the sales.

The straight-commission method has several advantages and disadvantages.

The advantages include the following:
- The income of a salesperson is directly due to productivity.
- A salesperson can earn a significant salary with no ceiling.
- A salesperson can easily keep track of performance and earnings.
- No company money is tied up because costs (exceeding a draw) occur only when a sale is made.
- A salesperson has maximum freedom and incentive to perform.
- Poorly performing salespeople usually quit on their own.

There are also some disadvantages to the straight-commission method:
- Salespeople develop little if any company loyalty.
- Salespeople must live with a great deal of uncertainty and anxiety about future income.
- There is a larger than normal turnover when business is low.
- Salespeople have little reason to do anything but sell.
- Salespeople tend to sell more product than the specific customer situation warrants, which can result in customers with too much inventory and can create customer dissatisfaction.
- There is a strong resistance to any change in the territories.

Straight Salary
Even though individuals with good selling ability are better rewarded (if they can perform) under a straight-commission plan, many people do not like to work under conditions of uncertainty and the potential for wide fluctuations in income. These more security-minded salespeople prefer a dependable, regular income rather than the larger amount of money possible with the uncer-

tain straight-commission plan. Security with a straight-salary plan is particularly important in widely fluctuating company and market situations and when sales are periodic or seasonal.

A company should consider a straight-commission plan in the following instances even though the incentive for higher sales volume may be reduced:

■ When a long learning period is needed for the salesperson to perform effectively, a straight salary is needed until commissions are large enough to provide an adequate living. Without a straight-salary plan, at least initially, it is impossible to recruit good salespeople.

■ For a major capital expenditure, when a long negotiation period is involved in completing the sale, a company may take more than a year to make a big a decision. Even though salesperson might be calling on and working with a company during this entire period to make the final sale, no commission is earned during this time.

■ Some sales, usually those more technical in nature, require team selling: A salesperson, a marketing support person, a technical engineer, and a person from upper level management. Because each of these individuals plays a role in the final sale, it is difficult to assign total credit to the salesperson. When this occurs frequently, a straight-salary plan is usually most effective.

■ When advertising, sales promotion, or a direct-mail piece has a significant effect on the final sale and the extent of this effect makes the salesperson's efforts difficult to evaluate, a straight-salary plan is usually best. The salary plan in this case rewards nonselling activities, commonly called *missionary selling*. These include providing customer assistance, setting up in-store displays, redesigning an entire area of a store, introducing a new line of products, or calling on potential new customers.

Because in a straight-salary plan a salesperson's compensation is not based on productivity, which is usually measured by sales, profits, or sales calls, this compensation plan provides salespeople with the most security and allows the company to direct all sales activities. This helps to ensure that the established objectives are reached. This is the primary reason that the straight-salary plan is used by many successful companies. In industries such as heavy machinery, aerospace, chemical, petroleum, and consumer nondurable goods, a straight-salary compensation plan is widely used. Sometimes the salesperson is called a consultant or engineer, and sales is not even mentioned in the title.

The straight-salary compensation plan has other advantages and disadvantages.

The advantages include the following:
▬ It provides security for the salesperson.
▬ It directs all the activities of the sales force.
▬ It provides flexibility and adaptability in territorial assignments and sales activities.
▬ It is very easy to administer.

The disadvantages of using the plan sometimes outweigh the advantages:
▬ It provides no financial incentive to increase productivity and the selling effort.
▬ It gives a fixed selling cost regardless of sales.
▬ It allows income inequities to develop, with the least productive salespeople being overpaid and the most productive underpaid.
▬ It tends to cause turnover in the most productive salespeople.

Combination Compensation Plans

A *combination compensation plan* combines the aspects of the straight-salary and straight-commission plans. The salary part of the compensation package is used to provide security and a base level reward for a required sales performance. The commission and/or bonus part of the compensation package is a reward for achieving or exceeding volume or profit goals. The critical factor in developing an effective combination compensation plan is the proportion of salary and incentive. The ideal combination is a salary large enough to attract talented salespeople with a large enough incentive plan to motivate them. Although the salary and incentive mix varies depending on the industry, the competition, and the nature of the selling task, a compensation package that is 70 to 80 percent salary and 20 to 30 percent incentive is usually considered balanced and attractive.

A single compensation plan is usually not flexible enough to work for an entire company or industry; in these companies, the combination plans tend to provide the greatest flexibility. There are four basic types of combination plans:

Salary plus commission is the most frequently used form of combination compensation. This plan allows a company to obtain a high sales volume without sacrificing customer service. It provides security for the sales force and yet motivates strong sales performance.

Salary plus bonus is the best combination compensation plan for achieving long-run sales objectives. It guides a salesperson to achieve a particular customer mix or to sell large capital expenditure items. A bonus differs from a commission in that it provides a lump sum of money (or stock) for a specified performance such as making a quota, making a certain profit, obtaining a specified number of new accounts, or selling a new product to a specified number of existing accounts.

A guaranteed salary plus commission is the best formula for a salesperson. If you give the salesperson a guaranteed salary and don't take anything away from the commissions, then you are giving that person the extra incentive necessary to turn in a good job. However, the salesperson's guaranteed salary should not be too large; it must be at a minumum level and in any event the salesperson must be monitored to avoid the "resting on laurels" syndrome.

Bonuses can be paid for individual or group performance and can be distributed in the next pay period, over several time periods, or deferred until retirement. Depending on the tax structure, the latter arrangement may be favored by highly paid salespeople or sales managers because the income may be taxed at a lower rate during retirement. Unless there is an overriding reason, it is better to pay the bonus a soon as possible after it is earned to enhance its effect in stimulating sales performance. Bonus plans provide flexibility in stimulating the sales force on an individual or group basis to achieve whatever objectives have been established.

Commission plus bonus is used for group sales. When a team effort is needed to call on a buying committee or a salesperson calls on a central buyer and another salesperson calls on a store manager, this plan is the easiest to administer and provides the fairest compensation to all involved in the sale.

Salary plus commission plus bonus combines the previous two plans. It provides the greatest flexibility while stimulating sales and providing security because it allows management to focus the sales force on achieving certain objectives such as new product introduction or specified product or customer sales. This compensation plan is particularly useful in eliminating inventory imbalances or minimizing extreme fluctuations in seasonal sales.

FRINGE BENEFITS AND EXPENSE ACCOUNTS

Significant aspects of sales costs and the sale compensation plan are fringe benefits and expense accounts. The fringe benefit package, in particular, is a way the company can provide job satisfaction and establish company loyalty, minimizing turnover.

Companies are also faced with significantly increasing selling expenses in the form of travel, meals, and lodging. These increasing selling expenses have significantly raised the average cost of a sales call and have climbed faster than any other sales cost. Although every company must understand that selling costs and entertainment expenses are part of the cost of doing business, these costs should be carefully monitored for compliance to company policy. They also should be reimbursed quickly because they often are personal outlays by the salesperson. The policy of most companies is to reimburse for such road expenses as travel, automobile, telephone, meals, lodging, drinks, and laundry.

The Expense Plan

Because expense reimbursement is examined very carefully by the salesperson, an expense plan should be carefully designed, taking into account acceptability, flexibility, and ease of administration.

By far the most important factor in designing an expense reimbursement plan is that it be equitable to the company and to the salesperson. The expense plan should reimburse all legitimate selling expenses incurred by the salesperson without any profit or loss occurring. Legitimate expenses should reflect regional cost differences in lodging, travel, food, and entertainment, as well as the costs of dealing with different types of customers, selling different products, or performing different selling tasks. A company can get a feel for the costs of doing business in a major metropolitan markets by looking at the yearly selling cost index (SCI) in *Sales and Marketing Management* magazine.

As with all aspects of sales compensation, the expense plan needs to be flexible. Constantly changing market conditions require that a salesperson have the freedom to respond, to maintain established customer and product bases as well as to obtain new ones. This may mean that a large potential customer may need to be especially catered to at a greater cost than is usually allowed. A sales expense plan needs to be flexible enough to allow and even to encourage this type of activity when needed.

Finally, the established expense plan must be easily understood and easy to administer. Some companies have in the past made their expense plans so full of "legalese" that they were difficult to understand and administer. Clear guidelines must be established so that a salesperson can easily understand which expenses are reimbursable. These expenses should then be reimbursed efficiently and quickly with minimum clerical costs and effort.

Types of Reimbursement Plans

Given the increasing burden of selling expense, it is important for a company to implement a good reimbursement plan when the expenses are not paid by the salesperson, which often occurs in a straight-commission reimbursement plan. There are three widely used reimbursement plans: Limited, unlimited and combination.

Limited reimbursement plan: A salesperson is restricted to a flat amount of money for a given time or a specified allowable amount per item. In the former case, a company can establish a fixed amount per day or per week, above which expenses are not reimbursed. With the specified amount per item, a fixed amount is established for lodging, meals, or cents per mile traveled, and the like. By establishing very clear guidelines, there is little chance of misunderstanding and expense-account padding. It also allows expenses to be predicted and budgeted more accurately. There are disadvantages to a limited reimbursement plan. It can make salespeople too expense conscious and they may avoid incurring expenses that could save a customer or product line. The benefits of larger expenses may far outweigh the costs incurred.

The plan can also damage the esprit de corps by giving salespeople the feeling that management does not have faith or trust in them. Frequent revision of the established expense figures is also needed, for example, in time of high inflation. When revisions are made, management must ensure that the changes are clear and the timing of their implementation well understood to avoid confusion.

Unlimited reimbursement plan: An unlimited reimbursement plan is the most widely used method for reimbursing all the necessary selling and traveling expenses. To be reimbursed, the salesperson must submit itemized expense reports with the necessary receipts. This flexibility allows the expense differences in territories, customers, and products to be taken into account. The sales manager must ensure that the salesperson does not operate too inefficiently or pad the expense account. The plan makes it very difficult to accurately forecast expenses.

Combination reimbursement plan: A combination reimbursement plan often provides flexibility and control. One combination plan frequently employed sets limits on certain items, such as food and lodging, but has unlimited travel expenses. Another combination plan relates the expenses to sales. A salesperson may be reimbursed for all expenses up to 3 percent of net sales and can also be rewarded with a bonus depending on the level of expenses below 3 percent of net sales. For example, if net sales are $30,000 and expenses $940, the salesperson would be reimbursed only $900 (3 percent of $30,000), not the $940 actually incurred.

CHAPTER PERSPECTIVE

Properly compensating the sales force remains the most effective means of motivation. Because various compensation methods can be used, it is imperative to fully understand the importance of sales compensation because it is directly linked to the well-being of the entire company. There are three basic methods of sales compensation. The straight-salary plan provides an individual with a fixed amount of money at fixed intervals. The straight-commission plan pays salespeople an amount that varies with results, which are usually measured in terms of sales or sales profits. A combination plan pays the individual a fixed amount of money and then an additional amount based on performance in the form of a commission or bonus. To determine the appropriate plan for a particular company, it is important first to analyze the job description. Sales objectives must be established from an analysis of the duties and goals of the salesperson.

These objectives make it possible to establish appropriate general categories of compensation. At this point a compensation plan can be developed and pretested. The plan is then implemented and should be evaluated. Whatever plan is chosen, there are many options for compensation. To provide further incentive and to motivate performance, stock options and other fringe benefits, such as club memberships and company cars or airplanes, can be used to add interest to a compensation plan. An interesting, solid compensation plan helps maintain a satisfied sales force, which is necessary for maintaining good relations with the customer.

Evaluating the Sales Force

INTRODUCTION AND MAIN POINTS

A major portion of the sales manager's time is spent evaluating the efforts of the salespeople. The process is complicated by the many factors, both inside and outside the organization, that can affect performance. It is also complicated by the fact that there are a number of elements in this thing called "performance." Although sales volume is critical, if that were the only thing to be concerned about, evaluation would be greatly simplified. The sales manager must evaluate not only the person's output but also the inputs. The salesperson needs to receive feedback not only on relative sales volume, but also on how that individual is doing in terms of servicing customers.

In the back of every sales manager's mind is the desire to ensure fairness in conducting evaluations. This leads to a heavy reliance on standardized forms. However, these forms often provide only a shallow understanding of a person's performance and the reasons for a given level of output. Additionally, the sales manager is plagued with the difficulty of attempting to translate that evaluation into some useful feedback for the salesperson.

After reading the material in this chapter:

■ You will recognize the different elements of performance that need to be evaluated.

■ You will understand some of the tools useful in the evaluation process.

■ You will gain some insight into the use of the evaluation as a forum for providing useful feedback for the salesperson.

■ You should be able to design a system of evaluation that will be applicable in your organization.

Performance evaluations are increasingly important for several reasons. First of all, they are used for a number of purposes:

Salary Adjustments

Promotions

Termination Decisions
Motivation
Training Decisions
Territory/Duty Assignments
Feedback

Strategic Planning

As performance evaluations will be used in these various applications, it is critical that they be as done as well as possible, and that they be designed to accommodate as many of these purposes as is practical. In addition to their widespread application, performance evaluations also must meet legal standards. As in hiring decisions, performance evaluations cannot be discriminatory in nature. Just as instruments used in hiring must meet tests of validity, reliability and so forth, instruments used in evaluations must meet such tests. Furthermore, the way these instruments are applied must not violate the intent of the law.

Elements in the Evaluation Process

There are five aspects of the salesperson's job that need to be evaluated. These are interrelated; however they are best evaluated separately. These five are:

Output
Customer Relations
Job Skills
Company Relations
Personal Characteristics

Output has to do with what traditionally is thought of as "productivity measures," such as sales volume, sales mix, sales costs, profitability, number of sales calls, allocation of effort, and so forth. Although sales volume has traditionally been viewed as the major measure of sales productivity, increasingly, sales managers recognize that simply being concerned with volume can lead to less profit being generated by the sales unit. Sales mix, the combination of products or product lines sold in a given period, has become much more of a focus of attention. This is because, without a good sales mix, the salesperson will not generate as much profit as possible.

Concurrent with this move away from simply looking at sales volume, many sales organizations have begun to treat sales territories as "profit centers" rather than as sources of revenue. While this may sound like semantics, it does provide a different view of the responsibility of the salesperson and the role of the territory in the overall plan of the company.

There are a number of approaches to evaluating the profitability of salespeople. The simplest approach is some sort of sales volume analysis. For example, Allied Electrical may evaluate a salesperson using the information from the Table 19-1.

Based on this table, the sales manager can get an idea of how salespeople are performing in terms of sales relative to each other. A sales manager can look at the information on this table and have an idea not only of overall sales but also of the relative success of each salesperson in increasing sales from the previous year relative to the overall increase. The person in Territory 2 had the highest overall sales, but had the lowest increase in sales, and was significantly lower than the overall increase. At the same time, the person in Territory 3 had the lowest sales volume with the highest increase. The person in Territory 2 may well have reached a plateau and may need some additional encouragement, while the person in Territory 3 may need some additional resources to develop his or her territory.

TABLE 19-1
Allied Electric Sales Figures

Sales in Thousands

Year	Territory	Sales	% Change	Company	% Change
1991	1	1,900	5.0	12,250	4.5
	2	2,050	2.9		
	3	1,400	6.1		
	4	1,750	4.5		
	5	1,550	4.5		
	6	1,850	5.5		
	7	1,750	3.0		

Obviously, the sales manager cannot rely solely on the information in this table in deciding on a definitive action. For example, if housing starts were down and the overall growth rate in the electrical supply industry were only 2.5 percent for this past year, Allied would be doing quite well and what appears to be relatively poor growth in Territory 1 may actually be quite good given the situation in the industry.

Sales managers have always evaluated the activity of the salesperson as a component of productivity. Hence, companies generally have had a system for reporting the number of sales calls, the number of new accounts opened, and the like. However, given the increasing cost per sales call, firms are recognizing that they need to increase their efficiency by a better allocation of effort. Therefore, the sales manager needs some way of making a relative evaluation of efficiency and effectiveness of salespeople. An approach growing in popularity uses the return on assets managed (ROAM) as a measure of output.

$$\text{ROAM} = \begin{array}{c} \text{contribution margin as} \\ \text{percentage of sales} \end{array} \quad \text{x} \quad \begin{array}{c} \text{asset} \\ \text{turnover} \\ \text{rate} \end{array}$$

$$= \text{profit contribution/sales} \times \text{sales/assets managed}$$

This measure provides the sales manager with some additional information. For example, Territories 4 and 7 show the same overall sales for the period. Are these territories equivalent in their overall output? Using the ROAM formula and the information in Table 19-2, we gain some additional insights into how well these territories are doing relative to each other.

Overall, Territory 7 has almost twice the ROAM as does Territory 4, which would indicate not only greater profitability, but also greater efficiency in the use of assets. As we look more closely at the figures, several things become apparent about the nature of this difference in the ROAM of the two territories.

First, although the sales are the same and Territory 4 seems to be increasing sales at a faster rate, it is doing so at the expense of profit margin. It would appear that the salesperson in Territory 4 is selling a large quantity of lower profit items. Additionally, although both territories are handling the same amount of inventory, Territory 4 accounts receivables are considerably higher which may mean that the salesperson is "stretching" the credit limits and terms of the customers. It should be noted, however, that the salesperson in Territory 4 does not have significantly greater selling costs than the person in Territory 7. Using ROAM, the sales manager has the opportunity to gain a greater depth of understanding of where the corrective action might need to be taken.

Aside from sales- and profit-oriented measures, there are several other facets of output that sales managers need to consider. For example, the number of new accounts is a critical aspect of performance because it affects the future viability of a territory. Salespeople are often hesitant to develop new accounts because of the difficulty involved and because many sales organizations do not reward such development.

Given the increasingly longterm nature of the relationship between suppliers and customers, an important measure of perfor-

TABLE 19-2
Territory ROAM Data

	Territory 4	Territory 7
Sales	1,750,000	1,750,000
-Cost of Goods	1,250,000	1,050,000
Gross Margin	500,000	700,00
-Selling Costs	160,000	150,000
Profit Contribution	340,000	550,000
Accounts Receivable	750,000	500,000
Inventory	850,000	850,000
Assets Managed	1,600,000	1,350,000
Contribution Percentage	19%	31%
Asset Turnover	1.09	1.30
ROAM	21%	40%

mance is the level of service being provided. Often companies use the "back door" approach to measuring this by considering the number of complaints the salesperson receives. While this does provide some information, there is a whole segment of the market that will not register a complaint with the salesperson's company, but rather, will take its business elsewhere. One approach to measuring this aspect of "output" is to periodically send brief questionnaires to a sample of customers in each territory. This not only provides information for the sales manager, but also sends a signal to customers that the company is concerned about providing good service.

For each company, there are unique aspects of output, some of which are more readily quantifiable than others. Most companies will wish to measure such things as the number of calls per day as part of output. A good evaluation system considers all the important aspects of output. If a company only looks at sales volume, the message is conveyed to salespeople that this is the only thing that is really important. The sales manager may talk at length about the need for salespeople to provide good service to existing accounts and the need for prospecting for new accounts, but salespeople will respond to those things for which they are rewarded.

The other four elements that the sales manager needs are Customer Relations, Job Skills, Company Relations, and Personal Characteristics. These are more qualitative than quantitative and, thus, present some additional difficulties in evaluation.

However, these are important parts of the sales job and are

typically part of the evaluation in most companies. Table 19-3 shows the results of a study of how firms evaluate sales forces.

TABLE 19-3
Qualitative Aspects of Salesforce Evaluation

Characteristic Evaluated	Percent of Sample Considering
Attitude	90
Product Knowledge	89
Selling Skills	85
Appearance and Manner	82
Communication Skills	81
Initiative and Aggressiveness	80
Planning Ability	78
Time Management	73
Knowledge of Competition	72
Judgment	69
Creativity	61
Knowledge of Company Policies	59
Report Preparation and Submission	59
Customer Goodwill Generated	50
Degree of Respect from Trade and Competition	34
Good Citizenship	23

Source: Donald W. Jackson, Jr., Janet E. Keith, and John L. Schlacter (1983), "Evaluation of Selling Performance: A Study of Current Practices," *Journal of Personal Selling and Sales Management*, (Nov.), 45-56.

The qualitative elements of the job are more difficult to evaluate because they require that the sales manager spend time with individual salespeople to form a first-hand opinion of how well the person is doing. Also, the sales manager is forced to obtain an evaluation of the person in relation to other salespeople and must do so in an impartial and legally-sound fashion.

Although there are a number of ways a sales manager might evaluate any one of these elements, generally some type of scale is employed. One popular form is known as a Graphic Rating Scale. For example, if the sales manager wants to evaluate the person on "Time Management," one of the elements in Table 19-3, the following forms of such a scale might be used:

	Poor					Exceptional	
Time Management	0	1	2	3	4	5	6

	Below Average	Average	Above Average	Exceptional
Time Management	1	2	3	4

Allocates enough time to the better accounts to provide them with a good level of service.

Almost   1   2   3   4   5   6   7   Almost
Never   Always

These scales allow the manager to make a value judgment with the aid of a numerical scale that can differentiate levels of performance. Although these do not eliminate bias, they at least force the manager to give a relative rating to the salesperson.

Another approach to evaluation that seeks to more specifically define the important elements of the sales job is known as the BARS (Behaviorally Anchored Rating Scale).[1]

This involves a multi-step process of delineating the behaviors related to a given aspect of sales. The following steps are involved:

1) Individuals familiar with jobs are asked to detail critical incidents of effective and ineffective behavior. This set of incidents is then reduced into a smaller set.

2) The group developing the BARS reviews the set of critical incidents and groups them into a smaller set of performance dimensions that are stated in general terms.

3) The set of critical incidents is presented to another group of salespeople, which is also provided with the performance dimensions outlined in Step two. It is asked to assign the critical incidents to the appropriate dimension of performance. A critical incident statement is retained if 60 percent or more of the group assign it to the same performance dimension.

4) The second group is then asked to rate the behavior described in the critical incident on a seven-to-ten point scale as to how effectively or ineffectively it represents performance on the dimension.

5) A set of six to eight incidents, determined by the group to have the highest rating as being related to the dimension, is then selected for the BARS.

The final product would be similar to that shown in Table 19-4 that uses the performance dimension of Time Management. The BARS approach to rating offers a number of advantages that the graphic rating scales do not. First of all, it involves several persons in the process of development, which means that the sales manager can take advantage of the expertise of others in the company. Related to that is the fact that when people become

[1] See: Cocanougher, A.B. & J.M. Invancevich (1978), "BARS Performance Rating for Sales Force Personnel,"/*Journal of Marketing,* Vol. 42 (July), 87-95.

involved in the development of the system in which they work, they will generally be much more accepting of the results of the system. The other major advantage of the BARS is that it provides concrete descriptions of behaviors related to a particular dimension of the sales job. That makes it easier for the sales manager to pinpoint how a salesperson should be rated on a given aspect of job performance.

TABLE 19-4
A BARS for the Dimension of Time Management

Time Management

Performance Categories & Definitions of the Dimension		Behavioral Anchor Statements
VERY HIGH This indicates a very good use of time management.	10 9	Allocates time well, gets reports completed when or before they are due, and uses scheduled appointments.
	8	Allocates time well, is seldom late with reports, and often uses scheduled appointments.
	7	Does a fair job with time allocation, gets many reports in on time, and occasionally
MODERATE This indicates an average level of time management.	6 5	uses scheduled appointments. Does not spend enough time with better customers, turns
	4	many reports in late, and seldom uses appointments.
	3 2	Spends excessive time on low yield accounts, turns very few reports in on time, and only rarely schedules appointments.
VERY LOW This indicates a very poor level of applying time management principles.	1 0	Does not prioritize accounts into a hierarchy, consistently turns reports in late, and does not schedule appointments.

All of these approaches to rating the performance of salespeople have both strengths and weaknesses. The sales manager must develop the approach and the tools that best apply to the company. The point of rating scales is to force the person doing the evaluation to break the job down into its components and to judge each of those components separately. This helps to eliminate any personal bias that the sales manager might bring to the evaluation table. Every person will have areas where he or she does well and areas that present problems. The evaluation process should result in the sales manager being able to provide adequate feedback to the salespeople and help them to make "mid-course" corrections. The only way to that is to obtain as specific information as is possible. The sales manager must develop the system that fits the company and the sales force.

Following are some considerations when evaluating salespeople:

■ Be aware of the "halo effect" masking the evaluation.

■ Base ratings of individuals on observed and not perceived potential.

■ Do not allow personalities to affect your perception of the person and his or her performance.

■ Do not rate the person on a few instances of good or poor work, but rather on their general success or failure in performing sales duties.

■ Recognize that all people will have some areas where they excel and other areas in which they struggle, and remember that these will often differ from your strengths and weaknesses.

■ Resist the temptation to make too close a comparison between the person and the top performer in the company.

■ Realize that over time people will change, and sometimes those changes can positively or negatively affect how the individual performs in certain dimensions of the sales job.

Providing Feedback

One of the most difficult things for a person to do is to provide feedback that is meaningful to the listener. This is difficult because the information must be couched in terms that the individual will relate to and understand. Another difficulty is that there is often a tendency to forget the purpose of providing feedback. Often managers have some things that they "want to get off their chest," which usually translates into blowing off steam. Feedback, however, should be for the purpose of providing guidance to the individual. The feedback session is the forum for developing future performance, and when used as such, can be a key to the longterm success of the sales organization.

Following are some guidelines that will be useful in the feedback session:

1) Evaluations should be discussed with each salesperson individually.

2) Any evaluation should contain positive suggestions for improvement in weak areas:

■ These suggestions should be in addition to the ongoing "coaching" process.

■ These suggestions should contain specific information and support for your assertions.

3) Evaluation meetings should be the forum for establishing goals for the next period and for developing plans for meeting those goals.

4) Avoid being overly critical of the individual, especially if that criticism begins with "when I was in your shoes."

5) If the evaluation process involves discussing a pay raise, it is better that the salesperson be given an idea of the average raise given. The person will then have an overall idea of how well performance compares with others in the organization. If you do not provide that information, there is a tendency to underestimate how relatively good a raise is if the person is doing well, and a tendency to underestimate the average if the person is doing poorly.

CHAPTER PERSPECTIVE

In this chapter, we discussed the quantitative and qualitative aspects of evaluating the sales force. In terms of the quantitative side, we discussed the problems with viewing sales volume as an adequate measure of performance. More and more companies are viewing salespeople as profit centers, and, thus, there is a need to look more at profitability and effective use of company assets. In considering the qualitative aspect of selling, we presented various approaches to evaluating performance. Those qualitative aspects are multifaceted and require an approach that takes into account the different elements in performance. We presented graphic rating scales as an approach to evaluating some of those aspects. We also introduced the BARS as a more in-depth approach. Finally, we discussed the issue of feedback, along with some tips on how to do so.

REFERENCES

Cocanougher, A.B. & J.M. Invancevich (1978), "BARS Performance Rating for Sales Force Personnel," /Journal of Marketing, Vol. 42 (July), 87-95.

Donald W. Jackson, Jr., Janet E. Keith, and John L. Schlacter (1983), "Evaluation of Selling Performance: A Study of Current Practices,"/Journal of Personal Selling and Sales Management, (Nov.), 45-56.

Ethical and Legal Issues

INTRODUCTION AND MAIN POINTS

Probably no single issue plagues people in the sales profession today more than ethics. In the world of business, the pressures to gain a competitive advantage and to attain a high level of performance are great. Often there is not a great deal of difference between the various products in the marketplace, and as a result, salespeople are constantly looking for a competitive edge. Striving for a competitive edge carries with it the temptation to compromise ethical standards.

The vast majority of people in sales act in an ethical and morally responsible way, but there are countless stories of unethical and sometimes illegal behavior on the part of salespeople and their managers. These stories serve to bolster the stereotype of salespeople as "sleazeballs," willing to do anything to make a sale. In the popular media, salespeople are portrayed not only as being inept, but also as being willing to "cut corners" when necessary. Such media creations as Herb Tarlick of *WKRP in Cincinnati* and the characters in movies like *Used Cars* and *The Tin Men* are not only humorous, but also subtly support popular misconceptions.

When a salesperson approaches a customer, this stereotype lurks in the back of the buyer's mind and, although the buyer may recognize on one level that the image is unfair, the individual will still be affected by it. When the salesperson does anything that verifies this image, the problems encountered in the sales process increase geometrically. It is not enough that salespeople behave within the law: They must be trustworthy.

Generally, most people have no trouble with determining what is right and wrong on major issues. Selling a product that is clearly defective, inadequate, or unsafe is blatantly wrong and is considered unethical by most people. However, ethical issues often arise in "gray areas," where right and wrong are not so clearly defined. An additional concern, of salespeople and sales managers alike, is the legal liability associated with making claims about products. There is often a fine difference between boasting about a product and misrepresenting that product to the customer. The sales manager today cannot afford to take a laissez-faire attitude regarding the ethics of salespeople.

After reading the material in this chapter:

■ You will understand the major approaches to ethics.

■ You will recognize the dilemmas facing an individual in the selling situation.

■ You will have insight into the implications of these various approaches for individuals.

■ You will have some understanding of the legal ramifications of certain sales practices.

THE BASIS OF ETHICAL DECISION-MAKING

There are two major schools of ethical thought popular today. One emphasizes the *consequences* resulting from making a choice—the ends—and the other emphasizes the *means* by which an end is accomplished. Everyone, whether conscious of it or not, makes decisions from one of those two frameworks. The framework chosen can have a dramatic impact on the outcome of the decision process.

Ethical Dilemmas

One of the problems facing sales managers is how to deal with ethical inconsistencies and ethical dilemmas facing their salespeople. These inconsistencies and dilemmas are the most pronounced in three areas.

Corporate Versus Individual Ethics

The process of ethical decision making is complicated by the fact that the individual exists within a corporation, the culture of which provides a standard of behavior based on the corporate ethic. This corporate ethic might not be in agreement with the ethics of the individual. It is expected that for a person to be truly a "part of the team," one accepts these standards and abides by them. Additionally, this corporate culture is *dynamic,* meaning it is subject to change with new leadership. The individual therefore faces the dilemma that a person's own standards may not correspond to the standards of the company.

The sales manager must be aware of this gap between corporate and individual standards of ethics. As mentioned in Chapter

14, training is a formalized socialization process. As such, it presents a forum for introducing new recruits to the ethical standard of the organization. By subsequent written and verbal communication, the sales manager reinforces this standard.

The *informal culture* in an organization is often more powerful in shaping a person than the formal. This may result in an individual who "hears" a different ethical standard than the company intends. For example, the company's executives may say, "This company is based on integrity and therefore we should always be completely honest with customers. We do not make false claims about our products, and we do not place undue pressure on our customers to make a purchase." At the same time, the salesperson in the field is told by peers that all the boss cares about is moving product and the only "completely honest" salespeople are ex-salespeople. The same salesperson is told by the manager, "You must increase sales volume—I don't care what you do to get sales, just don't tell me about it." The sales manager needs to be realistic enough to recognize the power of this informal socialization process and must be sensitive to whether the informal ethical atmosphere is in line with what is acceptable to the company.

Different Ethical Standards Within an Organization

Another ethical dilemma facing salespeople has to do with the inconsistent application of ethical standards within the company. A strong sense of ethics may be built into a corporate culture, and the corporation may support these ethics with a clear and concise code of conduct. However, no matter how formalized the ethical position or how well worded a document on ethics, it must be adapted for all the different groups within an organization. These groups may consist of different functional areas or different levels in the organization. The problem arises when the way the ethical standard is applied is inconsistent across the corporation. This leads individuals to question the ethical standards or to dismiss them altogether.

For instance, when upper management is allowed to conduct itself in an ethically questionable fashion and yet strictly applies its code of ethics to subordinates, the entire ethical system of the firm is undermined. Management may dismiss this as "rank has its privileges," but the message communicated is that ethics are not that important.

Another example is when the purchasing department is given restrictive guidelines about buyers accepting gifts, but the sales department is given license to buy gifts as well as to provide entertainment and meals for buyers working for their customers. According to a 1986 article in *Purchasing,* this is an all-too-common practice, and it tends to undermine the overall corporate ethical standard. Sales managers have the responsibility to ensure that their behavior is consistent with the ethical standard espoused by the company. Second, as part of the management team in the company, sales managers must work with other areas to ensure that standards are applied across the firm.

Espoused Versus Enacted Ethics

Argyris (1982) presented the idea that individuals often operate under two different sets of standards: One that they verbalize and one that actually guides their behavior. People assume that their espoused beliefs are those that direct their behavior, when in fact their behavior may, consciously or unconsciously, not be in line with espoused beliefs.

For example, an electrical components salesperson might believe that it is wrong to misrepresent the capabilities of the company's motors and that he should always try to sell a motor that meets or exceeds customer needs. In calling on a buyer of air-cooled heat exchangers, he finds that this buyer is particularly concerned about cost of components for a given job because the job was bid at a low margin. In looking at the specifications, the salesperson believes that a minimum of two horsepower is needed. However, the buyer has told him that the competition has offered "an underrated" one-and-a-half horsepower motor for a much lower price than his two-horsepower motor. Aware that the order is for 100 units and, therefore, a large order, and aware that his one and one-half horsepower motor is equal to the competitor's, he states that his, too, is underrated and will also do the job. On one level, this salesperson truly believes that all he is doing is matching the competition and giving the customer what he wants. However, whether he is conscious of it or not, he has violated his espoused ethic.

The sales manager needs to sensitize salespeople to the fact that the tendency exists to operate from two separate, often inconsistent frameworks. A heightened awareness on the part of salespeople means that they are more circumspect in the actions they take and the decisions they make. Often the ethical problems that arise for salespeople begin as insignificant events to which the person may give little attention or thought, but that "snowball" into major problems. The sooner the person recognizes what is happening, the less likely the event will turn into a problem.

ETHICAL AND LEGAL ISSUES FOR SALESPEOPLE

Many situations have possible ethical and legal implications. Some seem to be particularly troublesome for salespeople. In general, the difference between what is unethical and what is illegal has to do not only with intent, but also with action.

Gifts and Entertainment

Although gifts and entertainment are, in and of themselves, not ethical problems, they have the potential for abuse, which may lead to problems. In all likelihood, this is the area in which more problems arise than any other. According to Keichel, in a *Fortune* article, the value of all gifts and premiums given annually to organizational buyers is several billion dollars. Certainly, those figures have continued to rise since his article was published.

Sales managers are tempted to downplay the importance of a "gift." Many state that they are not trying to "buy" customers with a gift, they are simply rewarding faithful customers. Although a buyer may not be "bought" with a gift, the person may feel some level of obligation to the salesperson because of it. The problem, according to Keichel, is that the gift has the potential to alter the relationship and to make it more complex. Once the relationship moves away from providing the customer with good value for the right price, it moves onto shaky ground.

Traditionally, gifts have been given as a normal part of doing business. However, buying organizations are increasingly regulating gift taking. In a study reported in *Purchasing,* 66 percent of the respondents reported that their companies had a formal policy on accepting gifts. In fact, giving a gift to a buyer may place him or her in violation of company policy and, in turn, subject to disciplinary action. In one situation, when a vendor firm was found to have violated the gift policy of the author's firm, all orders with the vendor were canceled and the company was removed from the approved vendors list. The least that a salesperson should do is become familiar with the policy of the buying departments with whom the salesperson does business, and conform to those policies.

The major issue for salespeople concerning gifts and entertainment is where to draw the line: At what point does a gift become a bribe? What might be considered a nominal gift by one buyer or company may be considered a major gift by another. Much of the input for drawing this line comes from the industry.

In most industries, informal standards of practice provide insight into this issue. Giving gifts above and beyond these standards in all probability constitutes unethical behavior. However, those standards cannot become the final determinant of what the individual should do because they are often rather poorly defined and are subject to change. The sales manager is the person who can set the standard for individual salespeople. In setting this standard, the manager needs to consider the following issues:

▬ What is the purpose of the gift or entertainment?

▬ What part does it play in the overall approach to sales?

▬ How should gifts and entertainment be dispensed?

▬ How is the gift or entertainment likely to affect the buyer and the decision?

▬ What, if any, are the customer's policies on acceptance of gratuities?

▬ Does the gift or entertainment have the potential of compromising the professional image and behavior of customers?

Sales Puffery or Misrepresentation?

Sales is basically a process of communicating the reasons the customer should buy one product or another or from one company as opposed to a competitor. During the course of a sales presentation, the salesperson generally makes a number of statements and claims. A question arises about when these claims become legally binding: What is the difference between "sales talk" and misrepresentation? According to *Law for Business* (Barnes et al., R.D. 1991, p. 175), "The elements of misrepresentation are ordinarily given as: Misrepresentation of a material fact justifiably relied upon to the detriment (causing harm to) to the person relying." The authors go on to point out that the person making the claim is not excused because one "did not know" the statement was false. A salesperson's statement must be one of material fact—it was a major part of the decision for the buyer—if it is to be legally binding. Whether it is a major element in the decision depends on the circumstances.

Another major element in determining misrepresentation is whether the statement was one of fact or opinion. A *fact* is something that is knowable. Statements predicting the future ("The value of this property is bound to increase!") or opinions ("This is the nicest home in the neighborhood!") do not qualify as knowable. These are "puffery" or sales talk and as such are not legally binding.

The difference between puffery and misrepresentation is not

clear. For example, if the salesperson says, "This would be a great car to own," it is sales puffery. If the salesperson says, "This car was owned by an old widow lady who only drove it to church on Sundays," that person is probably guilty of misrepresentation if the car was owned by a Hollywood stuntman.

A salesperson should follow these rules about what is said in a presentation:

■ The person should be thoroughly knowledgeable about the performance and limitations of the product.

■ The salesperson must stress the important criteria and guide customers to a better understanding of how to make a reasonable choice.

■ The salesperson must be careful to accurately state the product's capabilities and performance parameters.

■ The salesperson must recognize the difference between statements of fact and opinions about the product and, when offering praise about the product, do so in general terms.

■ The salesperson must be familiar with local, state, and federal laws regarding price discrimination, warranties, and so forth.

■ The salesperson must recognize that he or she is an agent of the company and that statements made during the sales process can legally bind the company.

Anticompetitive Practices

In a number of instances salespeople face strong competition and, in the push to perform, engage in illegal acts. A common occurrence is *price discrimination.* According to the Robinson-Patman Act of 1936, charging different prices to similar customers is illegal. This sounds simple enough, but there are a number of exceptions that complicate this issue. For example, a company is allowed to offer discounts for large quantities of a product if the lower price is the result of cost savings brought about by selling in larger quantities.

A firm is also allowed to offer a lower price to a particular customer if it is doing so to meet a competitor's prices. A company may also charge different prices to a different classification of customers; for example, one price for contractors and another for the general public. Generally, it is up to the courts to decide if an act constitutes price discrimination, and their approach has historically been to apply the rule of reason.

Another action that may be illegal is a *tying arrangement.* In this situation a company refuses to sell one product line unless the customer buys another line of products. This can be illegal if two distinct and separate product lines are involved and the situation represents a restraint of trade. The exception would be when the two products are related and, if not used together, overall quality is harmed. Exclusive dealerships can also be considered illegal if they are deemed in restraint of trade.

Exclusive dealerships are situations in which a manufacturer requires resellers to carry only its brand. *Exclusive territories,* guaranteeing that a particular firm is the only firm with the right to sell a product within a given territory, can be illegal under certain circumstances. Usually, this is illegal if it can be proven that it lessens competition and restrains trade. The courts generally apply the rule of reason in such cases. This is positive because it gives a fair degree of latitude to the courts but negative in that there is no hard and fast rule to guide salespeople.

Sabotaging Competitors

The pressure to perform can lead to a dismissal of ethical standards. One practice that occurs all too often is interfering with competitors. An example takes place in the sale of consumer products to food stores. Store managers often allow a salesperson for a consumer products firm to have direct access to store shelves. This salesperson suggests a shelving plan for the products and also checks the shelves and replenishes stock for the store manager. A common, ethically questionable practice, occurs when the salesperson reduces the shelf facings of a competitor's products and replaces them with his own products.

Another instance of sabotage is when the salesperson spreads a false, damaging rumor about a competitor to the customers. Some defend both practices as "no big deal," but they constitute unethical behavior. The acid test of whether a practice constitutes unethical behavior is the question, "What is the consequence of my competitor's doing the same thing?" In the final analysis, for unethical behavior to work, only one of the parties engages in it.

Expense Reports

Selling is an expensive process. However, the expense is justified because sales is the most productive avenue to persuade customers to buy products. The salesperson is entrusted with company assets in the form of an expense account and often a company automobile. The policy on company expenses must walk the fine line between reasonable cost and fair reimbursement of the salesperson. When costs are out of line, already high sales costs are pushed even higher; and, if the reimbursement is not fair, the company invites salespeople to become liars. Filling out expense reports is viewed as "creative writing" by some salespeople, but the vast majority make a concerted effort to give an accurate account of expenses. In striving to hold down overhead, companies force salespeople to account for expenses accurately by paperwork (the bane of salespeople). Probably the best way to ensure that salespeople do not inflate their expenses is to instill in them a strong company ethic against such practices, and to develop a reimbursement program that fully repays salespeople for their expenses.

LEGAL AND ETHICAL ISSUES FOR SALES MANAGERS

A major portion of a sales manager's responsibilities revolves around developing and revising sales territories. This is particularly burdensome in regions that are experiencing drastic changes in their population composition. Although territory decisions may not be deemed ethical issues at first glance, they have a major impact on salespeople, and the way decisions are made and how they are communicated have ethical overtones.

Consider the salesperson who has done a good job developing a territory and who, without having been consulted, is told that the territory is being given to another salesperson. This situation is especially complicated when the person is told to relocate to another territory. In this situation, the salesperson may feel that the company is simply using him and has no conscience where employees are concerned.

Often this feeling is aggravated further by the way in which the decision is communicated to the salesperson. An example is the salesperson who receives a cryptic call from the regional office and is told to bring all territory files into the office on Friday, but is provided with no further explanation. Upon arrival at the office, the individual is instructed to leave the files with the receptionist and, in the privacy of the manager's office, is told to report new territory in two weeks. The company has the "right" to make such a decision, but because the person is not consulted and is not given warning, the company, in effect, views the salesperson simply as a tool, not as an individual with needs, wants, and desires beyond the workplace.

This approach probably indicates an underlying attitude within corporate management and, regardless of how much this management gives lip service to caring about employees, these kinds of actions communicate a very different message. Stories of such incidents spread quickly within a company and within an industry and, eventually, negatively affect the quality of people who are attracted to the organization.

Sales managers can soften the impact of territory decisions on salespeople:

■ Institute a stated policy regarding the decision to change territories and to reassign major accounts, and communicate this policy to the person when hired.

■ Involve the salesperson initially in the decision process when such actions are considered.

■ On decisions that involve a relocation, plan changes to correspond to the school year.

■ As best as possible, ensure that the person's territory has as much potential after the change is made as before. When taking away a key account, altering the person's territory may be necessary to ensure that the territory has adequate potential.

■ Do not reduce the decision to make such a change to a matter of formulas or numbers. Other factors are as important as the bottom line.

■ Make only those changes that are necessary (this may appear obvious, but it is amazing how many times changes are made with little rhyme or reason).

The Dysfunctional Salesperson

The *dysfunctional salesperson* is ill, has a problem with alcohol or drugs, or has severe personal or emotional problems. Many sales managers take the view that they are not social workers or wet nurses and do not concern themselves with the personal problems of their salespeople. This view goes even further, with the approach that if the salesperson "can't cut it," the individual needs to find employment elsewhere. This may sound good, but losing a salesperson who is a valuable asset is shortsighted and costly to the firm. Additionally, not being supportive of salespersons during personal crises can undermine morale and calls into question the company's ethics where employees are concerned.

Sales managers can help salespeople who are having problems:

■ Get to know your salespeople and how they tend to act and react in different situations.

■ Take notice of sudden changes in behavior and performance, especially if they involve a sharp increase in absenteeism.

■ Practice good listening skills.

■ Spend some time with people who exhibit changes in behavior, and try to determine the cause.

■ If the behavior continues over time and drug or alcohol abuse is suspected, confront the person with your suspicions and offer to help them get started in a treatment program.

■ For a salesperson who is ill or experiencing serious personal problems, attempt to temporarily lighten the load during recovery.

■ As much as possible, keep the matter confidential.

■ In general, show emotional support for the person involved.

Sexual Harassment

At one time, sexual harassment was thought to involve only the boss trying to force himself physically on a female subordinate. This certainly constitutes harassment, but we now recognize that harassment also involves many verbal actions that previously were considered innocuous. These verbal actions may include verbal suggestions and innuendos dealing with sex. Additionally, sex-related jokes that are repeated over time, and that are considered offensive and suggestive, may constitute harassment. Certainly, repeated advances after a person has been told they are not welcome is also sexual harassment.

In general, any nonprofessional behavior of a sexual nature toward a fellow employee falls under the purview of sexual harassment. Given that personal sales forces, especially in the industrial arena, have traditionally been made up largely of men and given the relatively recent entry of large numbers of women into sales, sexual harassment is an especially important issue for sales managers to understand. Change, even change for the better, often engenders resentment and fear and may meet with resistance. Buyers who in the past dealt primarily with men may be uncomfortable dealing with women and may exhibit inappropriate behavior. Male salespeople, especially in a sales force that has not previously included women salespeople, may make disparaging remarks or take other actions to intimidate their female colleagues. The sales manager must understand these dynamics and also the implications of these actions and set appropriate standards.

The sales manager can begin to address sexual harassment by taking the following steps:

■ Provide subordinates with written standards of behavior.

■ Set a *positive* example of professional behavior.

■ If a salesperson engages in questionable behavior, approach the individual, outline the specific behavior in question, and remind the person that he or she is expected to comply with company policy.

▬ If sexual harassment is alleged, investigate these charges thoroughly.

▬ During the course of the investigation, keep the information confidential and respect the individual's right to privacy.

▬ Deal with the facts of the case, and avoid relying on third-party information when drawing conclusions.

▬ Take the corrective action needed to halt harassment.

CHAPTER PERSPECTIVE

Many legal and ethical problems face salespeople and sales managers, and there are different approaches to ethics. A person needs to understand the different bases of ethical decision making so that one can gain insight into developing a code of ethics and administering an ethics program. Sales forces face ethical issues such as puffery and the giving of gifts. Often, there is a fine line between what is ethical and what is not. Salespeople often state certain ethical beliefs and yet will sometimes violate these when a particular situation arises. The sales manager must recognize the conflicts that salespeople face, and should develop a code of ethics that is feasible.

REFERENCES

Argyris, Chris (1982), "The Executive Mind and Double-Loop Learning," *Organizational Dynamics*, 11(Autumn), 5-22.

Barnes, A. James, Terry M. Dworkin, and Eric L. Richards (1991), *Law for Business*, Homewood, IL: Richard D. Irwin, Inc.

Keichel, Walter III (1985), "Business Gift-Giving," Fortune (January 7), 123-124.

Purchasing (1986), "Gifts: One Issue that Puts Purchasing on the Hot Seat," *Purchasing* (Feb. 13), 18-19.

Glossary

Ancillary product the element of the item that helps the buyer use it better.

Associative thinking process the method of making sense out of a new situation by recalling similar incidents from the past.

AVLs (Approved Vendor Lists) lists from which suppliers are drawn.

BARS (Behaviorally Anchored Rating Scale) a process of determining behavior related to a given aspect of sales.

BFOQ (Bonafide Occupational Qualification) where the requirements of a job necessitate specific limitations on the type of person to be hired.

Blind ads those ads that provide only a post office box number to which candidates reply.

Box-Jenkins method a computerized mathematical technique to select the model that best fits the past sales data and that would provide the most accurate forecast.

Buying center a group of people with major impact on any buying decision.

Buying signal any visual or verbal cue given by the prospect indicating readiness to buy.

Channels of distribution the wholesalers and retailers who handle the product between the company and the customer.

Circular pattern route making sales calls in a circle until returning to the office.

Closing the sale asking for the order.

Cloverleaf route similar to a circular pattern but a route that covers part but not all of the territory.

Cognitive dissonance the buyer's feeling that perhaps the decision to purchase was incorrect.

Coincident indicators those in harmony with fluctuations in product sales in order to establish marketing strategies in a product's life.

Combination plan salesperson receives fixed amount of money plus an additional sum based on performance.

Commercial organizations those entities that exist to realize a profit so that the business achieves a return on investments.

Core product consists of the benefits the product represents for the buyer.

Customer profile the available information on a company, buyer or individual that delineates who makes the buying decision.

Delineating the benefits a marketing plan that shows how the product benefits the customer, establishes the price, and indicates anticipated returns to the company.

Delphi method a controlled succession of brainstorming sessions among a panel of experts.

Demographic information data relating to buying patterns, buying characteristics and history of prior purchases.

Draw a sum of money paid to the salesperson against future commissions.

Drop-ins people who come unannounced and uninvited to an office in the hope of obtaining an interview.

Ego drive where a salesperson's self-image is tied to success in making a sale.

Employment agency a company that seeks employees for firms it represents or a job for a candidate seeking employment.

Exclusive dealerships where a manufacturer requires resellers to carry only its brand.

Exclusive territories guaranteeing that a certain company is the only one with the right to sell a product in a specific territory.

Facilitating exchange the procedure in which the customer gives up money for what the company has to offer.

Formal product the actual item being purchased.

Going concern concept where the company plans to continue to do business with the same or similar customers year after year.

Governmental organizations entities that exist for the purpose of serving the public and are budget-driven through taxes.

Hopscotch route starting at the farthest point in the territory and making sales calls back to the office.

Impression formation the manner of helping a buyer to form a correct perception about the product or service.

Increased production capacity ability to produce more and more units at a decreased per-unit product cost.

Institutional organizations entities that are budget-driven and are controlled by their funding agencies.

Jury of executive opinion a method whereby top executives of a company forecast future sales.

Manufacturer's rep not employed by the company as a salesperson on permanent staff but rather as an independent contractor to represent the company on a straight-commission basis.

Marketing a process of making decisions that satisfy targeted groups of customers as well as accomplishing the company's objectives.

Matrix organization where specialists are accountable to both a superior from their particular area of expertise and a coordinating or project manager.

Modified rebuy where the item has been changed somewhat but is no longer available from old sources.

OJT (On-The-Job Training) where the trainer and the new salesperson go out on sales calls together.

Open ads those ads that identify the company doing the recruiting.

Organizational culture determines the climate within which the buyer operates such as formal, rigid, informal, fluid.

Perception checking describing what the listener perceives to be the unspoken emotions or needs of another.

Performance unit plan where the salesperson receives stock or cash when specific long-range goals or objectives are achieved.

Physical distribution deals with moving the product from the company to the customer.

Placement center a firm that specializes in matching graduating students with interested companies.

Postpurchase anxiety concern that buyer made wrong decision on purchasing product.

Price discrimination charging different prices to similar customers.

Principle of 80:20 where 80 percent of the sales come from 20 percent of the customers.

Problem solving interview where the candidate has to resolve a problem posed by the interviewer.

Professionalism a salesperson's ability to deal with a customer or prospect in a businesslike manner.

Prospecting the act of obtaining names of potential customers.

Purchase dissonance the prospect's concern about buying.

RFQ (Request For Quotation) a process involving selecting vendors from which to request quotations.

Resilience the ability of a salesperson to shake off refusals and rejection.

Sales budget a financial sales plan showing the way resources and selling efforts would be allocated to achieve the forecasted level of sales.

Sales forecast predicting the amount of sales in a specific market.

Sales mix the combination of products or product lines sold in a given period.

Sales quota minimum sales requirement.

Sales territory a group of present and potential customers assigned to a specific salesperson or branch of the company.

Scalar principle starting at the bottom of a company, each level is subordinate to another level above.

Servicing the sale keeping the customer satisfied about the purchase.

SIC (Standard Industrial Classification Code) a uniform numbering system that classifies all companies according to the nature of the product produced or the services performed.

Socialization the beliefs and practices of a company that the new salesperson is to assimilate.

Spotter a person who is close to potential prospects and provides information on them for a fee.

Stock option the right to purchase stock in a company at a future date but at a preset price that is usually lower than the market value.

Straight-commission plan salesperson receives an amount that varies with sales results, usually measured in number of sales and amount of profits.

Straight-line route making sales calls in one direction until the end of the territory is reached.

Straight rebuy where the item being purchased is bought on a repetitive basis with little searching by the buyer.

Straight-salary plan salesperson receives a fixed amount of money at fixed intervals.

Structured interview using a questionnaire that contains a specific set of questions.

Suggestion selling a process of suggesting other products or services relating to the main product purchased.

Target group customer identified and selected to receive the thrust of the marketing activity.

Telemarketing using the telephone to generate leads in a selected target group, identify the best prospects to receive a sales call, and sell product.

Trading up the process of moving a customer to a better grade of merchandise or higher-priced product than the one selected.

Trial close an attempt to determine if the prospect is ready to buy.

Tying arrangement where a company refuses to sell one product unless the customer buys another line of products.

Unstructured interview open-ended questions where the candidate is encouraged to talk extensively.

Index